HILLARY RODHAM
CLINTON

On The Couch

Written by Psychoanalyst and Biographer

ALMA H. BOND, PH.D.

Although factual information forms the core of *Hillary Rodham Clinton: On the Couch* (see Bibliography at the end of this book), the author never served as Mrs. Clinton's psychoanalyst, and was never granted an interview by Mrs. Clinton. However, it should be noted that most biographers not only never get an opportunity to interview their subjects, but, unlike Dr. Bond, lack the education and training to professionally analyze them.

Published by Bancroft Press
Books That Enlighten

Bancroft Press
P.O. Box 65360
Baltimore, MD 21209-9945
(phone) 410 . 358 . 0658
(fax) 410 . 764 . 1967
bancroftpress.com

ISBN
978-1-61088-164-7 Hardcover
978-1-61088-167-8 eBook
978-1-61088-166-1 Kindle

Cover Photo: Harald Dettenborn, Munich Security Conference
Cover and Interior Design: J. L. Herchenroeder
Author Photo: Afton Monahan

Printed in the United States of America

HILLARY RODHAM CLINTON

On The Couch

Written by Psychoanalyst and Biographer

ALMA H. BOND, PH.D.

To my wonderfully gifted twins, Janet Bond Brill and Jonathan Halbert Bond; to their dearly departed brother Zane, who will always be in our hearts; and to my son-in-law, Sam Brill, the most generous man on earth.

Introductory Notes

I am Dr. Darcy Dale, psychoanalyst and author, whom you may know from my *On the Couch* series, written so far about Marilyn Monroe and Jackie Kennedy Onassis.

Some time ago, I decided to take a long overdue but only partial sabbatical from my practice to write a book about Hillary, about whom I have wanted to write for a long time. To do so, I had to rent quarters in Washington, to be closer to the scene of action. I rented an apartment, said good-bye to my friends, and began to pack my bags.

Why did I want to write about Hillary Clinton? I was rather tired of delving into the introspective musings of great celebrities who enjoy examining their navels. Hillary would be different, I surmised, and a difficult, if not impossible, subject. She was known for being obsessive about protecting her privacy and that of people near and dear to her. But I have never been a person to run away from a challenge.

Hillary Clinton was not the usual neurotic or psychotic person I often chose to write about, but a typical person like you and me, except she is a major political leader in the most important nation of the world. I thought it would be fun to try to discover how this otherwise normal woman who looks like the girl next door could possibly turn out to be among the most important people who ever lived.

I read whatever I can find about uncommon and exceptional women, for I am always looking for creative women to write about, both in professional journals and my books. As such, I first became interested in Hillary Clinton when she came upon the political scene campaigning for her husband, Bill, then bidding to become governor of Arkansas, and I carefully followed her career in newspapers, magazines, books, and other media ever since. Knowing as many facts as possible about her undoubtedly helped me understand her.

What I will relate here are summaries of private sessions I conducted with Hillary Clinton. At the end of each day, I dictated the highlights of my appointments with her as best I could recall them. Sometimes my dictation was lengthy. Sometimes it was brief. It depended on how much time I had that particular day for dictation.

In no sense are these summaries everything that she and I said during the traditional 50-minute sessions, or what I thought at the time—just what I considered most important.

August 19, 2013

Shortly before I was to leave for Washington, Rivka, my elfish secretary, came into my Manhattan office with a look of excitement on her face. I can always tell from Rivka's expression whether the new patient waiting for me will interest me or not. This time, I had never seen Rivka so excited, not even when she had shown Marilyn Monroe into my presence lo those many years ago. *Who can be more exciting than Marilyn Monroe?* I wondered.

"I'm not going to tell you who is waiting for you," she said. "I want to surprise you. Believe me, you'll be surprised!"

"I guess I'll find out soon enough," I said nonchalantly, not wanting to give Rivka the satisfaction of knowing that she had indeed aroused my curiosity.

I walked into the waiting room, took one look at the lone person sitting there, and almost gasped. There sat Hillary Rodham Clinton.

What a coincidence! I thought. But then Jung said there is no such thing as coincidences. Perhaps the powers that be had seen to it that we would meet. (Such sweet destiny!)

She was silently weeping into her handkerchief. When she saw me, she tried to disguise her tears by pretending to be blowing her nose.

To fully take in her appearance, I allowed her some time to recover. I was surprised to find that she was quite pretty, far better looking than in her photographs. Looking closely at her in such an intimate setting, I could see that she had good bone structure, lovely white teeth, and beautiful skin. Her shoulder-length blond hair softly curled at the ends.

I had read somewhere that she was 5'4" tall, weighed 115 pounds, and worked out regularly to keep in shape. *115? I would have guessed more like 130. A little white lie,* I wondered, *or might she just be lighter than she looks?*

Because her apparel has often been judged harshly since she

appeared in a velvet headband on *60 Minutes* in 1992, I was surprised to note that she was dressed in a sophisticated, although casual, outfit—a dark blue blazer with gold buttons in the shape of her earrings. Under the blazer, she wore a light blue cashmere turtleneck sweater that exactly matched her baby blue eyes. (I learned later they were so blue because of tinted contact lenses). From her appearance, she could have been a New York society woman who did her shopping at Bergdorf's.

"Mrs. Clinton," I said, stepping up to her, "I am happy to meet you in person. But I'm sorry to see you so upset."

She stood up and immediately reached out her hand. As I expected, her handshake was firm and rigorous.

"Sorry for the tears," she said, "but if you had just found out that your husband had begun a new affair, I imagine you would cry, too," she said, looking fiercely into my eyes. "I discovered that he has a mistress in Chappaqua, where we own our house in New York. And to make matters worse, I'm just so tired. After working as hard as I did as Secretary of State, I thought I'd finally get a minute to rest and recuperate!"

"I certainly would cry, too," I answered compassionately. "But let's go into my office and you can tell me about yourself."

"I suspect you know all about me already from the media," she said.

"The media and I have a very different interpretation of so-called facts," I said.

She smiled and said, "We may just get along."

We entered my office. Hillary did not look around but sat down on the chair across from my desk and carefully examined her knuckles. It was only later that I found out that not one aspect of the room or its decor had escaped her notice.

"Well, where shall I begin, Doctor? The new affair?"

"Not immediately, Hillary. May I call you Hillary?" I may have had nerve addressing the former First Lady by her first name, but since that was my habit with patients, I decided that I would treat her no differently. To her credit, she nodded, as though she expected nothing else. "Let us begin where your life began, at its very beginning."

"Is that necessary? I came here because of the problem with my husband, and I am a busy woman. I have no time to waste."

"Believe me, I am well aware of that. But to understand a problem, we have to know its origin, its place in your life, and why it has happened at the present time. I have to know more about you before I can help you overcome the difficulties that brought you here. I am also very interested in what you said about being tired after your tenure as Secretary of State." I sat back and waited.

Hillary was silent for several long moments, seemingly engaged in an inner struggle.

I felt sorry for this eminent woman who was finding it so difficult to talk about feelings that were important to her.

"Tell me about yourself," I finally said. "It doesn't have to be anything you think is consequential, just whatever comes into your mind."

She hesitated. "That's not so easy for me to do. I find it hard to talk about myself. Whenever I'm interviewed about me, I freeze up. When I have to give interviews, I find it much easier to discuss topics like poverty in Burma, the mistreatment of children, or prejudice against women. I don't even think about my feelings much. It's also very unusual for me to cry in front of other people, especially those I don't know," she said.

I pictured a door with several heavy locks on it, and with me banging on it without success. I thought: *She may be a wonderful woman, but her character structure certainly will make her a difficult patient. I remember reading somewhere that her high school newspaper labeled her "Sister Frigidaire." I know what they meant. People who close off their feelings so much are often impossible to know.*

Maybe she isn't treatable and I shouldn't be taking her on. I could never forgive myself if I accepted so important a person for psychoanalysis and failed to help her. Nevertheless, if she will let me, I will try—for her sake, for my own, and perhaps even for the sake of the world. Never mind writing her biography. It would be much more useful to her as well as our country if I can help her to function better.

In my mind, I mulled over the possible sources of her impenetrable psychological armor and hypothesized that she had painful experiences during and after childhood that she could not bear to remember, so she projects them onto the outside world. When she handles earth-shaking problems on a purely intellectual level, it's not Hillary who is in pain, but all the abused women and children on earth. Hillary lives in her head, not her heart, and maintains what she calls "a zone of privacy" about her inner life.

Hillary finally broke the silence. Throwing back her head, she said, "I totally dismiss unthinking emotion. In fact, I find it pitiful."

My heart sank. In my opinion, it is much more pitiful *not* to experience one's feelings. And given that seemingly unchangeable attitude, Hillary Clinton was, I decided, far from the ideal candidate for psychoanalysis.

"Let's try," I said, feeling helpless. "I will help you learn to tolerate your painful feelings."

Tears began to roll down her cheeks again. She turned her head away from me and hastily wiped away the tears with the back of her hand. "I'm not sure I'm up to it."

"Oh, Hillary," I said, "from everything I've read about and seen of you, I know how brave and straight-forward you are. You have lived through the worst kind of scandals, you've been abused by the media as no other First Lady ever has been, and yet you've survived, and quite well. I know you can overcome this challenge, too."

She abruptly stood up. "I hear through the grapevine that you'll be in Washington for a year. I presume you'll see patients while you are there." I nodded but didn't tell her that I'd had no intention of carrying on a full-time practice while I was in Washington, though I would certainly make an exception for her. "I want to leave now," she continued, "and I need to think again about whether I want to do this."

I was shocked at the suddenness of her decision. "Certainly, Hillary," I said, thinking I had bungled the initial interview. "Please call my secretary if you want to make another appointment. I will be here for another week, and Rivka will take messages after I leave."

She walked hastily to the door and, to my surprise, stopped, turned around, and smiled. *She may come back after all,* I thought.

After she left, I thought about what I had learned from the media about Hillary Clinton's character, about her sometimes puzzling behavior, and how it compared with what I had observed during this brief introductory session. Most of what I had just seen of her confirmed what I had read, although I must admit I found her more likable than she'd been portrayed in much of the media. I knew she was intelligent, and I had read somewhere that she had so much energy that she wore out much younger staff members. (Come to think of it, I was pretty tired, too, and I had only seen her for one short session!)

According to all reports, her organizational and leadership abilities were unsurpassed. She was highly ambitious, both politically and professionally, and almost certainly more so than she would admit. As I had already noted, she was remarkably charismatic when she chooses to be. Reputedly a deeply religious person, she was strongly committed to her family. I had been impressed many times by the love she had shown her husband and daughter, at least as captured on video and in photographs. I guessed that love of her family was the strongest feeling she would readily acknowledge to herself.

On the darker side, it was also well known, at least via the media, that she was impatient and has frequent outbursts of temper, that she is a worrier often overcome by anxiety, that she is the victim of a constantly philandering husband and, as the family breadwinner, may have cut some ethical corners at times to make an extra buck or two.

Although many people love her, that is hardly true across the board.

All in all, a very interesting woman, I thought, although Freud himself would have had trouble treating her.

August 21, 2013

Indeed she came back, just two days later.

She came into my office and greeted me with another sweet smile. *No wonder voters like her,* I thought. *I don't know what she's like in private, but she really can be charming and likable when she wants to be.*

"Good morning, Doctor," she said. "As you can see, I have decided to try this out, at least for a little while. But don't be surprised if I quit soon. Although I attended a few psychology classes at Wellesley, Sigmund Freud is not one of my heroes."

"What don't you like about him?"

"All his stuff about penis envy is bullshit," she said in a voice reeking of certainty. "I never wanted a penis. If I had one, what would I do with it? Do you believe in all that crap? If so, maybe I'm in the wrong place."

I smiled. "Women's studies have come a long way since Freud."

"Well, that's a relief! Maybe psychoanalysis will work on me, after all, but you'll have to prove it to me before I give you a gold star. Well, what do you want to know about me, Doctor?"

"Whatever you want to tell me."

"You're a big help, I can see!" She was silent for a moment, and then said, "I guess I should start with my birth. I am one of the first Baby Boomers. I was born on October 26, 1947, two years after the end of World War II." She stopped and then said, "I think I'd rather tell you about my father, Hugh Rodham, who was probably the most important person in my life. Is that all right with you, Doctor?"

"Certainly," I said. "Talk about whomever or whatever you want." I couldn't resist forming a new hypothesis: Her father was more important in her own life than she was, which already told me a great deal about her.

Her shoulders drooped, though her face remained emotionless. I waited patiently while she pulled herself together. She had let an actual emotion slip through and, I suspected, was already regretting it.

She retreated to practical matters. Her father, she began, was Hugh Rodham, the son of Welsh immigrants. What she then told me about him, she recounted in a monotone that horrified me. She described a sour-faced and crabby man who tyrannized his children with scornful, unrelenting sarcasm and embarrassing penny-pinching, and who forced the kids to watch as he constantly humiliated and mistreated their mother. She said he beat his sons, but didn't say whether he hit her, too. *Was she protecting him,* I wondered, *or was she simply his favorite who remained untouched?*

According to her account, he was, whatever his assets—and I'm sure there were plenty—an awful father. He was so brow-beating and humiliating a man I find it incredible that Hillary turned out as well as she has. How she grew up to be the person she is with so abusive and mean-spirited a father is beyond my comprehension. At this early point in our journey, I suspect we have her heredity and perhaps her mother to thank.

"I spent a lot of my time trying to please my father," Hillary said. "I was rarely successful. A typical example concerned my grades in school. I was always a great student and usually brought home a report card full of A's. One day, I took him a report card containing all A's and one B. I waited patiently, silently praying for a complimentary word. His response was, 'How come you got one B?' The next month, I showed him a report card that had straight A's on it. His reaction? 'You must go to an easy school.'"

No matter how well Hillary did, her father kept raising the bar. What a frustrated child she must have been, desperately trying to please a father who refused to be pleased! I can see why she might like to be elected president. A whole country full of people voting for her just might soothe memories of never having satisfied the one man whose opinion she most valued.

A neighbor once said of Hugh Rodham, "He was rougher than

a corn cob, and gruff as could be." He was not a nurturer, leaving that parental function to his gentler wife Dorothy, whose intelligence and abilities he frequently mocked. He was a crude man. (Like her father, Hillary, lady that she is, also can sound overly direct and brusque at times). Whenever Dorothy threatened to leave Hugh because of his abusive treatment of her and the children, his comment as often as not was, "Don't let the doorknob hit you in the ass on your way out."

What a way to treat a loving wife! I thought. *I wouldn't stay with such a man for ten minutes!* Sometimes the children laughed at his remark, said Hillary, but not all the time. Surely they must have been aware of the cruelty behind it, although they don't admit it publicly, even now.

At dinner, Hugh held forth in long monologues about life and didn't take kindly to being interrupted or challenged. Most of the family would quietly squirm as they pretended to listen. Only Hillary would argue if she thought he was wrong. Apparently, she alone was allowed to disagree with her father without suffering dire consequences, but if Dorothy tried to voice a contrasting opinion, she was subjected to the scorn and ridicule of her husband and tagged "Miss Smarty Pants!"

Yet as provocative and insulting as Hugh was to his wife, Hillary made it clear that the couple managed to impart to their children a sense of family and love for each other that determined much of her future life. Looking at their relationship in analytic terms, I would have to label it a sadomasochistic one, which for Hugh meant that in the words of Oscar Wilde, "Each man kills the thing he loves." I figured it must be the example of Hillary's parents' marital life that allows Hillary to put up with her husband's infidelities.

Nobody is all bad, though. Even Hitler loved his dog. Hugh Rodham's excuse for mistreating his family, Hillary said, was his belief in old-fashioned values prevalent during the mid-century—that hard work, discipline, and education at home, school, and church would make any child's dream come true.

Hillary was told that it was her obligation to use her mind in order to have some control over her life as an adult. Thus, she and the other Rodham children had to do well in school. Hugh Rodham's favorite remark was, "You get in trouble at school, you get in trouble at home." Despite his unpleasantness, Rodham's philosophy paid extraordinary dividends in the case of Hillary, if not that of her brothers. To his credit, he taught her that opportunities for success would not be limited by her gender. In this respect, at least, he was ahead of his time.

I decided to take a chance and send out a trial balloon. I said, "Hillary, you puzzle me. Here you are, telling me the most emotional things about your father, and yet you remain utterly calm. How do you manage to look so unaffected?"

"I've been through it so many times that I'm used to it," she answered. I was skeptical, but thought it best to drop the matter until a later time, assuming there would be a later time. She impressed me as being an angry woman—not all the time, but much of the time—who does all she can to hide it. From what I'd already heard, she had plenty to be angry about. But worse was yet to come.

"My father was a chief petty officer in the Navy during World War II. He trained recruits at the U.S. military's Gene Tunney Program, a strict and demanding phys-ed regime based upon the famous boxer's defensive techniques. When my father returned home, he must have missed the Navy, for he treated us like an extension of the service. He sat night and day in his living room recliner, barking out orders to us, ridiculing us, making light of our achievements, downplaying our accomplishments, continuously raising the standards for us, and doing what he called 'character building.' I never gave up trying to please him.

"He was aiming for absolute control over his household. When one of us defied him, he ruthlessly insisted on subservience to his orders. For example, if one of us inadvertently forgot to place the top back onto a tube of toothpaste, he threw it out the window and forced the miscreant to retrieve it, even if the ground was covered with ice or snow. And no matter how freezing the Chicago winter nights, my penny-pincher of a father insisted on turning off the heat until morning."

I shuddered to think what else this fascinating woman had lived through during her childhood. On the occasions of her father's brutality, it is hard to believe that even his daughter didn't harbor resentful feelings toward him, though to my knowledge nobody ever heard her voice them publicly. But as I said, I hadn't heard anything yet.

"I was crazy about my father, meanness and all, and thought he was as handsome as any movie star," she continued. "Once, when I was about five years old and madly in love with him, I said, 'Daddy, will you marry me?' I was shocked to have my 'proposal' met with a sharp whack on the butt. I ran crying into the kitchen, where my mother comforted me with a chocolate bar."

What an awful man! I thought. Every normal little girl is in love with her father and, like Hillary, harbors similar desires toward him. This is the well-known Oedipus Complex, or, in the case of girls, the Electra Complex. How unknowledgeable Hugh Rodham was, and how cruel! No wonder Hillary always had problems with men.

"That was very foolish of him, Hillary, and very wrong," I said. "You were only experiencing and saying out loud what every little girl feels toward her father."

Hillary's eyes briefly clouded over, but she showed no other reaction to my remarks. Indeed, they seemed to pass right through her.

"Didn't his reaction make you angry?" I pressed.

"No," she answered. "I thought I deserved the whack."

I shook my head sadly and thought, *Enough said on that subject, at least for now.*

"Some people grow more pleasant as they age," she went on as if intuiting my thoughts, "but not my father. As he grew older, his meanness became more and more obvious. He had few if any interests besides commanding his household, and little lightness of heart, for his brow-beating and grouchiness escalated."

According to Hillary, all the Rodham men were depressed. I was not surprised. Her father's younger brother, Russell, was a physician who tried to hang himself in the upstairs attic of his home. Hugh cut him down, saving his life. Russell then worked as a bartender, and descended into alcoholism and an ever deeper depression until he died in a fire caused by a lit cigarette. Hillary said she deeply sensed her father's agony over his brother's fate, although I never would have known it from her flat tone or lack of facial expression. Despite his mistreatment of the family, she always seemed to love her father and empathized with his problems. *She was a better daughter than he deserved.*

Willard, Hugh's older brother, spent thirteen years taking care of his father after their mother died. When his father passed away at the age of eighty-six, Willard was overcome with despair, and followed his father to the grave five weeks later. Hillary's youngest brother Tony conjectured that "he died of loneliness."

With both his parents and brothers dead, Hugh fell into a lengthy depression and withdrew further and further from the world. Although he was only fifty-five years old, he retired from his business and sank deeper into himself.

Given this history of Rodham family males, it is not surprising that Hillary's brothers spent their adulthood enveloped in a sea of melancholy.

As adults, Hugh's three children, Hillary, Tony, and Hugh, all tried to talk themselves into believing that their father's rigid standards of child-rearing were part of a grand plan to enable his children to become "competitive, scrappy fighters," to "empower" them, as well as to foster elements of "realism" in their privileged lifestyle. It is difficult to imagine that they interpreted his actions so generously, for they were, in fact, abused children. It is more likely that they used the defense mechanism of denial, in which one does not see what one wishes were not true.

I suspected the same mechanism helped Hillary get through the years of her husband's infidelity. As everyone knows, when Bill was president, the Clinton marriage survived a series of scandals, in particular the Monica Lewinsky affair. When the media made it known that the White House intern had performed oral sex on the president, Hillary vigorously denied the allegations, insisting on NBC's *Today Show* that they were the work of a "vast right-wing conspiracy" that aimed to remove Clinton from the White House.

That's ridiculous! I had thought at the time, and asked myself if she really had been so caught up in the throes of denial that she believed what she'd said or if she was just being a smart politician. At the time, I had the gut feeling that, deep in her heart, Hillary Clinton wanted the surface to be peeled away. Now, I was determined to help her find her core, no matter how difficult the search.

"My father was a giant," Hillary said. "He was six feet two inches tall and broad-shouldered, had a booming voice, and was as dominating psychologically as he was physically. We were terrified when he went into a rage, and everybody knew that my mother's life with him was painfully demeaning. Even I, his loving daughter, was known at times to chafe at my father's outrageous behavior and petty stinginess. Many times his tirades lasted for hours, beginning at dinner, lasting all evening, and continuing for hours in their bedroom. I would put my hands over my ears and duck underneath the covers to drown it all out."

Dorothy was not the only recipient of her husband's anger and violence, Hillary said. "Occasionally, he got carried away when disciplining us, yelling louder or using more physical punishment, especially with my brothers, than I thought was fair or necessary. But even when he was angry, I never doubted that he loved me. My father," she added with a smile, "was not one to 'spare the rod.'"

Why are you smiling, Hillary? I silently wondered. *Somewhere inside yourself, you must have been furious at his tyranny.*

Hillary never said how severely Hugh beat his children, on what part of their anatomy he hit them, or if she was also the recipient of his blows, so I did not know how she really felt when being "disciplined."

Hugh Rodham's child-training philosophy of "not sparing the rod" was not totally successful, at least in the case of Hillary's brothers, Tony and Hugh Jr. Rodham pushed them mercilessly to follow his example so they would be as successful in business as he was. Tony adjusted better than Hugh Jr., who never gave up his impossible dream of pleasing his father. He tried to follow in his father's footsteps by playing football and going to Penn State, but the harder he tried to win Hugh's approval, the more his father pushed him away. A family member who wished to remain anonymous once said that Hugh was toughest on Hugh Jr. because he was his first-born son.

Tony Rodham was very different from his older brother. He didn't seem to care what his father thought of him and did exactly as he pleased. As a result, he won much of his father's esteem at a young age. It is clear that Hugh Rodham respected Hillary and Tony more than Hugh Jr., because they dared to stand up to him. Hillary managed to get away with many minor infractions of household rules. Even when she was the one who engineered the scrape, it was the boys who were punished.

"She was Daddy's girl," Tony has said. "She could do no wrong."

For all his shortcomings, and although he would have indignantly denied it, Hugh Rodham was a feminist in a way. It was Hugh who taught Hillary that she was as good as or better than any male, including her brothers, and Hillary believed him. "In high school," Hillary herself said, "one of my smartest girlfriends dropped out of accelerated courses because her boyfriend wasn't in them. Another didn't want to have her grades posted because she knew she would get higher marks than the boy she was dating." These girls had picked up the subtle and not-so-subtle cultural signals urging them to conform to sexist stereotypes, to diminish their own accomplishments in order to not outperform the boys around them. "Thanks to my father, I couldn't imagine giving up a college education or a career to get married, as some of my friends were doing," she added.

"When Tony was nine years old, he suffered from rheumatic fever and was forced to remain in bed for a whole year. He was lovingly nursed and cared for by our mother, until he was well enough to go back to school. My mother's treatment of Tony was typical of her, the person the boys sought solace from when they were in trouble with our father. She was considered the heart of the household by all of us and served as referee between my brothers and father when he became too tough verbally or physically.

"I grew up between the push and tug of my parents' values, and my own political beliefs reflect the thinking of both," Hillary said. "The gender gap, much talked of in U.S. politics about then, was quite evident in families like mine. My mother was basically a Democrat, although she kept it quiet in Republican-dominated Park Ridge. My dad was a rock-ribbed, up-by-your-bootstraps, conservative Republican and proud of it. Tightfisted with money, he did not believe in borrowing money or using credit, and he ran his business on a strict pay-as-you-go basis. His ideology stemmed from his strong belief in self-reliance and personal initiative.

"I'm afraid I take after him in that latter respect," she continued with an embarrassed look. "I put uneaten olives back in the jar and refrigerate leftover pieces of cheese, no matter how small they are. I guess he got me as worried as he was that we would end up in the poorhouse."

All the time Hillary was telling me about her father, I continued to marvel that she spoke in such a flat tone, with so little expression on her face. I have listened to many such tales over the years, and know that practically all patients, male and female, break down into tears when they speak of such matters. Not Hillary. She could have been reading a grocery list.

Did she behave that way in front of her father, too? Little Hillary somewhere, somehow, found the courage to stand up to him and hide her terror. I suspect this toughened her up so that the adult Hillary was able to challenge her husband and hardened her to the viciousness of political combat.

Eleanor Roosevelt once said that to be in politics, one needed the hide of a rhinoceros. "Eleanor knew what she was talking about," Hillary said. "She learned to take criticism seriously but not personally. Mrs. Roosevelt famously said, 'No one can make you feel inferior without your consent.' You win one day, you lose another day, you don't take it personally. You get up every day and you go on."

What a wise woman Hillary is! I thought, at least in that respect.

Apparently she was already wise as a child, and understood that her father's crass criticism was not personal but simply part of the way he was. Father Hugh was instrumental in toughening Hillary's skin to the necessary thickness and thus helped her survive the slings and arrows aimed her way during her political life and career. Without his "contribution," she probably would have been unable to continue her work at the White House. How many of us have the strength of an Eleanor Roosevelt or a Hillary Clinton and can come through such dreadful ordeals so well? Not I. It is hard enough for me to endure the criticism of patients, whom I encourage to speak up.

Part of Hugh Rodham's problem was that, from his youth onward, he was a disappointed man. He wanted to be a first-string player at Penn State and told everybody he had been awarded a college football scholarship. Unfortunately, he lied. Records show that there were no football scholarships awarded during his years at Penn State (1931-1935). "He was a bullshit artist," a member of his family once said.

Hugh Rodham's father had been a loom operator in the big Scranton Lace Works, and instead of becoming a famous football player, his disgruntled son followed in his father's footsteps at an early age. His mother, Hannah Jones Rodham, was known to be hard-headed and gruff and, like her son, dominated the life of the family.

But Hugh had one great skill that stood out: He was a very effective huckster. "Dad was the world's greatest salesman," Tony Rodham once said. "I never saw him lose a sale." A tradesman who manufactured drapes and lace curtains for hotels, offices, etc., he evidently could talk anyone into buying his products. He sounds a lot like Bill Clinton in this respect, for it was said that Bill could charm the birds off the trees. Certainly Bill knew how to charm Hillary, who stood by his side throughout his scandalous behavior, just as her mother had stood by her father, no matter how demeaning his treatment of her.

"He invested his money wisely, as befits a penny-pincher," Hillary continued. "When I was three years old, he bought a mock-Georgian home in Pine Ridge for $35,000. He paid for the house in cash, for he did not believe in borrowing, most likely so he could save what he otherwise would pay in interest. He never had a credit card, probably for the same reason. He usually returned home by 3 or 4 P.M., and he plunked himself down on his recliner, with his bad leg stretched out in front of him. He spent his time watching television, drinking beer, and shouting out the chores of the day to his children.

"Through his family," says Hillary, "my father managed to remain the commander, even though he no longer was a petty officer in the Navy. Rather than pay tradesmen for the upkeep of the house, he saved money by making us do the required painting and patching. Not surprisingly, we didn't do a very good job, so the house was a wreck, according to the real estate woman who handled the resale years later. Naturally, he didn't pay us for helping. 'You get fed,' he told us. 'That's enough pay.'"

I guess we shouldn't blame Hugh Rodham too much for his

stinginess, I thought. Like other children brought up during the Great Depression, he had seen many people become homeless or on the verge of starvation, and was always afraid that he and his family would join their ranks. His most familiar refrain was "Do you want us to end up in the poorhouse?" He constantly reminded his children that they had many advantages compared to those of his generation. He drummed into their ears, "You'll never know how lucky you are," which Hillary heard more times than she wanted to count.

"If I dared to ask my father for extra pocket money or an advance on my meager allowance, I was treated to a lecture that money doesn't grow on trees. Pretty soon I stopped asking.

"My dad was highly opinionated, to put it mildly," she said. "In our family's spirited, sometimes heated, discussions around the kitchen table, usually about politics or sports, I learned that more than one opinion could live under the same roof. By the time I was twelve, I had my own positions on many issues. I also learned that a person was not necessarily bad just because you did not agree with him, and that if you had a strong belief in something, you had better be prepared to defend it. That has served me well as a political wife and as a politician."

Surely her feelings about money were affected by her father's omnipresent anxiety. I've heard it said that Hillary is tight-fisted, too. One of America's top columnists, *The New York Times*' Maureen Dowd, wrote that the Clintons have a reputation for mixing up money matters and looking greedy in the process. If this is true of Hillary, it is understandable. She suffered considerably from her father's stinginess and his constant economic anxiety. It must have been a great relief to her that she was able to make a considerable amount of money in the law firm, as a U.S. senator, and a national office-holder, and especially from her books.

As she tightly pulled her top lip back, Hillary's lower lip jutted out, confirming my feelings about her relationship with money. "My father," she said, "was especially stingy about our clothing. We seldom were allowed to purchase new clothes until those we had were too small to get into or were worn through with holes. Tony was usually decked out in his brother's hand-me-downs. As often as not, we looked like orphans or homeless children."

Hillary's mother Dorothy was indifferent to how she dressed. It was a good thing, at least for the marriage, because she had to be. Hugh had no interest in hearing that girls, when dressing, need to consider more than covering up their nakedness.

No wonder Hillary dressed in shapeless pantsuits before she was First Lady! I thought indignantly. She never learned to dress properly at an age when most girls are taught such skills.

"All the other girls in high school were clothes-crazy," Hillary said sadly, as if she had zeroed in on my thoughts. "My father thought that was a frivolous reason to spend money and forced me to dress unattractively. My mother wasn't much help. When I complained to her that all the other girls dressed better than me, she said she didn't give a fig what other girls were wearing. She told me I was a unique person and that I didn't have to do what everybody else did. 'You can think for yourself,' she said. I didn't tell her that, thinking for myself, I still wanted to wear pretty clothes. It wouldn't have done any good." Was that a tear I saw glistening in Hillary's eye?

"When it came time to go to my high school prom," she continued, "Dad made me buy the cheapest gown in the store. Next to me, all the other girls looked like fashion plates. Sometimes I think his cheapness sabotaged my sense of femininity, and made it hard for me to be comfortable with boys. Gradually, his stinginess and constant criticism led to an almost complete breakdown in our relationship."

Who could blame her? I thought. I'm only surprised it didn't happen earlier in her life.

"The breach extended far beyond how I dressed. We disagreed on the most elementary of matters, not to mention politics, the war in Vietnam, or feminism, and he became increasingly intolerant of my views." But being Hillary, she felt compelled to add, "But even though we disagreed on just about everything, I always knew he loved me."

Their house was a small, two-story brick home painted in subdued colors and surrounded by maple and elm trees. Many of the Rodhams' neighbors had come from Chicago to escape the influx of African Americans from the South. Rodham despised black people and spoke of them in the most derogatory of terms.

Unsurprisingly, no Jews, blacks, or Asians lived in Park Ridge near the home of his choice. Maine East, the high school Hillary attended through the eleventh grade, then had the largest number of Caucasians of any high school in the country. It is praiseworthy that despite her father's influence, she wasn't racially prejudiced—in fact, far from it. Judging by her efforts to help women of all races throughout the world, I believe her to be completely unprejudiced, despite some contrary stories that arose during her 2008 campaign for president.

Park Ridge was a completely different type of suburb than those along Chicago's exclusive North Shore. The houses were newer, built in the 1930s and '40s, and without the pretensions of the more exclusive residential districts. Of course, the price Rodham paid for his house was much less than the cost of the prestigious homes of the North Shore. As Hillary droned on longer about neighborhood homes, I suppressed a yawn. She was not always the easiest person to listen to.

"My father considered himself a 'Taft Republican,' who tried to force his political beliefs upon us," she continued. "In 1952, he made us watch the Republican National Convention on TV and refused to let us look at the Democratic convention. But I made sure to visit a friend's house when I knew the Democrats were on."

I wasn't a bit surprised.

Bill Clinton said that even after he became president, his father-in-law never gave up hoping he would become a Republican and totally abolish the capital gains tax.

I'm no political expert, but it is beyond implausible that Rodham still hoped that his son-in-law, Bill Clinton, the President of the United States and the heart of the Democratic party, would actually transfer his party allegiance at that point and become a Republican. How unrealistic can a person be?

"My father died on April 7, 1993 at the age of eight-two," Hillary told me in the dullest of tones. Only the glistening in her eyes signaled that her statement held any special meaning for her. "Despite his treatment of the family," she said, "I mourned him terribly. In fact, his death even forced me to take a public break while working with my health care reform task force."

I thought she mourned him even more deeply than she knew and suspected she was talking about him when she wrote later, "Every one of us has a choice. I think that in everyday ways, how you treat your own disappointments and whether you're able to forgive the pain that others cause you, and, frankly, to acknowledge the pain you cause to others, is one of the big challenges we face. I pray every day that I, as the Biblical admonition says, will learn to forgive my enemies."

President Clinton delivered the eulogy at Hugh Rodham's funeral. Did Hillary like it? Was she pleased? Did she think he could have done better? I'll never know. She didn't say.

Instead, she jumped up and said, "I have to leave now."

I'll bet you do, I thought. *Heaven forbid you should break down and sob.*

August 26, 2013

The next session took place in my new quarters in Washington, which I had furnished to look very much like my old Manhattan office—a place where I was so comfortable—even to the point of shipping in my old brown leather analyst's chair. Hillary entered as if there had been no change. As in New York, she made no comment about the office, but I knew by now that she had taken it all in.

"Today I want to tell you about my mother, Dorothy Howell Rodham," she said. Beginning with the facts, Hillary was less guarded than she had been when talking about her father. Dorothy Emma Howell's character was totally different than that of her husband. She was born in Chicago in 1919, the daughter of Edwin John Howell Jr., a Chicago firefighter, and the former Delia Murray. Dorothy's only sibling, Isabelle, was born in 1924. Their ancestors were English, Scottish, Welsh, French, and Dutch, and their paternal grandfather was an immigrant from Bristol in Gloucester. Many of her more contemporary ancestors had lived in Canada.

"My mother's childhood was so bad it could have been written about by Dickens," Hillary said. "I have nightmares about it."

"Can you tell me the nightmares?" I asked.

"I don't remember them," she answered.

I should have known better than to ask.

Hillary continued with her mother's story. "The family was boarding in an overcrowded home along with four other families, and my mother was frequently moved from school to school. Her parents had a miserable, dysfunctional marriage, and like *my* mother and father, often were involved in violent fights. They paid only episodic attention to their children before they divorced in 1927. Incredibly, my young mother and her young sister Isabelle were sent that year on a train by themselves, unsupervised, to live with their maternal grandparents in the Los Angeles suburb of Alhambra, California.

"Can you believe it?" Hillary asked, expressing the closest to an emotion I had heard from her yet. "How could anyone allow that? Didn't they care about the dangers young children might face, alone for days on a train with open doors in the company of total strangers? Had they no heart?" At the time, Dorothy, who was in charge of her younger sister, was only eight years old, and Isabelle just three.

I, like Hillary, was horrified and wondered how any parents (or grandparents) could be so heartless. I said nothing, but she must have seen the look of dismay on my face.

She smiled and said softly, "It is good to feel understood."

After a brief pause, she continued: "The sisters' lives did not improve at all in their new home, for they were harshly treated by their unloving grandparents from the moment they stepped through their door. Delia Howell had essentially abandoned my mother when she was only three or four, leaving her alone all day for weeks on end with meal tickets to use at a restaurant near their five-story walk-up apartment on Chicago's South Side. Can you imagine a three- or four-year-old child eating her meals alone in a restaurant? When I compare it to the loving attention Bill and I pay to Chelsea's every whim, my heart breaks for my mother." Hillary's eyes grew wide with pain.

No, I thought. *That's preposterous!* I've analyzed many people over the years, but never have I had a patient who was so neglected, and to think these were the great-grandparents of America's First Lady!

It seems that Mr. Howell, a laborer for the city, left the job of taking care of his children completely to his wife, Delia. Dorothy remembered her as a strict woman always dressed in black who would not allow the children to have visitors or attend parties and punished them for even the smallest infraction. Delia was a weak and selfish woman who, in her later years, spent most of her time watching soap operas on TV.

"The girls were subject to constant criticism, ridicule, and harsh punishment," Hillary said."After Mrs. Howell learned one Halloween that my mother had gone trick-or-treating, she was told she'd be confined to her room for a year and allowed out only to attend school. The punishment lasted for several months, until Mrs. Howell's sister fortunately came to visit and put a stop to Delia's cruelty."

What incredible punishment for such normal behavior! I thought. *The woman sounds psychotic or psychopathic.*

Hillary herself had a memory of her grandmother which, as well as anything, illuminates the kind of self-involved, uncaring person she was. "Delia was babysitting me and my brothers when my eye collided with a chain-link fence while playing in the schoolyard. Blood streamed down my face as I ran home sobbing in terror. When Delia saw me, she fainted. I had to run next door and ask our neighbor for help. When Delia came to, she was furious with me for making her fall, angrily telling me she could have gotten hurt. I had to wait for my mother to return before I was taken to the hospital to get stitches, while my grandmother sat and nurtured her grudges while watching TV."

Hillary picked up on her mother's story. "Although it was the height of the Depression, my mother was wise enough at the youthful age of fourteen to leave her grandparents' unhappy home to find a job as a three-dollar-a-week housekeeper, cook, and nanny in San Gabriel, California. Fortunately, she was treated more kindly by her employer, who recognized her intelligence and encouraged her to read and go to school. My mother told me that without her time with a kind, loving family, she wouldn't have known how to raise us."

Dorothy attended Alhambra High School, where she joined the Scholarship Club and the Spanish Club and was mentored by two teachers: Miss Drake, who taught speech and drama, and Miss Zellhoefer, the writing teacher. "She taught English and was very strict," Dorothy Rodham wrote in 1998 in a book celebrating the centennial of the school. "We came from her class with respect for her and a solid grounding in English. What made her special was her desire that we develop critical thinking."

These nurturing teachers certainly contributed to the educated person Dorothy became. This supposition seems corroborated by Hillary's remark that caring adults who are not a child's parents can fill his or her emotional needs. Nevertheless, Dorothy must have carried the painful scars of her parents' and grandparents' abuse and neglect all her life. Most likely she became a fine mother by learning from her parents and grandparents how *not* to raise children.

Upon Dorothy's graduation from high school, she was surprised to receive an invitation from her mother, now remarried, to return to Chicago, with a promise of money to attend a university. Dorothy was thrilled. "I'd hoped so hard that my mother would love me that I had to take the chance and find out," she poignantly told her daughter. But the promised love and university financing never were delivered; it turned out that the only thing Dorothy's mother wanted from the reunion with her daughter was a free housekeeper.

Her mother had married Max Rosenberg, a Jewish man, a fact which later must have devastated Hugh Rodham, the anti-Semite, who ironically had a Jewish step-father-in-law. The pathetic attempt at a reunion between mother and daughter was a total failure, leaving Dorothy disappointed and in greater despair than before, for she now knew for certain that her fantasies of obtaining her mother's love would never come true. This didn't stop her for long. The plucky young lady then took her life into her own hands and moved into her own apartment and found office jobs to support herself.

I'll bet Hillary would have done the same thing under such circumstances, I thought. *I can see where she got her strength and determination not to be squelched.*

"I attribute my own interest in children's welfare to my mother's early life," Hillary said with shining eyes. "I symbolically help her by improving the lives of desperate children all over the world."

"Good insight, Hillary," I agreed.

During her unsuccessful presidential campaign in 2008, Hillary said, "I owed my inspiration to one person: my mother, who never got a chance to go to college, and who had a very difficult childhood, but who gave me a belief that I could do whatever I set my mind to." Here, for the first time in her sessions, Hillary displayed some emotion. She added, "Despite the repressive atmosphere dominated by my father, my mother was able to encourage my ambition and my passion for learning. I have always credited my mother with giving me the tools and toughness to enter politics."

Dorothy Rodham used a unique method to teach her children how to remain calm in the midst of turmoil. She took out a carpenter's tool and said, "See this instrument? Well, imagine that it is inside of you. You must always try to keep the bubble in the center." She tipped the tool to demonstrate how the bubble could float upwards or downwards, instructing the kids they always had to bring it back to the center. She called it "emotional desensitization."

The technique may have saved Hillary's sanity during the difficult White House years. "Thank goodness for the carpenter's tool," Hillary said. "It taught me to stay focused while living in the White House in the eye of many a storm." But however well "emotional desensitization" may have served her in growing up with a father impossible to please, and as First Lady during difficult times, it certainly is detrimental to a successful psychoanalysis.

"My mother was a very unusual woman," Hillary continued. "I was proud of the fact that she had a social consciousness at a time when few people did. She always tried to help us understand what was fair and just. She encouraged us to speak out, not to worry about what other people thought about us, and just to be ourselves."

What a great gift she gave Hillary! No wonder she was able to speak so directly whenever she chose to.

Although a difficult father, Hugh Rodham also contributed to Hillary's political success. Hugh Rodham was a tradesman, and Dorothy Rodham just about managed to finish high school. Together, they projected onto their daughter a desperate ambition to better herself. Dorothy Rodham's passion for reading shows up in her daughter, who reads prodigiously. Incredibly, Hillary has read the biographies of *every one* of her forty-three First Lady predecessors. (She has even read the series of mystery novels Elliott Roosevelt wrote, in which his mother Eleanor appears as an amateur sleuth.)

According to Hillary, while applying for a job as a clerk typist at a textile company in 1937, her mother met traveling salesman Hugh Ellsworth Rodham, eight years her senior. After a lengthy courtship, they married in early 1942. It was to be an inauspicious mating which Dorothy regretted until Hugh's death. But she remained in the marriage, Hillary said, because she believed that nothing was more important for her children than to hold the marriage together.

I doubted that, but I was not about to tell Hillary. I believe that in some perverse way, Dorothy loved her husband, just as I think that Hillary loves Bill. For sadomasochists, love cannot be love without pain.

Dorothy became a full-time homemaker, raising her three children and spending her afternoons in libraries and museums. Hillary's eyes lit up when she said, "I give my mother full credit for encouraging a love of learning in me, a curiosity about the world around me that she had never seen, and a tremendous will to persevere. She was an expert at that. It is amazing that she could encourage me to love learning and to pursue an education and a career that she herself had never had. In contrast to my father's staunch Republican views, my mother was basically a Democrat, although she wasn't outspoken about it. In my early years, I was a staunch Republican like my father. But I later switched parties to become an avid Democrat. The change brought my mother and me closer than ever."

Mrs. Rodham insisted that Hillary stand up to bullies, a talent that has stood her in good stead during her political career. Dorothy pushed her children to hold their own against persecutors, Hillary said.

"Once, when I was four years old, I ran to my mother in tears after a neighborhood girl named Suzy had bullied me. I got no sympathy from my stalwart mother, who instead said there was no room for cowards in our family, that I can't be afraid. She also said I had her permission to hit back.

"She later told me," Hillary said, "that she watched from behind the curtain as I squared my shoulders and marched across the street. I returned a few minutes later, beaming from head to toe. 'I can play with boys now,' I said, 'and I can even play with Suzy.' In fact, Suzi and I became good friends, and still are."

Similarly, when she was a freshman at Wellesley College in Massachusetts, Hillary called her mother to say she didn't know if she had the ability to remain at and compete in the Ivy League college. Once again, Mrs. Rodham refused to allow her daughter to be a quitter. "'You can't quit,'" Hillary quoted her mother, "'You've got to see through what you've started.' So I did!"

It reminded me of another one of Eleanor Roosevelt's remarks: "We gain strength, courage, and confidence every time we look fear in the face. We must learn to do that which we think we cannot do."

Hillary listened to her mother, learned to look fear in the face, and grew stronger for it.

She stayed at Wellesley until she received her B.A. degree in 1969. She said, "I arrived at Wellesley carrying my father's political beliefs and my mother's dreams and left with the beginning of my own."

Wellesley taught her many valuable lessons through a diversity of sources. She melded these ideas together to form her own future goals, how she planned to go about achieving them, a strong work ethic, which had expanded beyond what she had brought to Wellesley, and the confidence that she could reach for the stars. She also left with awe-inspiring strength of character, which helped her stand up under the vindictive, brutal attacks the Republicans aimed at her during Bill's presidency, and the vicious Democratic slings and arrows shot at her during her 2008 run for president.

"One of the things Dorothy said was that Hillary always had the capacity, the confidence, and the tenacity to stare the Devil down," according to Hillary's childhood friend, Ernest Ricketts. Dorothy's dream was that Hillary would grow up to become the first woman on the Supreme Court. She later joked that, unfortunately, Sandra Day O'Connor had beaten her to it. But I imagined that, for Dorothy, Hillary's later accomplishments made up for a daydream that failed to come true.

What a wonderful mother Hillary had. She was as responsible as anything else for her daughter's great success and strength of character. "Dorothy Rodham is the person who shaped Hillary more than any other, and there is no way to know Dorothy and not see how she fashioned her daughter," Linda Bloodworth-Thomason, a Hollywood producer and close Clinton friend, said. A quiet woman, Dorothy Rodham was always there for Hillary and her family, psychologically always "standing behind the curtain," quietly supporting them.

Nevertheless, as much as Hillary and Dorothy loved each other, they were not close in a way customary of many mothers and daughters—they were not confidantes. Dorothy told a reporter, for instance, that she didn't discuss anything intimate with Hillary about her marriage, herself, or anything personal. She said they didn't talk about deeply personal things. It's hard to believe, but that is what Dorothy said. Frankly, I don't believe it!

Probably more correct was her statement: "Hillary was born an adult. She never seemed to lack discipline or drive. Once she settled on a track, she stuck to it like the wheels of an express train." If Dorothy meant that from the beginning, her daughter was a conscientious, rational perfectionist, her remark makes a lot of sense.

Sometimes I question whether people really change their characters much as they mature. I once saw a video of small babies in which photos of their activities as infants were compared with those showing their adult behavior. People had no difficulty matching up the babies with their grown-up selves. They hadn't really changed that much at all.

Dorothy Rodham was there for her friends as well as her family. "She was always there if you needed anything," according to her lifelong friend, Hazel Price. "Dorothy was present for children as well as adults, inspiring self-respect and confidence in neighborhood youngsters as well as her own children by her willingness to listen attentively to their problems and conflicts." Apparently, she was a better listener to the neighborhood children than she was sometimes to her adult daughter, if we can believe Dorothy's own recorded words on the subject.

Hillary sank back in her chair as she mused about other memories of Dorothy. "She wasn't always serious and careful. She had a terrific sense of humor. Both she and my father were great dancers; she loved dancing." Hillary's face actually lit up as she recalled her former neighbor's words about Dorothy, as if she couldn't get enough of them.

Mrs. Price's sentiments about her friend were repeated by many people, including the wife of Lackawanna County Recorder of Deeds, Evie Rafalko McNulty, who Hillary said remembers Dorothy Rodham as a kind, cordial woman who exerted a positive influence on her children and grandchildren. "She was a lady who could have had access to the world through her daughter and son-in-law, yet you would never think so to know her," Mrs. McNulty said. "She looked like the dedicated mother and grandmother she was. She never wanted to hog the spotlight. She just wanted to be Dorothy Rodham. That's who she was."

Like mother, like daughter, I thought. I believed that Hillary just wants to be Hillary, wherever that may take her. But I suspect she has a different approach from her mother about "hogging the spotlight."

The Rodhams attended the First United Methodist Church, four blocks north of their Wisner Street home in Pine Ridge, although Hugh was frequently absent from services on Sundays, saying that he would rather pray at home. I imagined that his praying played second fiddle to watching the television set. A devout Methodist, Hillary practiced what she preached. She and her church youth group often looked after the deprived children of Mexican migrant workers who picked crops a few blocks from her home. Hillary always found great comfort in a religion that she has enjoyed sharing with others since she was a child. At one point when Bill Clinton was Governor of Arkansas, she toured the state, speaking to constituents about what it meant to be a Methodist.

The newspapers were not always impressed. One ultra-conservative newsletter called Hillary "a radical feminist who has little use for religious values or even the traditional family unit." I wondered where it got its information.

At their national convention in 1992, Republicans accused Hillary of influencing her husband to carry out a secret, liberal agenda. They couldn't be more wrong. Hillary's religious beliefs helped to form her character, and are at the core of who she is. She believes in the Methodist philosophy of setting the world to rights through good works. She still carries her Bible around everywhere she goes and constantly reads and marks it.

As she did in many other areas, Hillary followed in her mother's religious footsteps. "To come from, as Hillary used to call it, a loveless childhood, to be so loving and dedicated, it just says what an indomitable spirit Dorothy Rodham was," former Scranton Mayor James Barrett McNulty said about Dorothy Rodham. "Hillary possesses the same spirit—tough, but at the same time very compassionate. When you see Hillary Clinton, you see Dorothy Rodham."

"She was there as well for her granddaughter Chelsea," Hillary said proudly. "Chelsea adored my mother and called her every day. She said she was amazed at how much her grandmother had overcome and how she was able to build a better life for her children despite the terrible difficulties life put in her way. Chelsea said she would like to emulate her grandmother and do the same for the children she hopes to have some day and in the work she would like to do on behalf of less fortunate people."

On September 19, 2011, Chelsea posted the following Facebook status:

"My parents and my grandmother inspire me every day, both in my work and personal life. I think about how best to live my grandmother's twin mantras that 1) 'Life is not a dress rehearsal' and 2) 'Life is not about what happens to you, but what you do with what happens to you.'"

"My grandmother has had a remarkable life and overcame challenges when she was a child that I cannot even imagine," Chelsea said, "and her determination to build a better life for her children, which taught my mother and my father how to build a better life for me, is something I feel elevated by."

In 1987, Mrs. Rodham and her husband moved to Little Rock, Arkansas, to be closer to their daughter and granddaughter. An excellent student as a youth, Mrs. Rodham finally was able to take college courses in subjects such as psychology, logic, and child development. She never graduated, because she didn't want to settle down and major in one subject. Her loving daughter never got over the fairy-tale ending of Dorothy's journey from an abandoned little girl alone on a train to the mother of the First Lady of the United States.

I thought it was an incredible story. She said, "I'm amazed at how my mother emerged from her lonely early life as such an affectionate and level-headed woman." Dorothy Rodham never stopped learning as long as she lived. Here, too, her daughter Hillary follows in her mother's footsteps, and continues to expand her knowledge every day of her life.

Hugh Rodham died in 1993, and I wondered whether Dorothy missed him greatly or found his absence a relief. She probably felt both. She remained active to the end of her life, but valued her privacy and rarely spoke to the media. As a result, the public knows very little about her. She made an exception when she appeared on *The Oprah Winfrey Show* in 2004. In 2006, she moved into the Clintons' large Whitehaven house in the Kalorama neighborhood of Washington, D.C.

In December 2007, at the age of eighty-eight, she made a rare public appearance in Iowa and other early primary states to campaign for Hillary in her presidential bid. Like her daughter, Dorothy appeared at events concerning women's issues and also in a Clinton campaign television advertisement. A highlight of her life occurred in January 2009 when the proud mother was present at Hillary's swearing in as U.S. Secretary of State. But most important of all, Hillary showed her deep love for her mother and how much she considered her an integral part of the family by having Dorothy appear with her and Chelsea on the presidential platform when Bill Clinton was sworn in as President of the United States.

Dorothy Rodham was ahead of her time in many ways. Unlike the mothers of Hillary's friends, Dorothy did not stay at home housekeeping all day, but spent any extra time she could find in libraries and museums. It has been reported that she became much closer to her granddaughter Chelsea after her husband died. She traveled to Paris with Hillary when the president went there on an official visit. It was Dorothy's first visit abroad.

"My mother loved her home and her family," Hillary said, "but she felt limited by the small number of options open to women at the time. It is easy to forget now, when women's choices can be overwhelming, how few there were for my mother's generation," she said, shaking her head.

If it weren't Hillary Clinton sitting before me, I would swear I saw the sparkle of tears in her eyes as she spoke. Hillary then described her mother as a woman with a terrific sense of humor, who was absolutely devoted to her family, and equipped with an enormous sense of adventure. Hillary said, "My mother was a warm, generous, and strong woman, an intellectual; a woman who told a great joke and always got the joke; an extraordinary friend and, most of all, a loving wife, mother, and grandmother." This time I had no doubt that there were tears in her eyes.

Dorothy Rodham would have been a good woman to pick as a mother. She certainly contributed mightily to her daughter's character and personality. Hillary said she grew up in the usual parental household where the mother is the helper and encourager and the father supplies the money for the needs of the family. Perhaps in differing ways, both parents were of equal importance in preparing their daughter to be Secretary of State of the United States.

When Hillary finished her campaign for president with a speech at Washington's National Building Museum in June 2008, Dorothy watched from off stage and was seen to wipe away a tear as her daughter conceded the nomination to Barack Obama. Mrs. Rodham looked very different a few months later, when she stood proudly by as her daughter was sworn in as Obama's Secretary of State.

Hillary canceled a foreign trip she had planned to London and Istanbul to remain at her dying mother's bedside. Mrs. Rodham passed away shortly after midnight at a hospital, surrounded by her loving family, in Washington, D.C.. The cause of death is unknown, and Hillary never told me specifically, but it is believed that she suffered from heart problems. Mrs. Rodham's death ended a long period in which Hillary devotedly looked after her mother.

Hillary's grief at the loss of her mother was so great that the workaholic Secretary of State was unable to return to her job for some time. Hillary deeply loved her mother. After Dorothy's death, life for Hillary would never be the same. Perhaps ever afterward, she has been a little lonely. Nevertheless, Dorothy Rodham lives on as the primary role model of mother, the teacher who showed her daughter how to be a fine parent, and the activist who seeks to improve the lives of children all over the world.

The Clinton Foundation sent this touching statement to the news media to announce the death of Dorothy Rodham:

"Dorothy Howell Rodham was born in Chicago on June 4, 1919 and died shortly after midnight on November 1, 2011 in Washington, D.C., surrounded by her loving family. Her story was a quintessentially American one, largely because she wrote it herself. She overcame abandonment and hardship as a young girl to become the remarkable woman she was.

"Dorothy is and always will be lovingly remembered by her daughter and son-in-law, Hillary Rodham Clinton and Bill Clinton; her sons and daughters-in-law, Hugh Rodham and Maria, and Tony and Megan Rodham; her grandchildren, Chelsea Clinton and her husband Marc Mezvinsky, Zachary Rodham, Fiona Rodham, and Simon Rodham. She leaves behind many friends from all stages and places in her life, friends from California she met in high school, friends from Little Rock and Washington with whom she explored the world, the people who were first her doctors and then her friends at George Washington Hospital, and the people she met through her children and grandchildren who became as much her friend as theirs. Her family is and will be forever grateful for the gift of Dorothy's life and for the memories they will treasure forever."

In Carl Bernstein's biography of Hillary, *A Woman In Charge*, he wrote that "Dorothy Howell imparted to [her] children a pervasive sense of family and love for one another that in Hillary's case is of singular importance." Dorothy drummed into Hillary that nobody in the Rodham family ever got divorced. She repeatedly said, "Don't give up on Bill Clinton. You can work it out together. You must not leave your marriage! A child must have a father."

"My mother taught me that holding the family together is the key to keeping the bubble in the center," agreed Hillary. "She said that if you are married for more than ten minutes, you are going to have to forgive your mate for something, and Bill is no worse than anyone else," Hillary said with a faraway look in her eyes. "I will never forget it."

As her husband grew weaker, Dorothy even became something of a free spirit, at turns sentimental, analytical, spiritual, and adventurous. But she never forgot her religion, and taught classes at Sunday school, as would her daughter later on.

Dorothy changed along with the times and kept growing as long as she lived. It is interesting that her favorite movies were not those of her childhood, but *The Adventures of Priscilla, Queen of the Desert* (an Australian drag queen romp), and the bloody classic *Pulp Fiction*.

"I like movies, too," Hillary said in response to my question. "So does Bill. Sometimes we see five o'clock, seven o'clock, and nine o'clock shows all in a row. It was hard for us to get away from the White House, so we watched them sometimes on TV. I loved it when we all three sat together and watched the movie with our feet on the fancy White House chairs and eating popcorn. I recently tweeted Rachel Horwitz, the senior manager of Twitter's communications team, to tell her that I, like her, am obsessed with the upstairs-downstairs drama, *Downton Abbey*."

"What do you like about it?" I asked.

She hesitated a moment before answering. "I can watch it and pretend that I, too, am the lady of the English mansion," she admitted. "In many ways, it's not too different from being First Lady."

I laughed and said, "I like *Downton Abbey*, too. Hillary, I am delighted to hear that you actually relax sometimes, like us ordinary folks."

"Oh, I do," she answered. "But my main relaxation is doing crossword puzzles. It adds to my brain power."

Oh, I thought. *I knew you wouldn't do something just for the fun of it.*

"When I was running for president in the 2008 elections," she continued, "I told the *Washington Post* that my hidden talent is solving crossword puzzles. I share my passion with Nancy Pelosi, who said she stays up late into the night doing *The New York Times* crossword puzzle."

As Hillary continued talking about her interests, I discovered that they are broader than I had known. In the White House, she sought self-understanding and inspiration from New Age feminists, therapists, and theologians like Rabbi Michael Lerner, anthropologist Mary Catherine Bateson, and psychologist Jean Houston, the latter of whom said, "In our time, we have come to the stage where the real work of humanity begins."

But the most surprising news came in a note concerning Hillary's law school experience—that one of her teachers at the Yale Child Study Center was Anna Freud! Who would have thought it? Hillary was full of surprises. But maybe I shouldn't have been so surprised. She did a wonderful job raising Chelsea. Perhaps she put to use what she learned from Anna Freud in this most important area of her life.

Not everybody thinks that Hillary is a wonderful human being. I suppose a psychoanalyst should look at all sides of the picture, so here is what one Hillary-hater has to say:

Camille Paglia wrote in *Slate*, "It's time to put my baby-boom generation out to pasture! We've had our day and managed to muck up a hell of a lot. It remains baffling how anyone would think that Hillary Clinton is our party's best chance. She has more sooty baggage than a 90-car freight train. And what exactly has she ever accomplished— beyond bullishly covering for her philandering husband? She's certainly busy, busy, and ever on the move—with the tunnel vision workaholism of someone trying to blot out uncomfortable private thoughts."

I must have been losing the objectivity every psychoanalyst should have about her patients, for Paglia's comments infuriated me!

I stood up and said, "I'm sorry, Hillary, but it's time to leave now."

She looked at her watch and said, "Already? I'm just getting into this thing. Can't I stay a little longer?"

"I'm afraid not," I answered. "Another patient is waiting to see me."

I gathered not many people say "no" to Hillary Clinton. She stood up with highly erect posture, stuck out her lower lip, and stalked out of the room.

Concerned that I wouldn't be able to help a person as outwardly oriented as Hillary, I went to sleep that night and had a dream. The face of Carl Jung loomed large before me. Nothing else, just his huge face with his elegant mustache filling the dream screen. When I woke up, I thought: Jung? Why Jung? I'm not a Jungian. I never have found his work very helpful. But then you might say I am a psychological opportunist who uses whatever school of psychology has to offer if I find it useful in my work. I set about trying to remember what I had studied about Jung many long years ago.

The first thing that came to mind was his early work on introversion and extroversion. Yes, yes, that must be the meaning of the dream, I thought with elation. Jung believed there are two opposing ways of being in the world: introversion—a turning inward away from external objects—in contrast to extroversion, which is a looking away from the inner self toward the outer world. I decided to see if I could find anything he had to say about extroversion that might be helpful in treating Hillary.

Despite the hour, I leapt out of bed and went searching for my early notes. They confirmed what I remembered, that the extroverted person is characterized by an outward flowing of energy, an interest in events, people, and things relating to and feeling dependent on them, to the detriment of knowing his or her own feelings.

I got more and more excited as I delved further into my notes. They said the extrovert is usually motivated by outside factors and greatly influenced by the environment; is sociable and confident in unfamiliar surroundings; likes organizations and parties; and tends to be optimistic and enthusiastic.

Such a person also has weaknesses, of course. These include the need to make a good impression, making and breaking relationships easily, considering reflection a morbid practice, avoiding self-criticism, disliking being alone, and accepting the conventions and morals of the day.

That certainly sounded like Hillary Clinton, I thought. Jung must have met her twentieth-century counterpart. I scrambled through the rest of my notes to see if he had any suggestions on how to treat such a person. I turned page after page, but to my great disappointment, there was nothing. Nor could I find such instruction in any of Jung's other books, which I spent hours perusing.

What good does a description of her character do for her or for me? I thought angrily. So she is an extrovert! I know that already. What should I do now? The woman is coming to me for help, and I don't know if there is anything I can do for her. I feel like a charlatan. As a matter of fact, I suspect not many extroverts come for psychoanalysis, since they avoid looking inside themselves, so *no* analyst may have any useful advice on the subject.

Dream or no dream, I was right back where I started! In despair, I thought I better go back to sleep and dream a more helpful dream.

August 28, 2013

Hillary greeted me with a pleasant smile. I was surprised she had returned at all, let alone with a happy look on her face. I decided to tell her my reaction. It was the first time she had shown even a hint of emotion, and I wanted to encourage her.

So I said, "You look pleased to be here, Hillary. Are you?"

"Yes," she answered. "I am."

I couldn't believe my ears. Not only was she glad to come for her session, but she even admitted it.

"What do you like about coming here?" I asked.

"I like that you really listen to me, and don't seem to be making any judgments. I can relax with you. I don't always have that rhinoceros hide, even if people think I do. It's a relief to know that you won't attack me, whatever I tell you."

"Thank you, Hillary. I am delighted you feel that way," I answered. And indeed I was. I thought, *Extrovert or not, maybe we will get some place after all.*

"What'll we talk about today, Doc? Can we get to Monica Lewinsky yet? Everybody else wants to," she said.

I thought she was teasing me and said, "I'd rather you tell me more about your life first."

Her face fell, but she proceeded anyway. "Okay, you're the doctor. How should I continue?"

"You told me about your childhood and your parents, but I don't know anything about you as a teenager."

"There's nothing to tell. I was just an ordinary girl . . ."

"I doubt if you were ever ordinary, Hillary. Try me, and we'll see." What I really thought was that she was afraid to open up the pain she had undoubtedly felt as an adolescent.

Once she began to talk, however, she spoke with relish. "When I think of adolescence, I remember school," she said. "From the beginning, I was always good at it, because I worked very hard and brought home straight A's from elementary school, except for the one B, which was in Phys Ed, and which I alluded to earlier. I guess I was the biggest overachiever in the class. That made my mother happy, and even my father must have been pleased, although God forbid he would ever say so. I was usually the teacher's pet, which made a lot of the kids hate me, but it was worth it.

"What wasn't so great is that I have always been very nearsighted, and the doctor prescribed glasses thick as the bottoms of Coke bottles for me when I was only nine years old. I tried to jazz them up by picking out red or purple frames, but it didn't help. The kids at school teased me mercilessly and called me 'Owl Face.' Sometimes when I was feeling vain or had to go to a party, I left the glasses at home, and a friend would have to pull me around like a seeing-eye dog. A lot of kids thought I was being snobbish because I didn't say hello. They didn't know I just couldn't see them.

"I wore those glasses until I got my first pair of contact lenses when I was thirty-three years old. I know I look better with the contacts, but would you believe that I still feel like 'Owl Face?' Sometimes the feeling is so strong I have to look in a mirror to check." She looked sad.

I felt her pain and said, "Hillary, no matter what you looked like as a child, you are now a beautiful woman."

Her face lit up and she said, "You wouldn't just say that to make me feel better, now would you, Doc? After all, you *are* in the shrink business and get paid to make patients feel good."

"No, Hillary," I answered. "When you know me better, you will find that I never lie. I may not always say what's on my mind, but what I do say is always the truth." It remained to be seen whether she believed me or not.

"Even though I couldn't see well," she continued, "I got to be a good athlete. I was clumsy at first, but my father would take me to the schoolyard and teach me hour after hour to play baseball and football.

We would practice so much that eventually I was able to hold my own even with the boys."

Isn't that just like Hillary? I thought. *She would never be satisfied at performing anything poorly.*

"Starting from the time I was in elementary school, I developed deep friendships with girls. The boys came after. In the sixth grade, Betsy Ebeling and I became best friends and did everything together, even taking piano lessons from the same teacher after I coaxed my cheapskate father to buy me an old upright. My classmate, Art Curtis, remembers that he and I stood outside of my house and discussed politics. He was amazed that I could talk about Barry Goldwater with him when most of the girls he knew were only interested in clothes and boys."

In high school, Hillary said she was running things for her Girl Scout troop, including neighborhood carnivals. By the time she reached Maine East High School, she was active in almost every extra-curricular activity the school offered: the newspaper, student government, the Brotherhood Society, the Cultural Values Committee, the Prom Committee, and the *It's Academic* quiz show team, whose members (including Hillary) competed with other schools on local TV. She also was selected as one of the school's eleven National Merit Scholarship finalists.

"At the time," she said, "I wanted to be a doctor. But I gave up on that idea the first time I fainted at the sight of blood. Then there were lots of other things I dreamt about doing during my teen years, to try out different lifestyles and personalities before settling down into who I wanted to be. I wanted to travel a lot—to Africa, Asia, Europe, and around the United States. I especially wanted to visit Northern California, where the 'hippies' were living—to just bum around anywhere I felt like going for a while.

"I also daydreamed about working in arts and crafts, being an actress in the theatre, on television, and in the movies, and to meet all kinds of people all over the world. I thought I would do all this the year after I graduated from college but before going to graduate school. It didn't occur to me at the time that my plans were a bit unrealistic. But isn't that what adolescence is for—to help a youngster decide what and whom she would like to be?"

"Exactly," I said. "You were right on the ball there."

She smiled.

"If I were asked to describe myself as a child in one word, I would say *ambitious*," she said. "I remember one time when I was sitting in a circle on the floor with a group of Girl Scouts, and the leader went around the circle and asked each of us what we wanted to be when we grew up. All the girls said practically the same thing—that they wanted to grow up and become a wife and mommy. When the leader asked me, I said I wanted to become a wife and mother someday, but that wasn't what I wanted to *be*. She was surprised and asked me what I meant. I said I wanted to be an astronaut, and would write to NASA and ask how to prepare. The girls all tittered, but that didn't bother me. I just felt sorry for them. Everyone should have a big dream.

"I did write NASA, and was very angry when they answered they weren't interested in women astronauts. My daddy always said that girls are as good as boys, and should be able to do anything they want to when they grow up. I believed he was right. The rejection hurt badly for a long time. I remember angrily tossing my pigtail and thinking, 'When I grow up, I'm going to see that all women can become anything they want to be.' I'm still working at it."

When Hillary was fourteen years old, an event occurred that was to considerably narrow her choices and change her thinking forever. Betsy's progressive grandfather took her and Hillary to hear Dr. Martin Luther King, Jr. discuss segregation in the North as well as the South. Hillary was shocked to learn that black children were among the poorest and most deprived people in the nation.

King's lecture had a profound influence on her, for she had never known a black person. From then on, her core conviction was that the tragedy of race relations in America had to be changed, and she would do everything she could to improve it. Later, many of her closest friends were black, and Marian Wright Edelman, the Children's Defense Fund founder who hired Hillary as an intern to improve the fate of poor and neglected children, became her professional mentor.

Though she was an early supporter of Martin Luther King, Jr., Hillary still considered herself a Republican like her father. When she was fifteen years old, she became a Goldwater Girl, who searched out registration fraud in Chicago's minority neighborhoods. A privileged adolescent, she was able to see firsthand how multitudes of impoverished African Americans lived. The knowledge shattered her to the core.

"Although I got a lot of pleasure from social activities," Hillary continued, "my relationship with my father was deteriorating badly. His stinginess got more and more on my nerves. For instance, he wouldn't let me take ballroom dancing lessons, although all my friends went to dance class every Friday night, and I've always loved to dance. He said he didn't want me to dance with boys, but I didn't believe him. He didn't object when we spent time playing ball, going to the movies together, or doing anything with boys that didn't cost any money."

"Boys didn't find me too attractive, anyway," Hillary went on. "For one thing, because of my father's stinginess, I dressed very badly, and in addition to wearing those terrible glasses, I had thick ankles and a womanly figure. The boys liked girlish-looking girls. I also had trouble with my hair. I still do. So what else is new? The boys thought I was too bossy and uninterested in sex and behind my back called me 'Sister Frigidaire.' That really upset me."

I thought of that unkind remark when I heard Jay Leno's errant joke on the subject, "I'm surprised that they did a portrait of Hillary. I thought maybe an ice sculpture would have been more appropriate." I hoped she hadn't heard the "joke," or she would have been even more disturbed.

"It troubled me," she continued, "because I hadn't developed much of a thick hide yet. The boys considered me a nerd. Although I was hurt at the time, I must say they were right. I'm still a nerd, although I've learned to disguise it better," she said with a smile.

November 1, 2013

"What I've told you so far about myself as a teenager probably makes me sound like a real goody-goody," she began. "Since you want to know all about me, I decided to tell you that I wasn't always above reproach."

Oh, I thought. *Does that mean she is human after all?* I began to listen with especially rapt attention, but wasn't prepared for the punch in the stomach I felt when she spoke. Apparently, there are more aspects to the personality of Hillary Rodham Clinton than I dreamt of.

"I have a confession to make to you, Doctor, if you promise never to tell Chelsea. You know that when Bill was asked if he smoked marijuana, he said he had, but didn't inhale. Well, my drug history is a lot more checkered than his. During the '60s, I began to explore the social taboos and experiments that characterized the lifestyle of the decade. I guess I was a child of my times, and became known as a 'hippie.'"

What? I could hardly believe my ears and tried to keep my shocked feelings from showing on my face. Whoever would have suspected that Hillary, the good little conscience-ridden Methodist girl, had such a past?

"When I was a teenager," she said, "my rebellion took the form of drugs. I had a friend, Lorraine, who took me to her house after school. She told me how her cousin Jimmy got high by slurping cough syrup. We searched her parents' medicine chest but couldn't find any. We did find a box of Sucrets and each ate three. I sat down and closed my eyes for fifteen minutes, but nothing happened. I decided nothing was going to happen, and prepared to go to the kitchen to eat.

"As I was getting up, the room suddenly began to spin like a merry-go-round, and I got real dizzy and fell on the floor. Lorraine talked so fast I couldn't make out what she said. After a while, I opened my eyes and everything began to slow down, like when you turn off a record player. Finally, it stopped altogether and I was able to catch my breath. I never was so scared in all my life. Still, we decided to take some more the next day.

"After that, we went on a Sucrets jag that lasted until the neighborhood druggist got suspicious and refused to sell us any more. We then tried sniffing Elmer's Glue, but it paled in comparison.

"I wanted to move to Chicago, where you could walk into any store and buy all the Sucrets you could afford. I also wanted to go there so I could meet a handsome boy and take Sucrets with him. At the time, my teachers were assigning us too much homework. Sucrets helped make it all tolerable.

"Despite these yearnings, I managed to stay clean for most of high school. In the fall of my senior year, however, worn out from after-school campaigning for Barry Goldwater, I started sniffing ditto paper to keep myself going. It started as an occasional thing, a last resort on extremely stressful days. Then I began carrying a freshly dittoed sheet around with me, to allow an instant fix whenever I needed it. The next step was to carry a whole sheaf of ditto papers in a manila envelope wherever I went. I guess you could say I became hooked."

"I guess you could say that," I said wryly.

"On the Saturday before Election Day, catastrophe struck. I was caught breaking into the principal's office to replenish my supply of ditto paper. Instead of calling the police, the principal, who admired me as an overall student leader, let me off with a strict warning to change my ways or else. It worked. Something in me was still the obedient scholar. I never sniffed ditto paper again.

"But then I tried Pez for the first time with my friend LaVerne. It taught me that I had just been fooling around with all that other stuff. LaVerne had me lie down on the couch. She pulled Mickey's head way back and a little yellow candy came out and fell in my mouth. I said 'hmm,' and asked if I could have more. LaVerne smiled and shook her head.

"Then I went back home. Mom had made meat loaf and mashed potatoes for dinner. I gulped it down. She was puzzled and said she'd never seen me eat so much or so fast. Afterwards, I was exhausted and went to bed. I hardly had enough strength to say my prayers before I was out like a light. I couldn't wait to see LaVerne the next day.

"With a Midol-No Doz combination that Wellesley girls called a Bloody Mary, I finally found my ideal stimulant. It had all the kick of Pez but none of the morning-after effects. There was no possibility of getting seriously hooked. I would 'trip' only once a month. Finding the Midol was no problem, either, as it was in every girl's medicine chest, and No-Doz could easily be gotten from the Harvard and Amherst boys, who swarmed all over the Wellesley campus every weekend.

"Law school brought a temporary stop to my drug habit. For most of my first two years at Yale, I abstained from drug use, except for the occasional handful of Good 'n' Plenty at an informal gathering in someone's dormitory room. Then, in 1970, I replaced my craving for drugs with an addiction to Bill Clinton.

"I quit Sweet 'n' Low cold turkey, and after a few weeks of Cremora maintenance under medical supervision, started drinking my coffee black, which I do to the present day. Marriage to Bill in 1975, and the obligations of a rising young lawyer and the wife of a prominent politician, sharply reduced my use of drugs. Then in late 1979, after learning of my pregnancy with Chelsea, and in preparation for my new role as mother, I completely stopped chasing kicks." She sighed and looked at me. "Well, Doctor, have I shocked you?" I smiled and was not about to tell her how I felt about it. Hillary is not the only one who can be a prude.

I repeated instead what a wise psychoanalyst had once said— that the drug culture is a sociological illness. Hillary found that very interesting and said, "So *I* wasn't sick. *Society* was sick!"

"You could say that," I answered.

Adolescence is a time when people psychologically move away

from their parents. Apparently, Hillary was so close she had to shut them out completely in order to become an individual. As a result, she apparently abandoned her internalized parents along with her actual ones. This left her with an inner emptiness she tried to fill with drugs.

Then I thought of something Anna Freud once told me. She said nobody could ever tell from observing an adolescent how he or she would turn out as an adult. Anna sure hit the nail on the head with Hillary. She was practically a drug addict. If I had known her then, I wouldn't have bet two cents on her recovery, and just look at her now!

November 6, 2013

"Let's talk about religion today," Hillary said.

From the sewer to the mountain top in one easy step, I thought. I actually preferred to hear more about her drug experiences and inwardly cringed, because I am an atheist. I believe, along with Pope Francis, that it's not the belief in God that counts, but "abiding by one's conscience," as the Pope told atheists in a letter written to the Italian newspaper *La Republica*, in which he responded to a query about whether God forgives "those who don't seek the faith." But of course I didn't tell Hillary any of that and responded to her remark with a simple, "Of course."

"My whole family is very religious," she said. "They walk with God, study with God, and argue with God, as I do—at least most of the time. It's good they never found out about my drug experiences. It would have killed my mother, who was so proud of my morality. She taught Sunday school all her life, and I regularly attended Bible class and belonged to the Altar Guild. When I was around sixteen years old, a very important man came to town: the Methodist Youth Minister, Reverend Don Jones, who remained my number one man until Bill Clinton came along. Don was only twenty-six years old, and didn't seem that much older than me. He had just been discharged from the Navy, and had graduated from Drew University Seminary.

"I had never met anyone like him before. He was very handsome and dashing, as he arrived in his red Chevy Impala convertible, and soon became for me a father, mother, brother, teacher, mentor, shrink, and fantasy lover, all rolled into one. He became the most influential person in my life, my counselor who greatly enlarged my concept of religion, who taught me how to grapple with adversity, and to save my soul by doing good works, which fit right into the philosophy of life I had already formed. He not only advised me on how to cope, but expanded my knowledge of art, literature, and the Gospel.

"One day, he brought us a copy of Picasso's *Guernica*, which frightened me to death and belatedly opened my eyes to the grotesque horrors of war. He taught us about Dostoyevsky, Tolstoy, and Salinger, and was an all-around Renaissance man not averse to playing Bob Dylan records. It was the summer of 1961, that very exciting time when the Freedom Rides were going on in the Deep South. When Martin Luther King, Jr. came to Chicago, Don took our group to hear him speak on 'Sleeping Through the Revolution,' which wove God's messages with matters of conscience."

Sounds like Pope Francis, I thought.

"I still return to his teachings whenever I need to," Hillary continued. "I've been writing to Don for over twenty years now, and he and his wife frequently visited Bill and me at the White House."

I silently chastised myself about cringing when Hillary brought up the subject of religion. Now, I was glad she had done so, for I had not known before just how central it was to her character. Ever since she was a child, she has prayed every night before going to sleep, and prayer has remained an invaluable source of consolation and guidance for her. Religion helped to make her a decent, law-abiding citizen, saw her through her drug addiction, and generally served her well. It explains the strength with which she attacks the forces she opposes, her extraordinary self-discipline, and how she gets herself through terrible times that would sink a weaker person.

She spent the summer between her freshman and sophomore college years working as a researcher for Anthony D'Amato, an ex-Wellesley professor editing a book about the Vietnam War, *The Realities of Vietnam: A Ripon Society Appraisal.* The Ripon Society was a liberal Republican movement which professed to believe that "the country's future would be found not in extremism, but in moderation." It is easy to see how their philosophy would have appealed even then to the young Hillary.

The former professor contributed further to Hillary's education by giving her books to read by Marshall McLuhan and Jesuit polymath Walter J. Ong, both liberal Catholics who appealed to Hillary because of their philosophical resemblance to her Wesleyan orientation. Ong wrote about the creation of "a global village," which would make it possible to stage the kind of electronic town meeting that Bill Clinton would later use to such profound political effect. Hillary believed that Ong's book was one of the most significant she had ever read. I silently wondered if the title of her book, *It Takes a Village*, was inspired by Ong's writing.

When I asked Hillary about her early relationships with men, she told me of her connections with the opposite gender during her high school years. She said that she and her friends of both sexes usually hung out after school at a Main Street luncheonette and went to the movies together on weekends. It was all very innocent. Not many couples "went steady," and most were inexperienced sexually.

"I didn't go in for heavy necking then," she confessed with a blush. "Maybe because not too many boys wanted to neck with me.

"When I got to Wellesley, activities with men were pretty much those from Ivy League colleges," she continued, "and consisted largely of walks on the Boston Common, train rides to Manhattan and New Haven, football games, and attending concerts and museums. We relied mostly on weekend mixers with undergraduate men from New England Ivy League schools, which occasionally led to more serious dating. On weekend nights, we rushed back to our dorms to meet the 1 A.M. curfew. Men were allowed in the Wellesley dorms only on Sundays from 2:00 to 5:30 P.M. The 'two feet rule' was in effect in the dorm rooms; two out of four feet had to be positioned on the floor at all times. I've always liked men," she said, looking directly into my eyes. I wondered what she was trying to tell me that she wasn't saying.

"My first important boyfriend was Geoff Shields," she went on."I met him on a double date at a party at Harvard when I was a freshman. While we were dancing, he whispered in my ear that I was a pretty girl, a great dancer, and interesting to talk to. I was thrilled to hear it—I'd never felt that men considered me good-looking or even interesting. I found it hard to believe that an attractive 'older man'—a jock and an all-state football star—was attracted to me. I wrote letters to him at Harvard that embarrass me now when I remember them. They were passionate, star-struck, and romantic.

"But in person, we mostly talked about politics and how to go about solving the problems of the world. Our dates usually would begin with a party at Winthrop House, where he lived. We would dance, cheek to cheek, to Elvis Presley or the Beatles, but I've always preferred to sit around and discuss politics rather than dance at a party or go to a football game. Football bored me. That's why I always took along a book when we went to a game, which horrified some of the jocks.

"It was a time of intellectual awakening for me. We often got into heated debates about the Vietnam War, civil rights, or racial matters. I admired that he had a black roommate, which was very unusual in those days. We discussed literature, politics, music, and philosophy—especially philosophy. I keenly remember one very heated discussion on whether there's such a thing as absolute morality, or only relative morality. It was good to have a male friend who could keep up with me intellectually. Most of the boys my age couldn't have cared less.

"My parents were very strict with me," she said wistfully, "and refused to give me permission even to stay overnight with a girlfriend, much less travel to New York. 'It's too dangerous!' they said. 'We can't have you running wild there!' If they'd only known about my drug habit! But in my sophomore year, I managed to sneak out from under my parents' wings and took off for a party weekend at Dartmouth. There I met a boy I liked and stayed overnight at Hanover. I was so proud of myself," she said with a smile. "Monday morning, I couldn't drag myself out of bed, even to go to Bible class. Despite my strict moral Methodist conscience, I was beginning to change!"

I grinned and thought, *Good for you, Hillary!*

By her sophomore year, Hillary was already a Wellesley leader, having recruited six classmates to move into a dorm to live with her. They took all their meals together in a stone gazebo, and developed what would later become known as a "sisterhood." Hillary has always wanted to know more about African Americans, and invited a black student to go to church with her. In those days, that was a daring thing to do. Friends chided her for doing what they considered a political stunt and not acting out of a wish for integration. Hillary wasn't so sure.

"I was testing myself as well as the other churchgoers," she said. "In my college class of more than four hundred students, only six were black, and there were no black faculty members at all. Eventually, I was to become a political ally of the black students, but at the time I was just a friend. Unfortunately, I was a not a part of the momentous civil rights events of my generation."

"Although I supported civil rights in my heart," she went on, "I did not join the sit-in kids from SNCC who went to Selma, Alabama because I felt that what they were doing was too extreme. I worked hard to learn all I could about blacks and issues of poverty in a cerebral rather than an experiential manner, because that is my way. Because of my very real concern with race relations, though, I was one of the first Wellesley students to enroll in an urban sociology class, which I found completely absorbing. Race relations remain one of the great interests of my life.

"D'Amato taught me that facts are the only tools for discovering the truth, and that subjective judgments must be ignored. It is the classic male scientific way of perceiving the world, and it makes a lot of sense to me."

His writings and teachings alienated her even further from her intuition and insights. I wasn't surprised when I read that many of her fellow students considered Hillary to be utterly devoid of introspection, and believed that when things went wrong, she always looked elsewhere to find the reasons. As long as she could bury her own problems by seeking to solve the difficulties of the world, she did not have to look into her inner self. She also could be aloof and impatient when people disagreed with her. She revealed little of her inner life to those around her. How could she, when she wasn't in touch with it herself?

When I read the comment in some book or other, little did I know this trait of Hillary's was to become the bane of my existence. How do you teach someone who habitually runs away from pain to look inside of herself? Lord only knows. I'm sure I don't.

There was one big problem that her way of looking at the world caused Hillary: She wasn't always sure who she was. "I wish I could meet her sometime," she said facetiously. "I'm sure I would like her."

"I know you would," I said.

This characteristic didn't seem to make Hillary's classmates admire her any less. She was known to be warm, funny, and a hard worker who knew how to get things done. She was both gracious and generous, and people liked to be around her. A natural born leader, she unselfishly praised others and remembered details of their lives that were important to them.

November 8, 2013

"What should we talk about today?" she asked.

"What's on your mind, Hillary?"

"I'm a person who likes order in my life. I seem to be telling you my life story in chronological order, so I guess I'll just continue that way. Is that okay with you?"

"Certainly."

"When it came time to choosing a college, I knew I wanted to go to a women's school so I wouldn't be distracted by men. I didn't want to spend my precious learning years worrying about whether the guy across the aisle thought I was pretty. I also thought I would like to go to one of the Seven Sisters schools because they were the best place at the time for a woman to get a fine education. I chose Wellesley."

"What made you pick Wellesley?"

She looked pleased at my question. "Oh, a number of things. A high school teacher I admired had gone there and highly recommended it. She said I would have more interesting classes at Wellesley and that the girls were smarter than at the other Sisters schools. Also, I had seen photographs of the college and was struck by its beautiful scenery, rolling green acres, tree-lined horse trails, and the beautiful Lake Waban. It reminded me of a cottage my grandfather built on Lake Winola in the Pocono Mountains twenty miles northwest of Scranton, where I had spent many delightful summers. It helped that the college looked just like the one I had pictured attending in my daydreams.

"But unfortunately, I had never imagined what the other students would be like. It soon became obvious to me that I had chosen a school full of glamorous and sophisticated young women who wore meticulous makeup even to class and dressed in evening gowns for weekend dances. I had arrived with a suitcase full of Peter Pan blouses and pleated skirts my mother had picked out for me, along with knee-high socks and moccasins.

"For a while, I was embarrassed to be seen by the other students and looked down at the ground whenever I passed by any of them, but 'times they were a-changing,' and I soon found out I could compete with them on an intellectual level. So I stopped worrying about my clothes and got down to work.

"Robert Reich, a friend who later became Bill's Secretary of Labor, described me to a mutual friend as wearing bell-bottomed jeans with long, ironed hair and no makeup at all. Not particularly flattering, but it helped that he liked me. We were reformers together. We marched for civil rights and demanded the admission of more black students to the college. We had high hopes of bringing the nation together, but had no idea how naive we were."

Pause.

"It was as a freshman at Wellesley that I first experienced depression."

My ears perked up. "Depression? Why do you think you were depressed, Hillary?"

"I don't know."

"Could it be because you missed your family?"

"I never thought of that, but I suppose that could be true. I had never been away from home alone before, even for a weekend. I called my mother and told her I couldn't cope with Wellesley and wanted to come home. She said in no uncertain terms that she didn't want me to quit, so I stayed. I was better for a while and made some new friends, but in my junior year, it hit me again. Even though I got all A's, was dating a popular Harvard man, and had a close relationship with a seven-year-old black girl I was tutoring, I often overslept, fell asleep in classes, and was convinced my teachers didn't think much of me."

"What did you do to get help for your depression?"

"I corresponded with Don Jones, who remained my counselor, spiritual advisor, and confidante. He convinced me that there would be grace in my life, and I should just carry on. He was right. After a while,

I just got better."

"He was a wise man, Hillary. It is good for you to remember that even the worst depressions eventually get better."

November 11, 2013

Despite her interest in Martin Luther King, Jr. and the Freedom Riders, the '60s pretty much passed Hillary by, except for her love affair with drugs. Although many hundreds of Yale, Harvard, Columbia, and Vassar students participated in the rides and marches, Wellesley women in general were less involved. For Hillary and other scholarly students, it was a time to listen and learn, and to participate politely in politics.

Rather than become a member of off-campus protest groups, she worked to keep matters under control and steered the anti-war movement at Wellesley and the student fury at the murder of Martin Luther King, Jr. away from confrontation with the authorities and school administrators that had swept like a tsunami over many university campuses. She became a leader of the Wellesley Young Republicans Club and, at the end of her freshman year, was elected president.

Nevertheless, she found herself moving away from her father's beliefs and toward the liberal wing of the party. Much to his dismay, *The New York Times* became her favorite newspaper. Hugh, meantime, became more and more antagonistic toward Hillary's views on feminism, equal rights, and the Vietnam War. When she came under the influence of John Wesley, his disciples, and such New Left theoreticians as Karl Oglesby, who later became a leader of the radical Students for a Democratic Society, Hillary found herself moving even farther away from Republican views.

"I was totally opposed to the Vietnam War," she said, "and my deep interest in both children's issues and racial inequality was already apparent when I started tutoring impoverished black children.

"When I brought a black classmate to church services in town, it was to test myself as well as the other churchgoers," she said. "But my father was not happy about any of this, and deeply regretted having allowed me to leave home for college."

Hillary and her Wellesley class were responsible for more changes than any other in the history of the college. When she arrived in 1965, no men were allowed in the dorms on weekdays, and students were not permitted to drive cars on campus. Jeans and slacks were forbidden in the dining room. By the time she was graduated, Wellesley seemed a different college altogether.

"It is hard to believe that so many changes could occur in so short a time, and largely as a result of our activities," she said with a look of wonder on her face. "Black Studies were added to the curriculum, and the number of black students admitted and black faculty members hired increased. Anti-war activities were allowed on campus, slacks and jeans were permitted, and grades were given on a pass-fail basis. I rarely missed a committee meeting, improved the system for returning library books, and developed an important plan to reduce the number of courses required for graduation."

According to her friends, Hillary soon became a pacesetter of unique stature on campus. She was concerned about social matters, pleasant in appearance and personality, and expressed herself clearly. She was a fun-loving person who toiled hard at her studies. Her fellow students revered her. She seemed aware of that and carried that admiration around as part of her identity.

In what little spare time she had, Hillary attempted to save the lives of endangered species. "Believe it or not, I have always been an animal activist," she said. "One day, while walking along the polluted Lake Michigan shore, I came upon hundreds of dead fish, their dead eyes glaring at me, as if to say, 'How can you let us just lie here exposed like this?' Before I could continue my walk in peace, I frantically set about covering them with sand."

While discussing her years at Wellesley, Hillary said, "The most wonderful thing that happened to me at Wellesley is that I was asked to give the first commencement speech ever given by a student at Wellesley. My fellow graduates and I decided that, in this age of student protests, a student should speak at our commencement, or none of us at all would attend.

"To our surprise, President Ruth Adams agreed, as long as she knew that the speaker was to be me. She said in her introduction to my speech that I 'was cheerful, good humored, good company, and a good friend to all of us.' How nice to hear such things said about oneself by the president of one's college! I thought it was a difficult description to live up to, especially the 'good humored' part, but I vowed to certainly try my hardest."

"What was the speech?" I asked, thinking it would give me some hints as to what the twenty-one-year-old Hillary was like.

"I'll bring you a copy of it next session," she answered.

November 13, 2013

Hillary's commencement speech at Wellesley followed an address by Republican Senator Edward Brooke of Massachusetts, at the time the highest-ranking black elected official in America, the only non-Caucasian member of the U.S. Senate, and someone for whose election Hillary had campaigned hard. Yet, the courageous Hillary thrust aside her prepared text and lit into the Senator, who, in her view, had made some bland, dispassionate remarks about empathy.

He had said that while he felt empathy for some of the goals of the anti-war and civil rights protesters, he disapproved of their tactics, which he called "coercive." To Hillary, he appeared to be defending not only the war but President Nixon's manner of prosecuting it. Hillary also thought it strange that Brooke, a black man, had failed to mention the assassinations of Martin Luther King, Jr. and Robert Kennedy, events which had defined the decade thus far.

I read her written speech. "We're not in positions yet of leadership and power, but we do have that indispensable task of criticizing and constructive protest, and I find myself reacting just briefly to some of the things that Senator Brooke said. Part of the problem with empathy with professed goals is that empathy doesn't do anything for us. We've had lots of empathy, we've had lots of sympathy, but we feel that for too long our leaders have used politics as the art of making what appears to be possible impossible. What does it mean to hear that 13.3% of the people in this country are below the poverty line? That's a percentage. We're not interested in social reconstruction; it's *human* reconstruction. How can we talk about percentages and trends?"

She continued with what she and her classmates had been like on arriving four years before. "The question about possible and impossible was one that we brought with us to Wellesley four years ago. We arrived not yet knowing what was not possible. Consequently, we expected a lot. Our attitudes are easily understood, having grown up, having come to consciousness in the first five years of this decade—years dominated by men with dreams, men in the civil rights movement, the Peace Corps, the space program—so we arrived at Wellesley and we found, as all of us have found, that there was a gap between expectation and realities. What we did is often difficult for some people to understand. They ask us quite often: 'Why, if you're dissatisfied, do you stay in a place?' It's almost as though my mother used to say, 'I'll always love you, but there are times when I certainly won't like you.'"

She went on to discuss the changes her class had brought about at Wellesley. "Our love for this place, this particular place, Wellesley College, coupled with our freedom from the burden of an inauthentic reality, allowed us to question basic assumptions underlying our education. Before the days of demonstrations orchestrated mostly for the media, we had our own gatherings over in Founder's Parking Lot.

"We protested against the rigid academic distribution requirement. We worked for a pass-fail system. We worked for saving some of the processes of academic decision making. And luckily, we were in a place where, when we questioned the meaning of a liberal arts education, there were people with enough imagination to respond to that questioning. So we have made progress. We have achieved some of the things that initially we saw as lacking in that gap between expectation and reality.

"Our concerns were not, of course, solely academic, as all of us know. We worried about inside-Wellesley questions of admissions, the kind of people that should be coming to Wellesley, the process for getting them here. We questioned what responsibility we should have both for our lives as individuals and for our lives as members of a collective group."

I found myself thinking how admirable that students themselves could bring about so many changes in their education. How different it was from my college days, when any suggestions made by students were promptly tossed into the nearest waste basket.

Hillary, who had long been overwhelmed with feelings about the disadvantaged people of the world, continued with her wishes for humanity. "Coupled with our concerns for the Wellesley inside here in the community were our concerns for what happened beyond Hathaway House. We wanted to know what relationship Wellesley was going to have to the outer world. One of the other things that we did was the Upward Bound program. There are so many other things that we could talk about; so many attempts, at least the way we saw it, to pull ourselves into the world outside. And I think we've succeeded. There will be an Upward Bound program, just for one example, on the campus this summer."

With her speech, Hillary wanted to describe her new life as an idealistic young woman, "Many of the issues that I've mentioned—those of assuming power and responsibility—have been general concerns on campuses throughout the world. But underlying those concerns, there is a theme, a theme which is so trite and so old, because the words are so familiar. It talks about integrity and trust and respect. We are, all of us, exploring a world that none of us even understands and attempting to create within that uncertainty.

"But there are some things we feel, feelings that our prevailing, acquisitive, and competitive corporate life, including, tragically, the universities, is not the way of life for us. We're searching for a more immediate, ecstatic, and penetrating mode of living. And so our questions, our questions about our institutions, about our colleges, about our churches, about our government, continue. We have seen them heralded across the newspapers. Senator Brooke has suggested some of them this morning. But along with using these words—integrity, trust, and respect—in regard to institutions and leaders, we're perhaps harshest with them in regard to ourselves."

I don't know about the other students, but it was and is certainly true of Hillary.

"Every protest, every dissent, whether it's an individual academic paper, or a Founder's Parking Lot demonstration, is unabashedly an attempt to forge an identity in this particular age," said the still adolescent Hillary, who was much preoccupied with forming her own identity. "That attempt, for many of us over the past four years, has meant coming to terms with our humanness."

(I wondered if she meant that she had forgiven herself for her own transgressions doing drugs.)

"Our perception of reality is that it hovers often between the possibility of disaster and the potential for imaginatively responding to men's needs. There's a very strange conservative strain that goes through a lot of New Left, collegiate protests that I find very intriguing because it harkens back to a lot of the old virtues, to the fulfillment of original ideas," said Hillary, "and it's also a very unique American experience. If the experiment in human living doesn't work in this country, in this age, it's not going to work anywhere.

"But we also know that to be educated, the goal of it must be human liberation—liberation enabling each of us to fulfill our capacity to be free to create within and around ourselves. To be educated to freedom must be evidenced in action, and here again is where we ask ourselves, as we have asked our parents and our teachers, questions about integrity, trust, and respect. Those three words mean different things to all of us.

"For instance, 'Integrity: the courage to be whole, to try to mold an entire person in this particular context, living in relation to one another in the full poetry of existence.' If the only tool we have ultimately to use is our lives, we use it in the way we can by choosing a way to live that will demonstrate the way we feel and the way we know.

"Trust: When I asked the class at our rehearsal what it was they wanted me to say for them, everyone came up to me and said, 'Talk about trust. Talk about the lack of trust both for us and the way we feel about others.' What can you say about it? What can you say about a feeling that permeates a generation and that perhaps is not even understood by those who are distrusted? All they can do is keep trying again and again and again. There's that wonderful line in 'East Coker' by Eliot about there's only the trying, again and again and again, to win again what we've lost before."

That line defines the adult Hillary as well as everything I know about her, I thought. What Hillary wants, Hillary strives for again and again and again.

"And then respect," her speech continued. "There's that mutuality of respect between people where you don't see people as percentage points. Where you don't manipulate people. Where you're not interested in social engineering for people."

Wouldn't it be great to have a president who believed this? I thought.

"The struggle for an integrated life existing in an atmosphere of communal trust and respect is one with desperately important political and social consequences, and the word 'consequences,' of course, catapults us into the future. Fear is always with us, but we just don't have time for it. Not now."

She ended her speech with a wonderful poem written by Nancy Scheibner, but Hillary could have written it herself. The last verse is:

You and I must be free
Not to save the world in a glorious crusade
Not to kill ourselves with a nameless gnawing pain
But to practice with all the skill of our being
The art of making possible.

I thought it was a marvelous speech, particularly when considering that the speaker was only twenty-one years old. I gave Hillary my opinion. She beamed and said, "I'm so happy you think so! While my father was at the graduation, it is one of the great regrets of my life that my mother was ill and unable to attend. I was so disappointed, after all she had done to ensure my success at the college! In some ways, the celebration was as much hers as mine. Your pleasure in my speech makes up a little for her absence."

I was startled. *Is she developing a mother transference to me?* I wondered. I had been unaware of it. In any case, I hope the answer was yes. She could take her analysis to much deeper levels.

Meantime, I thought I had better check my counter-transference, the reaction brought out in a therapist by his or her patient. *Why do I like her so much? I like her because she's likable, that's why. She is smart, she is funny, she is highly knowledgeable, and I learn a lot from her. She is more fun to be with than any other of my patients. Also, she is a celebrity, and I am highly flattered that she wants to come to me. Who says you can't like your patients? What kind of crazy business am I in where it is suspect to like your clients? I'd do better to be a cashier in a supermarket where nobody criticizes you if you laugh with your customers.*

In any event, the whole world, it seems, agreed with my evaluation of Hillary's speech. The editors of *Life Magazine* thought it typified what was happening on campuses all over the country, and featured it along with a photo of Hillary in her Coke-bottomed glasses and striped bell-bottomed pants. Only Hillary was unaware of how unusual her speech was. She was not sure she had said the right things.

When I finished reading Hillary's speech, I was overwhelmed by the depth, intensity, and wisdom of this still adolescent youngster. At her early age, she already was a great woman. No wonder *Life Magazine* featured her. If I had heard the speech at the time she gave it, I would not have been surprised if someone had predicted that one day she would be elected our first woman president.

November 15, 2013

"Well, Doctor," she began, "can I talk about Bill yet? I'm up to where I met him in this saga."

I smiled. "If you are ready," I answered.

"Ha! I've been ready since the minute I stepped in here, but you wouldn't let me."

I smiled again and said, "I doubt if anybody ever *stopped* you from doing anything!"

"Right you are there, Doctor!" She smiled back in agreement. "Okay. If you have anything to say to me, you'd better speak now or forever hold your peace, because once I start on Bill, you probably won't hear anything else from me for a while." I smiled yet again.

"I was sitting in the Yale library, reading Karl Oglesby's *Ravens in the Storm: A Personal History of the 1960s Anti-War Movement*, when I noticed at the next table this handsome guy who looked like a Viking, with his long hair and raggedy beard. He kept staring at me. I couldn't imagine why, as it was a time in my life when I wasn't exactly a cover-girl type. I was wearing bell bottoms, those huge glasses, and driving a beat-up old car with a mattress tied to the roof. I flung my arm in front of my eyes to block out the sight of him so I could continue reading my book without distraction.

"To my disgust, I wasn't able to concentrate. When I put down my arm, he was still staring. *Since I am not able to read anyhow*, I thought, *I better do something about it.* So I marched over to him prepared to say, 'What are ya looking at, Bub? Haven't you ever seen a lady before?' Instead, to my amazement, I reached out my hand, and said, 'You've been staring at me ever since I came in here. Do you want to know my name? It is Hillary Rodham. What's yours?'

"He smiled that gorgeous smile of his, put out his hand, and said, 'I'm Bill Clinton.' But when I went to take back my hand, he wouldn't let it go, but just kept holding it and looking deep into my eyes. We stood there, locked together for several moments, and I felt a shiver of fear run down my spine. Somewhere I sensed that I was hooked for life, and, indeed, from that moment on, we were inseparable."

No wonder she isn't an intuitive person, I thought. *When she does intuit something, it is so deep that it scares her to death. Better not to know something than to be terrified all the time!*

"I looked down at the hand holding mine, and it struck me that it was beautiful." She looked straight at me and said, "You look surprised, Doctor. Why? Don't I look like the kind of person who likes and notices beautiful things? Bill is gorgeous, and I still like to look at him. His wrists are narrow and his long fingers as elegant as those of a surgeon or a pianist. I love watching him turn the pages of a book, and I could watch him do that indefinitely. I'd never met anyone like him."

She continued, "This is not a guy who wastes any time! I sat down next to him without being asked, and right away he began telling me all about himself, the brilliance that had won him a Rhodes scholarship, his loving mother, his dead father, his lonely childhood, his ambitions, his everything. As if to warn me, he said he was going to turn down all the offers from big law firms and return to Arkansas after law school. He said, 'I am going to be governor.' Note that he didn't say he was going to *try* to be governor, but that he was going to *be* governor.

"Later, he told me he had been watching me ever since we both began taking the same class at law school. He said he had never seen me before and was sitting in the back of the class when he first noticed me. He said he was struck by my strength and self-possession and how I always knew the answers to the professor's questions. He said he began following me around the campus. Funny, I wasn't aware of it until he told me."

He told her right away that he liked being around her, and that she never bored him, and very early on in their relationship, he said that he would like to grow old with her.

"I was bewildered," she went on. "Even at the very beginning, fantasies of marrying him buzzed around inside my head—me, Hillary, who's always so controlled and cerebral! In my mind, he had already asked me to marry him, and I was considering the proposal. I realized that if I went along with his plans, it would be like signing up with a minor league baseball team in the hopes of someday being promoted to a major league one.

"On the other hand, if I followed my own star, I would lose him. The situation didn't sound very hopeful. Nevertheless, we sat there talking until the custodian had to throw us out of the library. I have always been ruled by my head, not my heart, but Bill Clinton is a very seductive man. As unlikely as it seems for cool and collected me, I went back to his room with him. Sometimes I think my parents should have tied me down with ropes."

I thought, *Bill supplies the missing part in Hillary. He is all heart, while she is all head. Together they make a complete person.*

"He immediately brought joy and sparkle into my prudish life," she went on, as if she had read my mind. "He turned me into a passionate woman. I became overwhelmed by emotions I couldn't control. The essential question in my life became: 'Should I choose pleasure or self-control?' For the first time in my life, my mother's carpenter tool went skidooing all over the place. I couldn't eat, I couldn't sleep, I couldn't even study. I didn't know what to do. All I was aware of was that we fit each other like a glove. It took three months before we were able to get out of bed.

"I decided to discuss all this with someone. I, who was famous for never talking about my real self to anyone, chose my former boyfriend, David Rupert, who was as clear-headed as anyone I knew, to give me advice.

"'I have a problem, David,' I said. 'I'm madly in love with this guy Bill Clinton who says he's going to be governor of Arkansas. He leaves no doubt in my mind that he *will* be. That's the kind of person he is. I would like to go to Arkansas with him. But then, what about my own ambitions? They are very important to me. I doubt if I could change the world from Arkansas. What should I do, David?'

"He wrinkled his brow and asked only one question, 'Do you love Bill?' Without losing a beat, I answered 'Yes!' He said, 'Then go for it!' I threw my arms around him and gave him a great big wet kiss, which already showed Bill's influence on me. David had said exactly what I wanted to hear.

"In my third year at Yale, Bill and I moved in together. We rented an off-campus, Victorian-style house with a porch surrounded by white pillars. But things were not as settled between us as I originally had thought. Shortly after I moved in, it seems our positions reversed. While I became more and more involved with Bill, he became very ambivalent about our relationship. He never lost sight of his lofty political ambitions. He was worried about being in love with me, he said, because he had to return home to Arkansas to be governor. I was worried, too. I couldn't imagine living in Arkansas, but I couldn't bear the idea of leaving Bill.

"Although I was scheduled to graduate in 1972, I was so besotted with Bill that I lived with him in New Haven for another year until he graduated. I spent the year taking courses in child development at the Yale Child Study Center. I wasn't going for another degree; I just hung around to hang on to Bill Clinton."

November 18, 2013

"A few months before his graduation, we took a trip to Arkansas, ostensibly for him to take the bar exam. He said I should take it too, 'just in case.' I did. We both passed. Although I don't think he knew it at the time, he really took me home to meet his mother. I was weary and dirty from the long drive, wore a babushka over my greasy hair, and had no makeup on when his mother and I met for the first time.

"No greater contrast between two people can be imagined. She was a flamboyant woman who worked hard at being glamorous. She even went to bed wearing makeup because, as she said, it took her so long to put it on. Her eyelids were striped in three different shades of eye shadow, and she had a silver streak dyed down the middle of her hair. To me, she looked like nothing so much as a skunk. I'll never forget the shock that came over her face when she first saw me. By her reaction, you'd have thought her wonderful son had picked up a homeless creature under a bridge somewhere. Maybe she thought he had.

"It wasn't just our looks that were so different. She was known as a pleasure-seeking lady, in major contrast to me. The reception she gave me was chilly and definitely un-Southern. I suspect she never got over that meeting. Neither did I.

"Bill is a great flatterer, and knows just the right words to say to make people feel good. No wonder! He learned at his mother's knee. The first thing she said to him every morning was, 'Nobody ever tells me how cute I am!' He would answer, 'Virginia, you're so cute you're adorable!' Thus he could make sure she would be nice to him for the rest of the day.

"One time, he was off in the clouds somewhere and didn't give Virginia the 'right' answer. She ignored him for hours. But little Billy was a quick learner. He never 'forgot' again. She taught him how to flatter and praise women, a lesson he applied the rest of his life.

"One of my favorite stories about Bill concerns his alcoholic, abusive stepfather Roger, who was very cruel to Virginia, especially when his rages were fueled by jealousy. Once, when Bill was in his early teens, he stepped into a room and saw that his stepfather had thrown Virginia on the floor, yanked off her shoe, and begun to beat her ferociously with it. Bill picked him up by his neck and yelled at the rotten drunk to stop, telling him that if he ever did it again, he'd have to deal with him."

"What a wonderful story, Hillary," I said. "A teenager who stands up to his father figure has resolved his Oedipus Complex and won't be afraid to compete with anybody in the world." Even as a young man, Bill did not hesitate to say he was going to be governor of Arkansas and then be elected president of the United States.

"Bill was his mother's idol, the sole redeeming aspect of her life, the Holy Grail into which she poured all her hopes and dreams," Hillary continued. "He, in turn, nurtured his stepfather and his brother, Roger. Bill was father, brother, and son to the whole family. His mother's adoration felt wonderful, but the burden was suffocating."

I've heard it said that a man marries a younger version of his mother. The person who said that never met Virginia Kelley and Hillary Rodham.

November 20, 2013

Hillary came into her next session still wanting to reminisce about her decision to marry Bill Clinton. She said, "I was madly in love with him but still conflicted about going to live in Arkansas. I couldn't decide if I should pursue my ambitions as an independent woman or take a chance that a partnership with Bill Clinton would take me where I wanted to go. So I decided to discuss it with my friend and mentor, Bernie Nussbaum, a man with a good legal head who would eventually become Bill's close friend and lawyer. I was hoping to get some good advice. I was only twenty-six years old and thought I needed it. Goodness knows I didn't know what to do on my own.

"Our conversation went something like this: 'I'd like you to meet my boyfriend. I think you'd like him.'

"He said, 'Oh? What's his name?'

"I answered, 'Bill Clinton. I met him at Yale Law School.'

"He said, 'Is he going to be one of those big-shot lawyers?'

'No, he isn't,' I said. 'He's going to be a politician. He's going to return to Arkansas and run for Congress right away.'

"'Run for Congress right away?' He looked at me strangely. 'Shouldn't he have a law practice and first get some experience under his belt?'

"I ignored his question and said calmly, 'After he runs for Congress, he's going to be governor of Arkansas. And then he's going to be president of the United States.'

"He looked at me incredulously, as if he couldn't believe what he had just heard. 'Hillary,' he said, 'I know you are in love with the man, but don't you think you're being unrealistic? Who becomes governor, let alone president of the United States, without any legal experience? Have you gone mad? Or, hopefully, has the vodka we drank gone to your head?'

"By now, I was fuming. Bernie knew me well and should have

realized that, vodka or not, I never talked out of the side of my head. I thought, 'Bernie's no help here!' and ripped up my prepared speech and threw the pieces at him. I said, 'Bernie, you're a nincompoop! How can you possibly have an opinion about a man you've never even met?'

"Without waiting for an answer, I got out of the car, slammed the door, and stalked away. Here I had asked for advice from a so-called man of wisdom, but was given a lecture. I was worse off than I'd been before. I decided not to consult any more 'friends.' They were of no help to me at all. When Nancy Bekavac, an old classmate from law school, asked me when I would know if I was going to marry Bill, I snapped, 'I'll know when I know.'"

Hillary continued musing, until it was time to leave. She got up and said, only half-jokingly, "I should have known you then, Doc! You would have believed me."

"I'm honored that you think so," I said.

Hillary put her hand over her heart and took a little bow.

November 22, 2013

She came into my office in a pensive mood and said, "You always seem surprised, Doctor, that I can go on functioning as well as I do when I'm constantly being attacked by the media."

I nodded. "It is a gift, Hillary. I doubt if I could do it."

She said, "To go along with my mother's carpenter tool technique, I learned from Bill how to manage my troubles. He taught me how to compartmentalize my difficulties. He said his mother taught him to banish his problems by locking them up in an airtight little white box. 'When bad things happen, and they will, construct a box in your head that's as strong as steel,' she told her children. 'Keep your secrets locked up inside the box and don't let anyone else open it.'

"He'd been doing that since he was a child, he told me. If he didn't, he wouldn't have been able to do so well when all the kids in school called him 'Fat Cat.' He must have felt the way I did when the kids called me 'Owl Face.' The 'little white box' still rules him. He tells me every day that we can't let people with their own agendas rule our lives or our duties, because they will if you let them."

I was impressed, and said so. "I'll have to get me a little white box, Hillary."

November 25, 2013

Hillary continued with her Billary tales as if no time had elapsed between sessions. "After Bill graduated from Yale, he kept his promise to return to Arkansas and immediately got a job teaching law at a local university in Fayetteville. I missed him terribly and decided I didn't want to spend another night away from him. Unbeknownst to anyone, including Bill, I had quietly begun preparations to move to Arkansas months before, so I already had a teaching job waiting for me at a law school there and a place to live. I made the decision to join him, and immediately started to pack a little suitcase."

"As I was packing, my friend Susan Ehrman wandered in and asked where I was going. I said something like, 'I'm going to Arkansas to marry Bill Clinton.'

"'Does he know it?' she asked.

"'Not yet,' I answered.

"She glanced at my overnight bag and laughed. 'How are you making out with the moving?'

"'Well, I have a minor problem. I don't know how to get all my stuff, like my books, the rest of my clothes, and my bicycle, to Fayetteville.'

"Are you sure that now is the right time to go?'

"'No, I'm not. But I'm going anyway.'

"Susan said: 'I'm against you going, Hillary. I've told you that many times. He's only a country lawyer in a small town. You don't belong there. You're a brilliant woman and could have a wonderful career on your own right here.'

"But *Bill* is there,' I answered.

"She offered to drive me and my stuff to Fayetteville. I guess she hoped to have enough time during the ride to convince me to return to my senses. No matter what she argued—and she is a very persuasive person—she couldn't convince me to change my mind."

I was not surprised.

"'You can just visit him,' she persisted, 'and then turn around and come back home with me, where you belong.'"

"As I'm sure you already know, Doctor, it's not easy to persuade me of anything I don't agree with. Especially about who to marry. But Susan was a good sport about it and retained her cool all the way down to Arkansas. But when we reached the desolate looking outskirts of the town, she broke down in sobs."

As a feminist of another generation, I found myself sympathizing with Susan, and thought that if I had been there, I might have done the same thing.

"I wanted to hook on to a political man, and Bill was that man," Hillary said. "Even before arriving in Fayetteville, I knew I shouldn't live with him, because of the local morés, so I went ahead and rented a room in an old professor's house. Not that I stayed in it very much.

"I frequently dropped by the Clinton Congressional campaign headquarters and was horrified by what I saw. It was run by a bunch of school teachers who were bungling the campaign. I soon took over, and headquarters immediately changed from fun-loving to dour-faced volunteers. They called me 'the drill sergeant,' but since when has name calling had any effect on me? Half of them quit. 'Good,' I thought. 'Maybe we can replace them with a higher quality staff!'

"Despite my arrival in town, I'm sorry to have to tell you that Bill continued the daily flings he was having. When I protested to the campaign manager that the staff was finding women for Bill, he told me that Bill was never going to change, that he needed a different woman every day to function, and that it had nothing to do with me, but it still made me feel awful.

"I must say there were times, the first of many to come, when I thought I had made a terrible mistake coming to Arkansas. But I loved Bill desperately, and decided to hang in there. I thought I could change him after we were married."

Sure, I thought. *And then you can buy the Brooklyn Bridge.*

November 26, 2013

Hillary opened this session with a sigh. "Well, it's time for me to get on with why I'm really here." She hesitated a moment and then proceeded. "Although I loved Bill madly, I hesitated a lot over whether I should marry him. One of the reasons, which you must certainly know about, was that he had and has a terrible reputation of being a womanizer. A so-called friend of Bill's took me aside and told me it was never going to work because I was too decent for Bill and that he'd break my heart. My eyes popped. I hadn't known it was that bad, although many people in Fayetteville said they had seen him around town with other women even after I arrived. Maybe I was looking at his proclivities in small doses, until I was able to see the whole picture without breaking my heart."

Did she learn that from me, or did she intuit it herself? I wondered. Either way, I was pleased. *She is getting more insight,* I thought. *Her treatment is progressing nicely.*

"I usually tried locking up the information in my 'little white box,'" she continued, "but then the next day somebody would blast it open when they said that they, too, had spotted him with another woman, sometimes in a compromising position. I once came across a list of his 'friends' in his desk drawer. I ripped it up into tiny shreds. Of course, you could say I deserved what I found, because I shouldn't have been snooping in the first place!"

I remained silent. I have to say I do not approve of snooping, and when it comes down to it, I can be as puritanical as Hillary. But this was not the time to tell her that.

"I knew the leopard doesn't change its spots," she continued, "but the megalomaniac in me was convinced I could change his behavior after we were married. Other times, I would think maybe it would be worthwhile to be with the man I loved all the time, even with his terrible character flaw. After all, nobody is perfect. In any event, if I did decide to marry him, nobody could say I went in with my eyes shut."

November 27, 2013

"Shall I start today with the good or the bad things about my relationship with Bill?" she asked.

I remained silent. She knew by now that she should talk about whatever she wanted. "Okay, Doctor. First the good things about our relationship," she said, starting in of her own accord. "When things were going well, we were in perfect balance, and still are. I seem to be the motor that energizes his leadership, and he blossomed under my approval. He behaved like I was his Rock of Gibraltar.

"I was his anchor; he was my sail. I was the realist, he the dreamer. I was the strategist, and he the executor of my plans. I'm tough and aggressive. He's gentle and wants people to love him. I have a killer instinct, but I lack his subtlety. He's slow to recognize the malevolence in people, and therefore is often taken advantage of, while I see through people's masks right away. Without me, he never would have become president. I'm very lucky. Bill and I started a conversation over forty years ago and have never stopped talking. He's my best friend, and there isn't anything I can't tell him.

"What I've learned over the years is that there is real glory in a good marriage. The feeling comes from knowing that no matter what trials and tribulations you've been through, you're able to look at your mate and still love what you see. I think Bill feels the same way.

"We long ago rejected the idea that marriage is a fifty-fifty proposition. Instead, Bill and I see it as a hundred percent commitment. Both partners must give their all, and persist through the crises and difficulties that invariably arise in any couple's lives."

"Sounds good," I said. "And now for the bad side of the relationship?"

"We fought all the time," Hillary said. "Any time we weren't making love, we were arguing. First, he and I would throw things at each other—I once threw a heavy ashtray at him and nearly broke his skull—and then each of us would slobber all over the other. 'Oh, darling, my sweetheart, I hope I didn't hurt you. Come give me a kiss!'" she said, pursing her lips.

"Our intellectual exchange was electrifying, but then it would always turn into a fight. And those fights would prove to be exhilarating *and* exhausting for both of us. After a few months of these 'I love you, I hate you' episodes, Bill said he was sick and tired of it all and was through with me. He told our friend Betsy, 'I tried to run her off, but she just wouldn't go.'

"He was right about that, Doctor. No way would I ever let him go! I thought about him night and day. And fights or no fights, nobody in the world mattered nearly as much to me as Bill Clinton. Our friend Max Brantley, editor of the *Arkansas Times*, was asked what he thought about our relationship. He said we really cared about each other, that nobody could fake the chemistry between us. When Max was asked how I handled Bill's promiscuity, he answered that Bill was maybe just a good liar or that I intentionally didn't pay attention, not wanting to face the big picture.

"The fights continue to the present day," she said wearily. "I did all in my power to change him over the years, but character is character, and I never could succeed. I guess he needs love so badly he really can't be good. When I think of how much he needs my love, nothing else matters."

I asked, "Why do you stay with him?"

"Because I love him and don't want to live without him." Her eyes filled with tears. She was genuine.

Even I was affected.

November 29, 2013

"I wanted to get married and 'suggested' it to Bill. His response wasn't much better than my father's when I proposed to him at age five. But at least Bill didn't hit me. He only hurt my feelings.

"But since Bill wasn't too eager to get married, I thought, 'I'll show him!' and decided to play hard-to-get. I went on a job tour of New York, Washington, Chicago, and Boston to see what the large cities had available for me that Arkansas didn't. I was offered an important job in a gold-plated New York firm, and went back to Arkansas to think it over. Should I be a big shot in Arkansas with the man I loved, or small potatoes in New York City?

"Bill was so upset about the possibility of my moving north that he consulted a friend, Jim McDougal, about it, telling him he couldn't get me out of his head and was seriously thinking of marrying me. Jim, who had just begun to date Susan, encouraged Bill to marry me, saying that it's good to be married to someone who's different than you.

"You wouldn't believe how I found out he wanted to marry me," Hillary said next. "I had casually admired a simple wood-and-glass cottage on the way to the airport. When Bill picked me up on my return, he stopped the car at the house.

"'Why are we stopping here?' I asked.

"'You said you liked this house, so I bought it,' he said. 'You'll love it. So I guess you'll have to marry me.'

"Bill has always had exquisite taste—much better than mine. The house was a tiny simple jewel with a back porch overlooking the river and forest. He said, 'Can't you just picture us growing old together and sitting here in rocking chairs overlooking the beautiful river and forest?'

"I loved the house, but not enough to get married. Bill moved in himself, and when the kitchen was overrun by field mice, he put out breadcrumbs for them."

November 30, 2013

"Despite Bill's purchase of the new house, the struggle between my head and my heart continued. I loved Bill passionately, but my lifelong ambition to do some good in the world persisted. I didn't know how much good I could do in Arkansas, and I just couldn't bring myself to take the leap.

"Circumstances came to my aid. Nixon's Watergate scandal was just breaking, to the detriment of the party's ability to find any Republican candidate likely to win a Congressional election in Bill's district, so he began considering running for the office himself. If Nixon were to be investigated by the House Judiciary Committee, impeached by the House, and tried by the Senate, the process would take at least a year. As my stature as a lawyer was soaring, I was offered a job on the impeachment inquiry staff.

"My job would be to collate procedural information about former impeachment proceedings, something that I would be excellent at because of my organizational skills. Then Bill and I could be Washington's new hot young power couple. I liked the idea. We decided to go for it and see what happened.

"One day, about two months after his first marriage proposal, I looked into his beautiful eyes and thought, 'I can't live without this man.' So in the end, like millions of women before me, I married for love. I decided to travel the traditional path of my mother's generation and follow my man. I would be his partner, his manager, his advisor. I would listen to my heart.

"I refused an engagement ring and planned a simple home ceremony in Fayetteville without any fanfare. No wedding invitations were sent out. The wedding was set for October 11, 1975, in the living room of the pretty little house Bill had bought. On the eve of my wedding, my mother asked me what dress I was planning to wear. 'Dress? What dress?' I answered. What I would wear was irrelevant to me.

"What was important was that Bill and I were finally getting married. My mother was horrified and rushed me down to Dillard's, the only store in town that sold wedding gowns. I reached onto a rack and pulled out the first dress I saw, a Jessica McClintock in a Victorian lace style. Without trying it on, I said, 'This will do.' I wore it. I didn't hear any complaints."

December 2, 2013

"At the tender age of thirty-two," she began, "Bill was elected the youngest governor in the history of Arkansas. The constituents idolized us for bringing youth and beauty to the governor's mansion, which, of course, I loved to hear. But my parents were not happy about my marriage and new locale. They would have liked me to marry some rich doctor or lawyer.

"His mother wasn't happy about our union either," Hillary continued, "and made no bones about it. She either complained about me or treated me like an interloper. On one of our visits, Bill told her off. 'Look, Mom,' he said, 'I don't need to be married to a sex goddess or a beauty contest winner. I'm a politician, serving the public, and I need a wife like Hillary who's willing to work alongside me. I wish you'd treat her with a little warmth and respect. You better be happy it's Hillary,' he added, 'because it will be Hillary or nobody at all.'

"All Virginia could answer was, 'I'd like to sit her down on the edge of the bathtub and give her a few lessons on how to put on makeup. She has a pretty face, but you'd never know it to look at her.' To my everlasting gratitude, Bill answered, 'To me, she is beautiful! She has the most beautiful eyes and the biggest heart. Diane is her middle name. It means *gorgeous and loving*. The name fits her perfectly.' At least that's how he said the conversation went.

"I was not interested in being instructed by Virginia, in the bathtub or anywhere else. I was determined to change the world and not to be a 'face girl' who wasted time on her appearance.

"My father wasn't much happier about Bill than Virginia was about me. When I first took him to meet my parents at our cabin on Lake Winola, Hugh made my long-haired and bearded boyfriend sleep out on the porch. Maybe he was afraid Bill had bedbugs. But unlike Virginia, who never accepted her son's choice of a mate, Bill's charm eventually won my father over, as it did everyone else.

"The wedding itself, like my wedding gown, was hastily arranged. It was a short ceremony, and there wasn't a wet eye in the house, because it was as close to an undramatic non-event as I could make it. Nobody there was happy except for Bill and me, and I'm not so sure about me. The climax actually happened afterward when I announced that I was not going to take my husband's last name. Virginia threw a fit, saying, 'I have never heard of such a travesty!' Then she started to cry."

"Why did you want your wedding ceremony to be a non-event?" I asked Hillary.

"I guess I was still ambivalent about the marriage. I thought the papers wouldn't make a big deal about it if it was a nondescript affair, and I could later get out of the marriage easier if I wanted to. I needn't have given it a thought. Despite my parents' apprehensions and Virginia's scorn, we have been married for thirty-eight years and are still going strong."

"Tell me, Hillary, if you had to do it over again, would you make the same decision?"

"In a minute!" she replied, without missing a beat.

"Shortly before I married Bill in 1975, I tried to join the Marines, probably to make a political statement. I was rejected by the Marine recruiter on the grounds that I was 'too old, couldn't see well enough, and was a woman.' I felt just as bad then as when NASA had rejected my childhood application to be an astronaut. Who was it who said, 'The more things change, the more they remain the same?'"

I Googled it. "Jean-Baptiste Alphonse Karr."

December 3, 2013

"I guess I should tell you a little about the Arkansas years," Hillary began.

"Certainly, if that's what *you* want to talk about."

"As you know, I'm a compulsive kind of person, and I don't want to leave out anything important."

I nodded, thinking I would prefer her to speak spontaneously, but that is not Hillary Clinton's way.

"The first year Bill was governor was a special time in our lives," she said. "I had already been recruited by Rose, Nash, Williamson, Carroll, Clay and Giroir, the second largest law firm in Arkansas, and was to be made a partner when I was only thirty-two years old. It was quite a triumph for a woman, especially one so young, because the firm was known for being a corporate power and was associated with old money. Vince Foster, an old friend of Bill's, had recruited me. We became dear friends, although our friendship, as you probably know, was eventually to result in one of the great tragedies of my life. But I'll tell you about that another time."

Of course, I thought. *You'll tell me about it in its proper chronological order.*

"Prestigious as it was, I considered my position at the Rose law firm merely my day job. I worked there mainly because we needed the money—the governor of Arkansas was paid a measly salary. At no time before Bill was elected president was I *not* the major bread winner in the family. My heart, however, was focused on my own agenda, which, as always, was improving the lives of women, children, and the poverty-stricken. I was especially interested in the plight of mistreated and neglected children. I saw a connection between the abuse my mother had suffered as a child and the horrendous things some parents were doing to their kids. I wanted to be the voice of the children of America. By helping them, I symbolically undid my mother's terrible childhood."

I was impressed with Hillary's insight, and thought, *Surprise! We really are getting somewhere!*

She went on, "I set up a legal aid clinic at the university where Bill and I both taught, and I flew back to Washington every few weeks to attend board meetings of the Children's Defense Fund. I also made a lot of money in the stock market, gambling a thousand dollars on risky cattle futures, which earned me an easy $10,000 by the end of the year. Unfortunately, although I had done nothing wrong, the deal was to come back and bite me later on."

I must have looked at Hillary a bit skeptically, because she protested, "You probably read about that, Doctor, but I swear to you I was strictly honest and was just lucky enough to fall into a windfall."

I nodded. *Who am I not to believe her? As far as I know, she has been scrupulously honest with me thus far.*

"My pet project as First Lady of Arkansas was educational reform, which became the signature accomplishment of the Clinton governorship. While teaching law at the state university, I was upset by the substandard education being made available to Arkansans. The students needed far better than they were getting if they were to make any kind of decent life for themselves. I insisted that they be given a greater variety of subjects, broader exposure to the arts and sciences, and many more internships. Eventually, every single one of my recommendations was adopted. Then I launched a summer program for gifted high school juniors, which was modeled on the University of Life program at which I had met Martin Luther King, Jr., and was instrumental in helping me shape my life goals. Several students have since contacted me to thank me and to tell me how much the program influenced their lives for the better. It feels good. I remember thinking that if I never accomplished anything else, I had earned my place on earth."

She beamed. I smiled too and congratulated her.

"I also was appointed by Bill to serve as the head of his health care advisory committee," she continued. "He had run into trouble during his first term when he appointed an out-of-state health commissioner who proposed that nurse practitioners be allowed to serve as doctors in areas of the state where there were few physicians. The state medical society created an uproar when they learned that their high Medicaid profits were about to be devoured by lay practitioners. Bill appointed me to solve the problem of delivering health care to the poorest counties in the state without taking a bite out of the doctors' pockets. I used my Washington contacts—you scratch my back, I'll scratch yours— to obtain federal money to pay for rural health care in Arkansas. It worked. Four rural clinics immediately opened, construction began on three others, and midwives and nurse practitioners were permitted to practice.

"When I feel low, I think of the good things I was able to bring about for the people of Arkansas, and I feel better."

"You have every right to feel proud of yourself," I said. "It seems as if you contributed a great deal at an early age."

A look of pleasure lit up her face. Even a First Lady needs a compliment now and then. "I began to get a national reputation as a social reformer," she said after taking a moment to savor the praise. "President Jimmy Carter heard about me and appointed me to the independent Legal Services Corporation, a national group of politically active lawyers whose job was to distribute money to programs that provided legal help to the poor. I soon was elected to chair the board. One thing led to another, if you will excuse the cliché, and my appointment to deal with the impeachment of our obnoxious president, Richard Nixon, came through. I won't go into it deeply, except to say that I loathed him at the time. I thought he was an evil man, and I had no doubt that he should be impeached. It will always be a source of pleasure to me that I managed to help in that regard."

I didn't say so, but I was delighted to hear it. Besides being a psychoanalyst, I am a human being who also happens to despise Nixon and surely can be excused for my all-too-human reaction.

December 4, 2013

"In his first term as governor of Arkansas," Hillary told me, "Bill proposed modest reforms in education and pollution control, but unfortunately, his biggest initiative, a highway construction and improvement program, was very expensive, and made Bill extremely unpopular among truck drivers, timber company owners, garden-variety motorists, and others, because, to pay for it all, he had to raise auto license fees, and the anger over that cost him the next election.

"As governor that first term, he also experienced several instances of pure bad luck, including rioting among Cuban refugees temporarily interned by the federal government at Fort Chaffee, Arkansas. Unfortunately for us, the voters elected Frank White, a politically unknown Republican savings and loan executive who didn't measure up to Bill's little toe. My husband thus became the youngest *former* governor in American history.

"The two-year span between Bill's governorships was one of the most miserable periods of our lives. When Bill is miserable, everybody is miserable, especially me. The biggest baby in my life is not Chelsea. He moans and groans and cries until I can't stand to be near him. It was at that time that I also became depressed and decided to bow out of his political life for a while. I withdrew, and spent lots of time reading in bed, working out at the YWCA, and blasting out in anger at whoever annoyed me, which was practically anyone around. You haven't seen it yet, Doctor, but when I get mad, my rebukes sting, and people tell me they never get over it."

"Is that a warning?" I asked. "If so, you don't scare me."

She smiled and continued, "To tell you the truth, the fact that I had refused to change my name to Clinton annoyed many a conservative Arkansan and was partly responsible for Bill's re-election defeat. I still don't understand why they chose to so express their disgruntlement with me, but I decided that much as I hated to give in to their prejudice, I'd better change my name to Clinton when Bill ran again, for I knew he certainly would run again. Another problem that bugged them was the way I dressed."

I looked at her in surprise and said, "You look lovely to me, Hillary."

"Thank you," she answered, but you should have seen me then! I had long stringy hair, went without makeup, still wore those awful glasses, and as often as not wore jeans and great big fisherman sweaters. One time during Bill's first term as governor, I even went dressed that way to a fancy ball, where all the other women were decked out in designer gowns. Boy, did I get dirty looks! I could practically hear them saying, 'Can you imagine? *That creature* is our governor's wife!' But can you imagine not voting for a man for governor because his wife didn't wear makeup or dressed differently? How shallow can you get?"

"Why did you dress like that? Surely a woman as intelligent as you could have figured out how to dress properly."

"It has nothing to do with intelligence. You should know that, Doctor. As I told you, I didn't want to become known as a 'face girl' who wasted her time on appearances. My last name broadcast that I was still me. Where other women worked on changing their looks, I wanted to change the world. So I deliberately dressed like a pseudo-hippie. I am *me*, and if people won't accept me as I am, I don't need them." She gave me a look that could kill, which clearly said, "And that includes you!"

She quickly realized that I certainly accepted her for who she was, and proceeded with the session. "I soon found that for those who were angry about the Clinton administration in Arkansas, I had become a lightning rod. When I was told I was an eyesore that might cost Bill the next election, I decided I didn't want that on my conscience and did something about it. I researched current styles at the library, much as I did my lawyering work. Although I hate to admit it," she said almost shyly, "I do enjoy looking nice.

"I secretly felt I had contributed to Bill's defeat, and we lashed out at each other continuously. I blamed him for his unfocused agenda, the tax and fee increases, and giving in to President Carter's pressure to dump the Cuban refugees in our backyard.

"Bill was bleeding from his loss. It's a moot question who was more devastated by it, he or I. The press continued to drag us over the coals, and Bill refused to be interviewed by them. I was worried that he was losing it. He would walk up and down the corridors of supermarkets, asking customers where he had gone wrong, and read everything he could get his hands on to find out the answer.

"Although close to being destroyed by his defeat, Bill eventually went to work for a Little Rock law firm where he spent most of his time campaigning for reelection. He boyishly admitted his mistakes as only Bill can do, so the voters fell in love with him all over again. How can anyone resist Bill Clinton when he turns on all his charm? Just ask me. I know! He used TV ads brilliantly to convince people to give him another chance. He promised major strides in education and avoided saying he would raise taxes.

"It worked. He not only won in 1982, but again in 1984, and for two four-year terms in 1986 and 1990. He kept his promises to the best of his ability and did a lot of good for the state. During Bill's tenure as governor, for example, the Arkansas Board of Education adopted stiff new accreditation standards.

"By this time, the two of us were beginning to be seen as a package deal. Our promise to improve the lives of Arkansans did much to bring about his repeated re-elections. He strongly pushed for educational reform. My biggest job as the wife of the governor was to head some of his more important study commissions. It was a job I loved. One of his important proposals called for competence tests for all teachers, a policy that succeeded in stirring up a national furor. Our sweeping education reforms changed Arkansas schools forever, causing a decrease in the dropout rate and an increase in college entrance exam test scores. I will always be proud that I helped to raise the educational level of the people of Arkansas.

"I also helped to form policy and to review candidates for Bill's staff. Pretty soon, it became impossible for even his staff to know which one of us had originated an idea. The 'two for the price of one' era had begun.

"But that is not all we accomplished during Bill's terms as governor. Our welfare reforms pushed recipients out into the workforce after two years, rather than permitting them unending, open-ended periods of welfare assistance. Bill believes in extending a 'hand up,' and opposes carrying around an able-bodied adult on our backs forever. He's a man who is genuinely without racial prejudice rather than one performing lip service to win votes.

"With my backing, of course, Bill also promoted affirmative action. He appointed more African Americans to commissions, state boards, and important agency posts than all of his predecessors combined. Bill is a highly creative man. He originated a style of government that resembled a permanent election campaign. He advocated legislative agendas based upon public opinion polls, and then built support for our policies through sales campaigns that used every public relations strategy available to pressure state lawmakers.

"I'm proud of what my husband and I accomplished for the people of Arkansas. My goal in life is to improve the lives of humanity. Thus I can safely say that being the First Lady of Arkansas helped me toward achieving my lifetime goal.

"But even at its best, my life with Bill Clinton wasn't all good," she observed. "All during his first governorship, rumors reached me of Bill's dallying with what I'll call floozies. He loved being on the road and out of my sight, where he could carry on as much as he pleased, which was plenty—women were drawn to him like flies to fly paper.

"I soon became not only suspicious of his every move, but infuriated with him. Even though I had known what I was getting into when I agreed to marry him, I was as hurt by each of his new women as I was by the first of the lot. I learned to live in a state of quiet humiliation. But I loved this man-child and was determined to stay with him whatever the cost. Besides, there was always the hope that he would settle down and realize that he loved only me . . . which is true."

At the end of the hour, our eyes met as she got up to leave. She saw the look of admiration and respect in mine and returned it in kind. We gazed at each other for a long moment before she turned the doorknob.

I thought, *What a lucky psychoanalyst I am! Not only am I analyzing the former First Lady of the United States, but she actually is doing quite well.* That night, I locked the office door and strode home wearing a smile.

December 5, 2013

"After the 1980 election, I first realized how weak my husband is," Hillary began. "I discovered that this handsome, virile, brilliant man was a little boy at heart who still cries for his mommy. Do you agree, Doctor?"

"Absolutely. Jung talks about the eternal boy archetype, who is stuck at an adolescent stage of development and greatly depends on his mother. These men are seductive toward everyone, women as well as men. Everybody must love them, or they can't love themselves. This eternal youth often brings about fateful crises, in which the man turns to a powerful woman to rescue him."

"Sounds like Jung knew Bill," she quipped. "Bill himself says that he was born at age sixteen, and will always feel that's how old he is."

"How old does he think you are?"

"He says I was born at forty, and that's how old I will always be." We both laughed.

She became serious. "You're the doctor," she said. "Tell me what to do about my sixteen-year-old husband."

"I wish I knew, Hillary. I can only suggest encouraging him to begin psychoanalysis. That *might* help. But with a man like Bill, who is so successful in life despite his weaknesses, there are no guarantees."

"Psychoanalysis, Doctor? You must be kidding. I'm lucky if I can get him to brush his teeth." She sighed. "I knew I would have to teach him how to fight, and that if I couldn't, nobody could. He has no boundaries and is gregarious to a fault. He is too idealistic, and lacks self-discipline and toughness, to put it mildly. He may be ambitious, but he is very laid back. He never could have gotten up the steam to campaign for governor if I hadn't taken control. He needs a hard-as-nails manager. I don't have to tell you, Doctor, that I am hard where he is soft. So in 1981, I became the back seat driver of our joint political careers.

"Bit by bit, inch by inch, I began to put Bill's shattered political career back together again. To do so, I had to ask myself first if I was willing to put aside my own career temporarily. I decided that yes, there were certain advantages to doing so. I have always known I am a political leader. But I was still stinging from the vicious attacks of politicians and journalists, and I wasn't even the one running for election! With Bill, I could vicariously live the leadership part of my identity without subjecting myself to the slings and arrows of nasty politicians. I thought, 'Let Bill have the darts thrown at *him* for a change, and allow me to recover my self-esteem in peace!'

"On February 27, 1982, I stood next to my husband as he announced his candidacy for the 1982 gubernatorial election. After deciding that I would stop at nothing to become Bill's political doppelganger, I became a changed woman. I was now Mrs. Bill Clinton. It was a calculated change. I had my hair lightened, exchanged my Coke bottle glasses for contact lenses, and wore a silk, form-fitting print-dress in which I tried to look like a fashion maven so the constituents would stop bugging me about my appearance. I steeled myself never to look back.

"When a reporter asked Bill why I had to change my name, he relinquished the podium, letting me speak for myself. I told them that I didn't have to change my name. I used my maiden name for my law practice, but since I was taking a leave of absence from the firm and helping Bill campaign, it was expedient to use his name."

"Have you ever regretted changing your name?" I asked.

She hesitated a moment and then said, "Returning Bill to office and working on education and health care were more important to me than retaining my maiden name. It was a deal. I would take his name in exchange for his promise to take me to the White House, where I would serve as co-president." Tears filled her eyes. "But I must confess that sometimes when I hear the name Mrs. Bill Clinton, I think 'Mrs. Who?' I get a little homesick for Hillary Rodham. But I suppose she's waiting patiently inside me, and I can always pull her out when necessary, such as if I ever get a divorce."

"Have you ever considered divorcing Bill?" I asked. "Nobody would blame you if you did."

"Yes, I have, many times. Whenever I feel humiliated by Bill's escapades, it helps me to think I can always divorce him. It would serve him right. My feelings about divorce and its effects on children, however, are like my mother's. She felt, and I agree, that it is necessary to put the interests of the entire family before that of one person."

Hillary got up to leave, and then turned her head and added, "Then, too, I realize how much I love him, and that I need him as much as he needs me, and I vow to put up with his affairs and stick it out a little longer."

I nodded compassionately and watched her walk dejectedly out the door.

Poor woman, I thought. *First Lady or not, I would never, ever trade places with her.*

December 6, 2013

"I want to talk today about the balance of power between Bill and me," she began.

I looked up with interest and said, "Of course." To tell the truth, I had been getting a bit bored with the story of the Clintons' Arkansas adventures and welcomed the idea of Hillary talking more about their relationship.

"1982 marked the beginning of the Rodham Regency. If you will excuse my lack of humility, I really ran the government in Arkansas, feeling much as a European regency does when a sovereign is too young to rule. There wasn't a single major political decision Bill made without consulting me. After all, didn't we agree, using Jung's analysis, that Bill was the eternal boy archetype who's stuck at an adolescent stage of development and greatly depends on his mother? In this case, the mother was me.

"I sat in on all of his strategy sessions; I was the major breadwinner. I campaigned for him; I gave him many of his best ideas. I kept him on the straight and narrow as much as one could say that he kept to it. I cleaned up his messes, which easily could have knocked him out of office. I acted as his conscience. It was as if I perched on his shoulder like Jiminy Cricket, keeping him on the path he had promised his constituents.

"There were lots of times he would have preferred to go home and read a book or watch a football game, but I always had a list of things that needed to be done. Sometimes he would protest and say, 'Why can't you just be a nice little wifey and let me alone?' But he always gave in and did what I thought he should, because that is what he really needed to become Bill Clinton. Most important of all, I gave him a perfect child. But I will have to devote many later sessions to talking about Chelsea, the love of my life.

"I must confess that some of my absolute power over Bill was based on his sense of guilt about his philandering. He knew I could leave him at any moment if his womanizing upset me enough, and he knew that he couldn't function without me, so he gave me any job I wanted in his government to keep me happy. It was a kind of a bargain; he kept his women and I controlled the reins of our relationship. Not the best situation for a happy marriage, but for us it seemed to work."

She looked suspiciously into my eyes. "You disapprove, Doctor," she said angrily. "It is written all over your face."

I was devastated that my feelings showed so blatantly and tried to rescue the situation. "I am not here to judge you, Hillary," I said, "but to help you understand yourself."

That seemed to soothe her enough for her to continue talking to me.

December 7, 2013

"I mentioned last time the balance of power between Bill and me," Hillary began. "It goes up and down like a see-saw. The downside happened after Bill's victory in 1986, which changed the relationship between us. The legislature had passed a four-year term of office for future governors, so Bill would not have to run again until 1990. He was carried away with himself, as only Bill Clinton can be. He had defeated his rival, was now serving a four-year term of office, earning a decent salary for the first time, and acting like the Pharaoh of Egypt. He no longer felt he needed me to rescue him, and he made it clear that I was not welcome any longer at his strategy meetings, so I stopped attending them. The power I had enjoyed during the Rodham Regency had fizzled away.

"I was very depressed. But Bill still needed my financial help—in 1991, I was earning $175,000 a year at the law firm, in contrast to his annual salary of $35,000. I also kept up my self-esteem by chairing the Children's Defense Fund and serving on the boards of a dozen organizations for social justice and education. Although my spirits were low for a while, I knew Bill, and I knew that if I waited patiently, the time would come when he would desperately need my help again.

"That happened sooner than I expected. After his triumph in the fall of 1986, Bill began to think seriously about running for president. I had dreamt of being First Lady ever since I was a little girl, and in spite of my anger at his treatment of me, I decided to throw my whole weight behind getting us to the White House. I was thrilled when my old friend Don Jones introduced me to his religious class as 'the future First Lady of the United States, because her husband will soon be running for president.' It was the first time I had been introduced in this manner in public, and it intensified my desire to the point where I decided to work night and day to put us there.

"I flew into New York to visit my old friend on the Watergate

Committee, Bernie Nussbaum, to talk to him about it. I told him not to commit to any other candidate because Bill might run. He laughed and said Bill was too young to be president. I smiled knowingly and answered, 'He who laughs last laughs best.' Bill had called a press conference to announce his plans to run for president. Everything was set for a private luncheon at noon on July fifteenth in the Excelsior Hotel ballroom. But go figure my husband! You never can tell what he will come up with next.

"Reporters were anticipating confirmation that Bill was announcing his candidacy, but the lunch soup got cold while everyone waited for him. Finally, he came into the ballroom and said with a grimace, 'I'm not running!' Everyone was shocked. He mumbled something about the conflict between his head and his heart. What could possibly have happened for Bill to change his mind at the last minute about something he had wanted all his life? It was a mystery to everyone, especially me.

"I spoke to Betsy Wright the next day. She was his Chief of Staff, and she clarified the issue. She had compiled a list of over one hundred women with whom Bill had had sex. They discussed each woman, how many times they'd had sex, where they were now, and how likely they were to talk publicly about the affairs. When they finished, Betsy told Bill that he absolutely could not run for president, that he would destroy himself if his sordid outside-our-marriage record became public. At first, Bill resisted. He protested that not many people knew about his affairs, and he wanted to proceed as planned.

"Betsy screamed at him, saying it would demolish me and ruin his relationship with Chelsea forever. According to Betsy, Bill sulked, and then promised her that he would drop his plans to run for president. He discussed the situation with his friend, Carl Wagner, who echoed Betsy's thinking that it would decimate his family.

"Apparently, Betsy and Carl convinced him. Bill stepped to the podium and announced that although it was his dream to run for president, it would be too hard on Chelsea if he and I were on the road for long stretches of time. He said he was sorry to disappoint everyone, but he had to be faithful to his family and his responsibilities.

"I was shocked, furious, and devastated. Tears surged down my face faster than I could mop them up. In fact, there wasn't a dry eye in the house, including Bill's. That night, as we lay back-to-back in bed, we both sobbed aloud, doubting that our shared lifelong dream—to occupy the White House—would ever come to pass."

December 9, 2013

"After Bill punctured our mutual dream, we both believed that he was going nowhere, and were deeply depressed. I felt I was even losing my identity as First Lady of Arkansas. Fortunately, not everybody agreed with me. One day, I was visiting a museum in Washington, thinking that if I didn't know who I was, no one else would either, and I could fade anonymously into the works of art. Suddenly, a woman came up to me and said, 'You sure look like Hillary Clinton.'

"'So I'm told,' I answered.

"Bored and restless, brooding night and day about his lost dreams, Bill practically ignored his governorship. He sought escape in the arms of willing women who for a little while made him feel important again. As a result, his marital indiscretions became more frequent and obvious. I tried to ignore the rumors, knowing I was his true love, and thinking at my better moments that, at this low point in our lives, anything that alleviated his misery was fair game. His sources were ecumenical and included a former Miss Arkansas and Miss America, a childhood friend, a municipal judge, a beautiful black TV anchor, the wife of a prominent judge, a staff member in Bill's office, and even a woman who sold cosmetics at a Little Rock department store. It didn't seem to matter to him what class the woman came from, as long as she had open arms and open legs.

"The most important of his paramours, Gennifer Flowers, surfaced at this time, seeking fame by claiming that she had carried on a longtime affair with the governor. She ended up on a list of his alleged lovers in a 1990 lawsuit intended to remove Bill from the presidential race. Betsy Wright came to Bill's rescue and had Flowers run out of town. She smugly refused to tell us what method she had used, but it was enough to know that it had worked, although the name of Gennifer Flowers sullied Bill's reputation later and for many years to come.

"Difficult as it was for me to tolerate his philandering, worse was yet to come. I had always known that Bill loved only me, and that his series of mostly one-night stands was emotionally meaningless to him. Then he had an affair that was different from all the others and shattered my soul; Bill fell in love with another woman."

As if she felt feverish, Hillary lifted her hand to her brow. She looked at her hand and seemed surprised to find there was no sweat on it.

She shook her head in despair and continued. "She was a tall, slim, blonde divorcée of about my age named Marilyn Jo Denton Jenkins, who had the seductive voice of a small-town Southern woman. I first saw her turning up at all of Bill's receptions and fundraisers and wondered for a while what she was doing there. Knowing Bill's habits, that wasn't too difficult to figure out. I was able to obtain Bill's phone records, and there were an incredible number of calls made daily to the same unlisted number.

"What hurt me the most was that on the same day he had made one brief three-minute call to me, he had spoken with Marilyn at 1:00 A.M. for a full ninety-four minutes! He told Danny Ferguson, a trusted state trooper, that it was tough to be in love with two women. Maybe it *was* tough for Bill, but I assure you the situation wasn't nearly as tough on him as it was on me.

"I asked Danny what he thought her attraction was for Bill. The trooper answered without missing a beat with something like: 'Everybody always wants something from Bill.' Then he dared to add, 'You asked me, so I'll tell you. Even *you* want something from him. You want him to be president. Marilyn apparently wants nothing but his company. Bill seems to glory in being loved for nothing but what he is.' Just what I needed to hear—that it was my fault that Bill loved another woman! I was so depressed I went to bed for a week.

"Bill is a narcissistic man, and rarely lavishes his love upon me. He really is emotionally unavailable most of the time and lives on campaign flattery and casual affairs. When I became furious with him, as I did during the Jenkins affair, he showed me some physical warmth and intimacy. At such times, he also awards me political benefits, usually giving me any job I want. I have what I consider an unusual ability; I know how to separate the personal from long-term goals. I am able to get mad at him and then sort that through in a matter of hours. I invariably end by realizing that I love him in spite of his behavior.

"And, at that time, I could offer Bill what no other woman could; I could neutralize the transgressions that had kept him from running for president. But the one thing I would not condone was Bill maintaining a meaningful, ongoing relationship with another woman. I told him he would have to give up Marilyn and realize how desperately he needed me, or I would divorce him. If he agreed, we could rededicate ourselves to the marriage and to capturing the presidency. Bill consented to my terms and promised to work on straightening himself out. We made a commitment to work on our relationship and save our marriage.

"And that was the end of Marilyn Jo Denton Jenkins, to the best of my knowledge, anyway."

December 10, 2013

"When Bill won his sixth term as governor, I had mixed feelings. I was sick and tired of being an Arkansan, and yearned for bigger things for us. I was sitting next to Skip Rutherford, a political junkie like me, and watching Chelsea cover third base, when he said he thought George Bush would be re-elected. I responded that I wasn't so sure about that.

"I *was* sure, but I wasn't about to tell Skip why I was so sure.

"In May 1991, Bill delivered perhaps the most important speech of his life. He was the keynoter at the DLC National Convention in Cleveland. He and I had worked all night on laying out the plans that would become the distinguishing characteristics of the new Democratic party. We were bound together again by what we both love most: the wish to change the world for the better. Before speaking, Bill wrote down three words on a small piece of paper: opportunity, responsibility, community. He proceeded to spontaneously deliver a passionate speech to a thunderously applauding audience. Nobody can orate as well as Bill when he speaks from the heart. They ate it up.

"Bill was talking to his friend Max Brantley when Max asked him if he was going to run for president. Bill answered, 'Hillary wants me to run.' 'Well,' Max said, 'I guess that means you will run.' Bill smiled and didn't deny it.

"As I said, I was sick and tired of being a governor's wife, and needed something bigger. I wanted to make my platform national. I was sitting up in bed early one morning and looking at Bill, who was still snoring away. I nudged him and said he had to do it.

"He yawned and said, 'Do what? You mean run for president? Hillary, do you know how tough that will be?'

"'I know,' I said. 'I'm ready.'

"But there still was the matter of Bill's infidelities to take care of before we could proceed. Unfortunately, Gennifer Flowers seized that moment to accept $100,000 from the *Star* tabloid to tell her disgusting tale of what she said was her twelve-year affair with Bill. The headline screamed out, 'They made love all over her apartment!' She spoke about Bill as being a wildly successful lover but not especially well-endowed. I felt as though I had been punched in the stomach, but decided it would be better not to come to Bill's defense. There was no Betsy Wright this time to tar and feather Flowers and chase her out of town.

"Bill and I talked it over and decided that the best thing would be for him to confess publicly that there had been some infidelities in his past, and that he regretted them very deeply. We felt this would serve as a kind of public immunization.

"My close friend, New York lawyer Susan Thomases, flew in to advise Bill not to deny having had an affair with Flowers. Polls showed that nineteen percent of voters would have reservations about voting for a man who had been unfaithful in his marriage, but that those numbers would lessen considerably if his wife accepted him in spite of his indiscretions. Who better than Bill's poised, brilliant, blond, Wellesley- and Yale Law-trained wife to say so?

"During a TV interview on *60 Minutes,* Bill acknowledged he had done wrong and caused me pain. He regretted his actions and apologized, promising it would never happen again. He said we'd still be together thirty or forty more years, whether he ran for president or not. It was a great performance! Bill missed his calling. He should have been an actor.

"Then the interviewer asked for specific details of his affairs. I quickly jumped in and said that he didn't have to be more specific. It was a private part of our lives.

"Betsy Wright gave me a score of one hundred for my remarks, and said I had shown that I was not a victim of Bill's behavior. And, as a result, we would be able to move on." Hillary smiled and said, "I have to tell you, Doctor, that I was pretty proud of myself, too. Even though my heart was breaking, I was able to do the right thing and make it possible for Bill to get elected president of the United States. There are many ways for a woman to show love for her mate. One is slaving over a hot stove to cook his favorite dishes.

"Another is going out with him until late at night when her aching bones are crying out, 'I just want to go to bed.'

"And a third way is to give parties for his colleagues when she hates to entertain. I stand behind Bill unconditionally even when I disapprove of his actions, to help bring about what we both want more than anything in the world. As my mother used to say when we misbehaved, and as I say to my child-husband, 'I don't like what you are doing, but I will always love you anyhow.'"

What did I, the analyst, think about Hillary's philosophy of love? Most of my colleagues would call her an enabler, that by seemingly condoning his behavior, she was giving him permission to continue it. I couldn't predict how I would feel about it in the future, but at that moment I could only look at her with admiration and think that Bill Clinton was indeed a very lucky man.

December 11, 2013

Hillary's pleasure in immunizing Bill from all allegations of marital infidelity didn't last long. She opened her next session with, "Do you know this line from Shakespeare, Doctor? 'When troubles come, they come not in single spies but in battalions.' Well, it certainly describes the life of the Clintons."

I said, "Oh? I'm sorry to hear it, Hillary. What happened?"

"We no sooner had put the matter of Bill's infidelities to rest than *The New York Times* began to pick on me. They called me unethical because, at the Rose law firm, I represented legal clients who had dealings with the state. The reporter, Jeff Gerth, also doubted whether Bill and I had the right to do business with Jim and Susan McDougal, whose savings and loan was regulated by the state. Our partnership with the McDougals involved the Whitewater real estate investment, and opened up a whole new can of worms you probably have read about.

"As you know, I am a very private person, and my integrity is very important to me. From early childhood, I have thought of myself as a virtuous person who is morally beyond reproach. I can think of no greater insult than to have my ethics questioned. My very character was under attack by a Washington society that seemed totally bereft of anything decent or principled.

"I believed that the clients I chose to represent, and what I did with my investments, was nobody's business but my own, so I refused to answer Gerth's questions. They said that I was being arrogant, regarding myself as beyond the sphere of questioning. The gist of the furor was that, if I had nothing to hide, I would have answered Gerth's questions, instead of adopting what has become known as the 'Fuck you, Jeff Gerth' strategy.

"It was speculated by White House appointee Lanny Davis that the whole chain of events which led to the Whitewater investigation, which led to the appointment of special prosecutor Ken Starr, which led to the investigation of Monica Lewinsky, which led finally to Bill's impeachment, can be traced back to Jeff Gerth's article in *The New York Times.*"

"Wouldn't you know," she cried, "that I would be blamed for Bill's impeachment? He took his fun wherever he could, and I always rescued him, and yet I am the one blamed for the whole mess! Most people in this town have no pain threshold. No one can say that about Hillary Clinton, though most people don't believe it. They call me ruthless but have no idea of all the sleepless nights when I toss in pain. I ask you, Doctor, is that fair? I repeat, is it fair?"

I felt sorry for this illustrious woman, who has been treated so vengefully by both the Republicans and the press. I said, "I agree with you, Hillary. It is rare to find anyone in this life who has gotten what he or she deserves."

She looked at me inquisitively and asked, "Not even you, Doctor?"

I smiled. "Not even I, Hillary." She grinned and wiped away her tears.

"After a while, things picked up a bit, as they usually do," she said. "It's a good thing they did, or I don't know where I'd be today. The voters of New Hampshire were touched by Bill's extra-marital confessions, not only forgiving these indiscretions but apparently even my zest for privacy, and in the end, we did well enough to stay in the race.

"In the presidential primaries, he fought his opponents to a tie in Colorado and moved on to decisive victories in South Carolina, Illinois, and Michigan.

"Unfortunately, the Texas businessman Ross Perot threw his hat into the ring, and shoved Bill down in the general election polls, behind both Bush and Perot. But New York newspapers like *The New York Times,* the *Post,* and *The Daily News* picked up the slack when they enthusiastically endorsed Bill, and he easily finished in first place in New York's primary. I do love that state! He helped secure his nomination by winning New Jersey, New Mexico, Montana, and even California, where he defeated the popular Jerry Brown in his own state.

"With this deluge of victories behind him, Bill and I exulted in a convention of triumph at Madison Square Garden, when his name was placed in nomination by top Democrat Mario Cuomo. Bill gave a very touching acceptance speech in which he focused on 'the forgotten middle class, those who work and pay their fair share of taxes so their children can enjoy a better life.' Tears streamed down my face as he spoke of the night Chelsea was born. I remember what he said well: 'I was overcome by the thought that God had given me a blessing my own father never knew: the chance to hold my child in my arms. Somewhere at this very moment, a child is being born in America. Let it be our cause to give that child a happy home, a healthy family, and a hopeful future.'

"Nobody can be as moving as Bill when he speaks so passionately. His speech brought down the house, with applause that thundered on throughout the hour-long speech. No one clapped longer or harder than me, overflowing as I was with love for my husband, the president to-be of the United States."

December 13, 2013

"In the Electoral College, it was Clinton, Clinton, Clinton all the way!" Hillary said exuberantly. "Bill won with 362 votes to Bush's 168, with thirty-two states in the Clinton column. Despite all the setbacks en route, we the Clintons had prevailed again.

"Tom Brokaw of NBC News helped set the tone for the Clinton presidency when he asked me what I thought Bill and I would do the first morning when we awakened in the White House. I said, 'We'll pull the blankets over our heads.' I must have known something even then!

"Sure enough, nothing went smoothly with the Clintons! Almost from the moment we were elected, we found ourselves knee deep in problems. The first was that we couldn't seem to settle on who would be the director of the transition team. Mickey Kantor, a dear friend of Bill's and his campaign chair, seemed the logical choice. I disagreed, because I felt he was taking over too much. I had a fit, and yelled at Mickey about trying to steamroll Bill. Exhausted from the last days of the campaign, Bill did nothing to thwart my wishes. Disappointed, Mickey flew back to California, his tail between his legs.

"Then Bill appointed Warren Christopher, a nice guy who would go to any length to keep the peace. But keeping the peace was not what was required. We already had a keeper of the peace in the person of Bill Clinton. What we needed was a firm, tenacious person who was not afraid to make decisions. The choice was between a tough guy who could bark orders versus a system in which everybody could speak his or her piece. We made the wrong decision.

"As a result, Stephen Hess of the Brookings Institute called ours 'the worst presidential transition in modern history.' The problem was, who was going to run the presidency? Of course Bill was the one who had been elected, but he had promised me that we would be co-presidents—the old 'two for the price of one' deal.

"This didn't sit very well with Al Gore, the vice-president, to whom Bill had also promised a leading role. So here we had three people competing for authority and no one in charge. Confusion was the order of the day. Unfortunately, I seemed to be at the center of it all. I was not about to yield the power I had been promised. I thought for a while of becoming chief of staff myself. Dick Morris, Bill's longtime political advisor who was to become counsel to the president, vetoed the idea, saying that the chief of staff served as the lightning rod for all the president's unpopular decisions. On thinking it over, I decided that was one job I definitely did not want!

"'What about nominating me to be Attorney General or Secretary of Education?' I asked. Again Morris demurred because he said it would be seen as nepotism and not reflect well on Bill's presidency.

"'How come Bobby Kennedy served successfully as his brother's Attorney General?' I asked. *His answer?* 'Times have changed.'

"He suggested instead that I take charge of a major domestic issue such as health care, just as I had handled education in Arkansas. His proposal was in line with my major interest in children and family and felt right to me. I would lead a social change comparable to Social Security and Medicare—something that would transform the nation.

"But there was trouble with Al Gore. Bill had promised him that he would play a decisive role in government and, as his ultimate confidante, would consult with him before making any important decision. There was only one problem with this: That position was already filled—by me. Al and I jousted with each other for power all through Bill's two terms, albeit in a superficially polite way.

"I insisted on having office space in the West Wing, the first wife of a president to occupy an office at the center of power, but that upset Al and cut into his space. Neither of us was willing to give in, partially because of the symbolism that came from which one of us was given a larger area and whose office was closer to the president. I wanted to be in the West Wing. Having an office side by side with the top leader of the country says a lot about the relative status of women versus men in the U.S., I believe. In the White House, I was acting out the drama of what was going on in offices and homes all over America, and I hoped to set an example for women everywhere.

"Despite my excellent reasons, Al was not impressed, and we kept on fighting with each other as long as Bill was president. A strong chief of staff would have resolved that problem once and for all. But seeing that there was no strong chief of staff, no resolution was achieved there, or anywhere else, for that matter.

December 16, 2013

Hillary continued with the difficulties experienced in the White House. "The problems didn't end there. Unfortunately, everything that possibly could go wrong did. From the moment I tried to bring about some order out of the chaos, I created hostility by barring the press from the press secretary's office. There were ongoing problems in the Justice Department, failed cabinet appointments, and the controversial executive order to permit gays to serve in the military. Then there was a disorderly staff. Nobody was in charge. There was no focus, order, or discipline in the new presidential administration. As one observer said, most members of the Clinton team felt as if they were starting their presidency amid a howling gale. I was one of them.

"I tried to take charge, to bring about some order. Not everybody was happy about it. Carl Bernstein, for example, commented that soon after arriving at the White House, I had become the first warrior First Lady. Now I ask you again, Doctor: Was that fair? Here the White House was a raging mess, and I was the only one who tried to bring some order to the administration, yet was criticized as 'America's first warrior First Lady.' Two weeks as First Lady and I was ready to resign!

"One good thing happened amid the chaos, however, or at least so it seemed to me at the time. Bill appointed me as chair of his task force on health care. As you know, I have always been interested in expanding health care to include the poor and downtrodden women and children of our country. Vice President Gore had told Bill that he wanted to head the task force, but I objected to his appointment, thinking that he certainly would try to hog the entire agenda. Of course, Bill stood by *me*.

"I don't mean to imply that no other good thing happened during that first year. Bill signed into law the Family Medical Leave Act, which allowed employees to be given up to three weeks of unpaid leave to handle family emergencies. He immediately overturned Reagan and

Bush's twelve years of prohibiting government support for programs that disseminated information on birth control or the termination of a pregnancy. Can you believe in this day and age that *two* U.S. presidents were so reactionary? I'm still puzzled that so many American women couldn't see past their noses and voted for those two regressive gentlemen. Couldn't they see that they didn't give a tinker's damn about them but were interested only in promoting their own political ends?

"Despite a stalemate with Republicans on most issues, Bill succeeded on two other major projects. In 1985, when he was governor, he had advocated a major overhaul of the welfare system to encourage work. And in his 1992 campaign, he had promised to 'end welfare as we know it.' When Congress approved a harsher version of his proposal in 1996, he signed it into law over the objections of many in his own administration and his party. Bill had vetoed two earlier measures that were even grimmer. The law limited lifetime welfare benefits to five years and required adult recipients to work after two years on welfare.

"In 1997, Bill worked out a compromise with Congress that included tax and spending cuts aimed at balancing the budget. The legislation also began a new children's health insurance program that expanded Medicaid coverage to millions of children from low and middle income families. I was so proud of him. That was the man I'd married! He also signed into law bipartisan measures to combat terrorism, including more funds to fight it and making it easier to deport foreigners suspected of being terrorists.

"I rejoiced that whatever his flaws—and we know he has plenty— at last we had a president who genuinely cared about the people of his country."

December 17, 2013

"On March 19, 1993, a terrible thing happened," Hillary said with deep sadness in her voice. "My father had a stroke. I took Chelsea out of school and flew immediately to his bedside. He was 82 years old, and had been in deteriorating health for some time. He had undergone a coronary bypass and been confined to a wheelchair. Even so, I was not ready for him to go. I sat beside my dying father and was overcome with feelings about him and our life together. Grief for his passing changed me. It made me a different person."

"You are wise to know that, Hillary," I said.

"Who would have thought that I would begin to remember unpleasant incidents about him at his deathbed, such as when he made us search for toothpaste tops in the snow and ice and that he would never say, 'Well done, Hillary,' no matter how hard I had worked or how well I had done. I remembered that the White House staff didn't like him, and considered him rude and nasty. Some members of that staff have called me a tyrant, too. I don't think I am. I am just a person who tries in every way to get the best results from them. But I can see that I sometimes come across as a despot, and if I do, we know where I get it from. I realized then that my mother's willingness to tolerate her husband's abuse had shaped my entire approach to marriage and to life itself.

"My father's death changed me. I began to question the very meaning of life and of death. When does life begin? When does it end? Or does it? I turned to my religion for answers and decided there were more important things in life than the search for power. I knew then that I wanted to teach people about the common ground we all share, especially people who now saw themselves as mortal enemies. It took the death of my father to teach me the truth. I talked to my followers about 'the spiritual vacuum at the heart of American society, this tumor of the soul.'

"While I was in the hospital, I suddenly found myself in the role of a family member of a mortally ill person who faced incredible costs, incomprehensible insurance rules, and confusing forms, and all of this while I was so overcome with grief that I was unable to think. I talked to other patients and their family members and to hospital personnel. I was told again and again by doctors that many of their patients couldn't afford to pay for necessary medicines, and often skipped doses of it to make their prescriptions last longer. All this reinforced my sense of how important it was to reform health care.

"In the meantime, my health care task force was at a standstill. After a two-and-a-half week absence, I decided I would have to return to Washington for a short while. Despite the long hours I had spent with him, I was not able to be at his side at the very moment when he passed. True to his character to the end, Hugh Rodham was never able to give me his final blessing or to tell me he loved me, nor was I able to tell him how much I loved him and of the hurt he had caused me.

"My father was dead," she said between sobs. "Whether or not he was a tyrant, I loved him and miss him terribly. I wasn't able to return to work for weeks. I mourn him to the bottom of my being. Don't *you* be like everybody else and tell me I will get over it," she said, looking at me hostilely. "Because I never will. I will never be the same again."

Analyst or not, I went over to Hillary and gave her a maternal hug. She cried against my shoulder for the remaining moments of our session.

December 18, 2013

"My dear friend, Vincent Foster, and I were soulmates when we worked together at the Rose law firm. He was Bill's childhood friend, and my best friend at Rose. We spoke together for long hours, ate lunches with each other, and giggled about vicious gossip. Having Vince as a friend made working at Rose fun and compensated for some of Bill's deficiencies.

"There was talk, of course, that Vince and I were lovers, but that wasn't true. We were just good friends. Vince came to the White House as deputy counsel to the president as well as our personal lawyer and mopped up a lot of our personal messes, which I won't go into fully now. It is enough to say that when I worked at Rose, we weren't supposed to take on clients who did business with the state. I regret to say that I sometimes forgot or ignored this rule. But Vince's new position caused an awful shift in our relationship.

"From being close personal friends, we became boss and employee, with me barking out orders in my habitual manner like, 'Take care of it, Vince!' Our friendly meetings, lunches, and gab sessions ended. Sometimes he was a counselor, and sometimes a fixer, but we no longer were intimate friends. Also, Vince was a bit slow about following my orders, which made me angry.

"I'm not happy when things don't go the way I want them to. For instance, I gave him the job of erasing my name from all references to the firing of travel office personnel, called Travelgate by the media. I didn't feel guilty about it, but thought that taking my name out of it might save us trouble later.

"I was so right! He did it but had compunctions about my actions. He just wasn't able to get things done as fast as I wanted, and he knew that I wasn't happy about it. He considered quitting the job but was too proud to allow himself to fail at anything. We were both heartbroken about the situation. He did all he could for me as First

Lady, but it became impossible for him to be my real friend anymore.

"One terrible day when I was visiting my mother, Vince went to work as usual. He left in the early afternoon, telling his office personnel that he would be back soon. He drove to a park in Virginia, took out a gun, and shot himself right between the eyes. When I heard the news, I fainted from the shock and blamed myself that I had not seen it coming and done something to stop it. Bill and I mourned Vince together, and Bill did his best to convince me that it was not my fault, and that given Vince's fragility, there was nothing I or anybody else could have done to prevent the tragedy. I don't believe it. I think Vince killed himself because he thought I didn't care about him anymore. Nobody will ever persuade me otherwise.

"A few days later, we found a suicide note Vince had left. It said, 'I made mistakes from inexperience, ignorance, and overwork. *The Wall Street Journal* editors lie without consequence. I was not meant for a job in the spotlight of public life in Washington. Here, ruining people is considered a sport. The public will never believe the innocence of the Clintons and their loyal staff.' I'll never forget it.

"Tell me, Doctor: How do you get over the suicide of a close friend, especially when you think it's your fault?" The tears rolled out of her eyes and down her cheeks. "The pain is unbearable," she said through sobs. "I can't get out of my mind the image of that gun firing a bullet through his head. It stays with me always. I see it as clearly as if I had been at the shooting, and it makes me feel as if I myself had pulled the trigger. Why won't it go away and leave me in peace? Didn't he realize how much his killing himself would hurt me? Why didn't I call him that morning? Why didn't he call me? Why didn't I realize how desperate he was? Why did I tease him, like when I said, 'Keep on moving at a glacial pace, Vince! You know how much that thrills me!' Didn't he know I was only kidding? Why? Why? Why?" Her voice slowly trailed away until I could barely hear her.

What could I say that could possibly help? All my years of study and practice couldn't prepare me to answer that simple question. Drowning in feelings of inadequacy, I responded much as anyone else might have.

"I'm so very sorry, Hillary. I know how awful you feel, but I don't believe you or anyone else is to blame. Vince was a sick man, a weak man, who couldn't pull himself together enough to realize that even the darkest of times will pass. That is why he killed himself."

She nodded but continued sobbing.

"There is another thing you should know, Hillary. Like you, I will quote William Shakespeare, who said in Sonnet Thirty, 'With old woes new, wail my dear time's waste.' He meant that every new loss brings back all the old ones. So with each loss, you are grieving for all previous losses, as well as the fresh one. At that point in time, you had recently lost your father. You were crying for him as much as for Vince."

She nodded again, and suddenly energy seemed to flow back into her voice. She said, "You're right! I've wondered why I keep superimposing my father's face upon Vince's in that image that won't go away! Thank you, Doctor. You have helped me when I didn't think anyone could." She dried her eyes, arose from her chair, and crossed to the entrance with dignity. She hesitated at the threshold for a moment and then turned her head and said warmly, "Thank you again, Doctor. I am glad I know you."

Hillary's grief awakened my own "old woes" as well as hers, and tears dampened my face as I wept for my son, my husband, and my parents. Unfortunately, I had only ten minutes to get myself together before the next patient was due. It helped to staunch my tears when I realized what a long way Hillary had come. It is real progress when a woman who keeps her feelings in a locked box her whole life finds herself able to mourn so deeply.

December 20, 2013

"From the beginning of Bill's presidency, and mostly because of our difficulties with the press, we felt alienated from the elite of Washington, which mainly revolved around the *Washington Post*. Nobody in Washington seemed to like me. To make matters worse, the White House staff, including the cooks, ushers, servants, and even the Secret Service, took a disliking to us. It all began the day after the inauguration, with breakfast served at 5:30 A.M.! Two Secret Service teams had to be on duty early in the morning, in case Bill wanted to go out jogging. Since he also liked to play cards and talk late into the night, that meant longer hours for the staff, who resented it. You have to remember they were used to staid old couples who kept normal hours. You can imagine how unpleasant it is to be around people who snarl at you all the time. So I remedied the situation by hiring mainly Arkansans.

"Nowhere was the strain in the relationship between us and Washingtonians greater than in 'Travelgate.' That involved the White House staff who, for years, made all the arrangements for trips, flights, and hotel accommodations for the press corps when the president had to travel. It all began when our close friends Harry and Linda Thomason told me they thought the travel office was crippled because of 'gross financial mismanagement.' Thomason even had a replacement team headed by a cousin of Bill's all ready to step in.

"Vince became worried about the firings that we were about to implement and ordered a review by KPMG Peat Marwick. They discovered that the in-house travel agency kept an off-book ledger, had $18,000 of unaccounted-for checks, and kept chaotic office records.

I saw the unexplainable expenditures of cash by the staff as an excellent opportunity to get rid of workers who were inefficient, if not actually dishonest. In May 1993, we fired all seven employees of the travel office. I was so angry with them that I made the mistake of not giving them a hearing or a chance to defend themselves. It set off a clamor in the media that has not subsided to this day. The story was picked up by the press, and centered not on the irregularities of the office, as it should have, but on what they called our 'management style.' It was only the first major ethics controversy we had to deal with.

"Further inquiries by the FBI and the Department of Justice, the White House itself, the General Accounting Office, the House Government Reform and Oversight Committee, and the Whitewater Independent Counsel all took place over the next few years. At one time, there were thirty-nine investigations going on at the same time. It felt like the Spanish Inquisition. You can imagine how this locked me into a state of tension and kept Bill and I at each other's throats for years, each blaming the other for getting us into the mess. Travel Office Director Billy Dale was charged with embezzlement but, to my surprise, found not guilty in 1995.

"In 1998, Independent Counsel Kenneth Starr exonerated my husband of any involvement in the matter, so we could breathe a little easier. To my fury, heavy media attention forced us to reinstate most of the employees into other jobs and to remove Clinton personnel from the travel positions. I still think I was right to fire them, but it certainly did not make me Miss Popularity of Washington, D.C.!"

"When Kenneth Starr issued a subpoena calling me before the grand jury to testify about missing billing records, I was frantic and regressed again to my depressed mood. I am a very conscientious person, and it hurt badly to have my credibility questioned in front of the entire nation, if not the world. I also was worried that my testimony would reflect badly on Bill's presidency and destroy voters' trust in us. I wanted to be his helpmate, not a load around his neck, and told him so. He felt very bad about it for me and told me not to worry. I deeply appreciated his support.

"We are a family that sticks together when one of us is in trouble. Chelsea also was very worried about me. She was now a young lady and closely followed the news about the investigations, sometimes to a degree I wasn't happy about. But as the old adage is true: 'What goes around comes around.' I had comforted and protected her for so long that she wanted to return the favor. I originally tried to avoid troubling her with what I was going through but relented when she said she felt better when I told her what I was feeling.

"Around that time, to add to our difficulties, Davis Maraniss' book, *First in His Class*, was published and exposed to everyone the problems Bill's indiscretions had caused in our marriage. I was in a fury, mostly at my 'friends' Betsey Wright and Dick Morris, who had divulged the details of our marriage to Maraniss. I was so upset that I turned on my 'Frigidaire' qualities. I refused to talk with Bill for weeks, and made him sleep downstairs on the couch. I tried to avoid him whenever I could, leaving a room if he came into it. I didn't want to be anywhere near him or have anything to do with him. Even Chelsea was mad at her father for the first time in her life. I wanted to wring Bill's neck but thought I had better not. Besides being my husband, he was my president."

Except for the one comment I had made early in the session, I said practically nothing during the hour. I felt Hillary just needed to vent. She didn't seem to notice my silence and left in a seemingly better mood.

December 23, 2013

Hillary's White House problems continued to grow, as she explained at our next session. "To my despair," she began, "the Vince Foster suicide quickly became a political time bomb. The media continually offered up conspiracy theories, speculated about treason, and even delved into so-called death plots. It never seemed to occur to any of them that sometimes life is just so hard that a person doesn't want to live. I feel that way too sometimes, when the whole world gangs up on me."

I looked at her in alarm.

"Don't worry, Doctor," she said. "I wouldn't do that to Chelsea."

I believed her and was greatly relieved.

"Six days after Vince's death," she continued, "the suicide note was found by White House employees."

"Vince got it right," she said sadly, wiping away a tear. "Life in Washington is one big fox hunt. And I am the number two fox. At a time when the whole country should have mourned the loss of an important public servant, as they did JFK, people actually believed we had planned the tragedy as part of our effort to become dictators of the United States. Are they kidding? Compassionate, warm-hearted Bill a dictator? How unrealistic can you get? But people still believe it.

"Bill and I endured verbal abuse for months that was heavier than what even Nixon had suffered. It got so bad we had to push each other out of bed in the morning. As most things do, the uproar gradually subsided to the point where normal White House living, if there is such a thing, resumed. Bill's domestic agenda was doing well, our poll numbers had risen, and it began to look as if we would be able to rescue the presidency from the vicious onslaught of the media and of Republicans.

"I will briefly remind you of just a few things we accomplished in those early years, as I imagine much of it will be familiar to you. Bill signed a law he proposed that required companies with more than fifty workers to give employees up to twelve weeks of unpaid leave every year to cope with family problems. He understood how important it was that I could stay home for four months after Chelsea was born.

"He established a national service program called AmeriCorps, which enrolls adults in intensive community service to help others and meet critical needs in the community. Bill has a big heart, and establishing AmeriCorps is just more proof of that.

"He also knows how to think in terms of huge amounts of money, even though he never has been able to balance our checkbook. Money means practically nothing to Bill. He doesn't mind having it and isn't averse to my making it (the only time I wasn't employed since I was thirteen were the eight years we spent at the White House), but is happy as long as he has enough money to buy books, go to the movies, go out to dinner when he wants to, and travel. I, on the other hand, am like my father, and feel more secure when our bank account is full. I learned early in our marriage that if we were to have any bank account at all, I'd have to be the one to fill it.

"During Bush's last fiscal year, the nation's deficit had reached $290 billion. Bill reduced government spending over five years by $255 billion and increased taxes on high incomes by $241 billion. Under his presidency, the annual deficit decreased sharply and completely disappeared in 1998. Bill had succeeded in balancing the budget for the first time since 1969!

"He also expanded the Earned Income Tax Credit, which provided extra income for millions of families earning less than $30,000 a year.

"As far as foreign affairs are concerned, Bill tried to arrange peace between religious and ethnic rivals in the Middle East and in Northern Ireland. His interventions brought religious strife in Northern Ireland to a standstill, and brought about an agreement between Israel and Jordan to end their perpetual state of war. When the Mexican peso collapsed in 1995, threatening the failure of Mexico's economy, Bill devised a $20 billion loan package to restore world confidence in Mexico, which they paid off three years ahead of schedule.

"Bill's major interest in foreign policy was not military intervention, for which the people of the United States should be grateful, but in strategic improvements in trade and the economy. He completed negotiations of the North American Free Trade Agreement, which reduced tariffs, and worked on a comprehensive world trade agreement called the General Agreement on Tariffs and Trade. In my opinion, prejudiced as it may be, and as angry as he makes me at times, Bill Clinton is one of the greatest presidents ever to grace the Oval Office.

"As you know, Bill was among Arkansas' most productive governors, and with my help, brought about extensive reforms in public education. His long tenure ended with a prolonged period of job creation and economic growth. As president, he succeeded in improving the economic well-being of low-income working families by $20 billion a year, supplying health insurance for their children, and providing tax credits for work and college expenses. Bill's presidency marked the longest period of sustained economic growth in the nation's history, including four consecutive years of federal budget surpluses. He was president at the peak of U.S. supremacy in the world, which was no coincidence, and he can be excused if he enjoyed personally basking in unprecedented global admiration.

"The country has never had it so good as during Bill Clinton's presidency. But what do citizens of the United States first think about when his name is mentioned? Monica Lewinsky!

"Whatever his childish proclivities, Bill Clinton was a great president. Sometimes, people don't know when they are well off. What a pity that the president who immediately succeeded him did not follow in his footsteps. If George W. Bush had, our country wouldn't have gotten into the mess it later did."

Even I, who always admired Bill Clinton, had not realized he had accomplished so much in his presidency. I told Hillary this, and said, "You must be very proud of him."

She beamed. "Oh, but I am! I have always known he had it in him to be a great president. That is the main reason I married him. I am afraid it will take a hundred years before the people in the United States catch up with my opinion of him."

I could only agree with her and hope that her estimate of time was exaggerated.

"Well, Doctor," she said as she arose from the couch. "I guess it's time to get off the soapbox!"

December 24, 2013

"Despite Bill's good work and the greatly improved state of the country, we were bombarded by accusations of wrongdoing throughout his presidency. What is the matter with people?" she said, raising her voice. "Why wouldn't they let us alone? I will never understand it, although my hunch is that the Republicans knew he was doing a wonderful job and wanted to tear him down before the next election. Doctor, do you know Bob Dylan's song 'Stoned?'

> *Well, they'll stone ya when you're trying to be so good*
> *They'll stone ya just a-like they said they would*
> *They'll stone ya when you're riding in your car.*
> *Then they'll stone ya when you're playing your guitar.*
> *But I would not feel so all alone*
> *Everybody must get stoned.*

"Dylan must have been listening in at the White House. And like him, Bill and I felt all alone. After the Republicans gained control of the House of Representatives and the Senate in the 1994 elections, they appointed congressional committees to conduct seemingly endless investigations of alleged misconduct in the White House.

"And the accusations kept on coming: that a White House aide had improperly raised funds privately while he ran Bill's wonderful agency, AmeriCorps; that Bill's first Secretary of Agriculture had accepted gifts from companies regulated by his department; that the Secretary of Housing and Urban Development had lied to Congress about the size of payments he made to his mistress, like that was any of their business; that his Secretary of Commerce had engaged in illegal financial deals; that Bill's Interior Secretary had lied to Congress about his role in granting a license to a gambling casino; and that our Secretary of Labor had taken part in an influence peddling scheme while he was an aide in the White House.

"Interesting that none of the investigations came up with any *evidence* of illegal activities. Why waste the taxpayers' money? I suspected the Republicans responsible for the investigations didn't even believe the allegations themselves but were merely trying to annoy Bill and to prevent him from bringing about things that would benefit the people of the United States."

Hillary had raised her voice so high I was afraid people in the corridor would hear her. I was happy the double doors to my office kept in most of the noise. "Didn't they have anything better to do?" she shouted. "Instead of attending to the affairs of the country, those sons of bitches wasted their time and the government's money hounding us!"

Tired by her own outburst, Hillary arose to leave. Her parting words were said in a more gentle voice: "Considering what Bill accomplished under all that stress, think what he would have done under ordinary circumstances. His face would have been carved on Mount Rushmore by now."

She looked at me. "Happy holidays," she said.

"You, too," I said.

December 27, 2013

"The congressional battle that still makes me sick to my stomach was over national health insurance," she continued in her next session. "As you know, Bill appointed me chairperson of the task force to study health insurance and to recommend a plan that would guarantee coverage for everyone. Under our proposal, people would join an alliance in each state to contract with insurance companies which would offer various policies.

"I worked night and day, along with a task force of five hundred members, to prepare the best possible health plan to cover everyone in the United States at a price all could afford. We finally worked out a program that pleased me. In fact, I was ecstatic about it, but my rapture didn't last very long. It took only one year for me to go from euphoria to depression. Did Congress pass our health plan? Is the Pope Jewish?

"Democrats had been trying for generations to pass such a law. Many impoverished people were uninsured and couldn't afford to take proper care of their health, some even losing their lives because of it. By putting his personal stamp on health care reform, Bill gave the Republicans the incentive to defeat it and humiliate him rather than agree on a compromise. Of course, it was not only our plan that was defeated. Every other health care reform proposal—the Cooper, Moynihan, Mitchell, Chafee, Cooper, and Grandy plans, to mention only a few, also were killed off by Congress.

"Instead of being concerned about the health of millions of Americans, the opposition focused on what those with good health care might lose. The insurance companies objected to our plan, and each generation of Republicans fights the passing of national health insurance more viciously than those preceding them.

"I am heartbroken that all our hard work and good intentions were for naught. Even today, the Democrats have enacted health care for all that the Republicans are still opposing. I badly wanted Bill's presidency to be remembered for what we did for our people, but what would have been our greatest contribution was flushed down the sewer. In my opinion, the failure of our proposed health care reform will go down in history as the greatest lost political opportunity of the century. It is a story of unaccepted compromises, deals never completed, and members of both parties failing to back proposals that they themselves had co-sponsored."

"From this great defeat, did you learn anything about health reform?" I asked.

She thought for a moment. "We made two mistakes: trying to do too much at one time, and taking too long. As a result, we ended up with nothing. If I had to do it over again, we would have taken on less and perhaps even compromised with the Republicans. As President Franklin D. Roosevelt once said, a politician must learn to compromise. If I had to do it now, I would compromise. The danger of doing nothing is greater than the risk of compromising. On the political agenda, it is unfortunate that health care had to give way to other priorities. During the transition period and his first year in office, the battle of the budget threatened Bill's presidency, and he had no choice but to focus on it.

"The task force and I were thrilled when Bill threatened Congress with a veto of anything but universal coverage. Like others in favor of reform, we failed to recognize that, by doing so, we risked losing everything. We naively assumed that changes for the better couldn't lose. To my regret, we learned that strategy and speed do matter in politics. On the positive side, changing times brought new possibilities. Even with Obamacare, I suspect that health care will remain at the heart of American politics for a long time to come.

"The failure of our health care proposal was probably the worst defeat of my life—even worse than my loss of the presidential nomination in 2008, and it hurt millions of Americans along with me. I will never get over it."

December 30, 2013

"I told you about the terribly distressing investigations that hounded us all during both of Bill's terms as president," she began. "The most troublesome one was a real estate deal we innocently went into in 1978, while he was attorney general of Arkansas. The investigation became known as 'Whitewater,' after the name of the land development company, Whitewater Development Corporation, which we formed with James and Susan McDougal of Little Rock. I can't think of the name without shuddering. We four purchased two hundred and thirty acres of wilderness near the White River and Crooked Creek in Marion County, then lost money when we were unable to develop and sell the lots.

"Even so, they persisted in accusing us of benefiting from the operations of a Little Rock savings and loan association that McDougal had formed in the 1980s, which eventually went bankrupt. Can you believe it? We were found innocent, of course, but the independent counsel kept right on prosecuting us! Pulling scabs off old wounds, they expanded the investigation to look into Vince Foster's suicide as well as the firing of the White House travel staff.

"Yielding to Republican criticism, Bill asked Attorney General Janet Reno in 1994 to appoint an independent counsel on Whitewater. Her appointee, a Republican lawyer named Robert Fiske, was removed by a panel of Washington judges and replaced with Kenneth W. Starr. Starr had been solicitor general under George H. W. Bush. Starr picked on an innocent man who was doing his best to improve the country.

"I have to stress to you, Doctor, that although they continued to persecute us, neither us nor any others in our administration were ever implicated in any wrongdoing in Whitewater-related activities. The investigations also concluded that Foster had committed suicide and that the firing of the travel staff involved no wrongdoing. You'd think that would have gotten Starr off our necks, but no, he proceeded anyway, and with a vengeance.

"Starr's agents had been conducting prolonged inquiries into reports of Bill's marital infidelities, as though they concerned anyone but us. A former employee of the Arkansas Industrial Development Department, Paula Jones, filed a lawsuit in 1994 alleging that my husband had made unwanted sexual advances toward her in a Little Rock hotel room in 1991, and the U.S. Supreme Court foolishly ruled that trying the suit would not distract Bill from his duties as president.

"In 1998 during his presidency, Linda Tripp, a confidante of Monica Lewinsky, gave Starr recordings in which Lewinsky talked about performing oral sex on the president. Bill is such a little boy! He really believed that not having actual intercourse meant he didn't have sex with her. In his mind, he was not lying. Although the Lewinsky affair was unrelated to any of the Whitewater issues, Starr justified the continual widening of the investigation by saying it was all part of a pattern of obstructing justice at the Clinton White House. In September of 1998, Starr gave the House of Representatives a lengthy printed report on Bill's indiscretions with Lewinsky, including his efforts to cover them up during testimony before Starr's grand jury and during a deposition that he gave in the civil case brought by Paula Jones.

"To my horror, the House Judiciary Committee accused Bill of 'high crimes and misdemeanors,' which are grounds for impeaching and removing a president, and brought four articles of impeachment against him. How we ever survived that, I will never know. In December, voting largely along party lines, the House adopted two of the articles—perjury before the grand jury and obstruction of justice—by votes of 228 to 206 and 221 to 212. Democrats, including me, believed that the impeachment proceedings were a Republican vendetta to destroy a popular president.

"Fortunately, only the Senate, by a two-thirds vote, can remove a president. In February of 1999, after hearing lengthy arguments presented by Republican members of the House and defenders of the president, the Senate voted down the perjury article, 45 for and 55 against, and the obstruction of justice article, 50 to 50.

"Starr said he would seek criminal charges against Bill for the Lewinsky affair after the president left office, but on the day before that, Bill, at my urging, issued a statement in which he apologized for giving erroneous testimony to the grand jury, and Starr closed the investigation. Owing to his admission of giving false testimony and proceedings instituted by the Professional Ethics Committee, Bill, to my despair, was forced to surrender his license to practice law in Arkansas.

"People wonder how I ever endured the terrible attacks on Bill and me. Someone asked me how I could even get up in the morning, knowing the charges were meritless. They have no idea how hard it was. My heart was broken, and everybody knew it.

"In an agonizing decision, I chose to stand by Bill, at least for the moment. I decided to rescue him one more time, both for his sake, our family's sake, and the country's sake. I didn't come to my conclusion the way some little woman like Tammy Wynette 'stood by her man.' I stood by Bill because I love and respect him and honor what he'd been through and what we'd been through together.

"If that's not enough for some people, then so be it. Also, I must confess that I needed him as much as he needed me, for personal reasons as well as our political future. If he went down, he would have taken me with him. So I swallowed my rage and humiliation and 'stood by my man,' at least publicly. Privately, he was relegated again to sleep on the couch for two months.

"After coming to that conclusion, I supported Bill publicly whenever I got the chance. As the House vote on impeachment drew near, I begged everyone to practice reconciliation rather than trying to get revenge. When asked by Richard Gephardt to speak to Congressional Democrats before the vote for impeachment took

ALMA H. BOND, PH.D.

place, I gave what I am told was an impassioned and effective speech imploring Democrats to stand behind their president. I said I loved and supported my husband, though I wasn't happy with his behavior. I said I didn't believe impeachment was the answer because Bill had been a wonderful president. I thought we should allow him to continue to produce changes that enrich the lives of Americans.

"Apparently my speech touched their hearts. Not a single Democrat crossed party lines to join Republicans, who were knocking themselves out trying to impeach Bill. This was in great contrast to the events of twenty-five years earlier, when Republicans joined Democrats who wished to impeach Richard Nixon. But then, despite his sexual transgressions, Bill Clinton is a goodhearted man. He was no Richard Nixon. Thank God for small favors!

"I appreciated more than ever Eleanor Roosevelt's advice that in politics you need to develop a hide as thick as a rhinoceros. While my armor was far from difficult to penetrate, it had hardened over the years as the criticisms kept pouring in, so that I barely recovered from one when the next one hit. I knew how a prizefighter must feel before the last punch knocks him out. You don't just wake up one day and say, 'I'm not going to let them get to me today.' Each day was harder to endure than the day before.

"To my surprise and delight," Hillary added, "I also was worried that my hardening surface might mask my underlying feelings that you are always griping about. You think I am unaware of them, but I constantly watched myself for evidence that I no longer could access my emotions. I had to know what they were so I could act on them."

Did she learn that from me? I wondered, *and not want to give me the satisfaction of saying so? Or was she really aware of it at the time? Who knows?*

"At a speech I gave about that time at Goucher College in Baltimore, somebody asked if I thought the charges against Bill were false. I stopped in my tracks and said that of course I did, but added that it was still painful when someone you love is subjected to such attacks and criticism.

"Then they asked why Bill was being attacked in that way. I remember my answer well. I said that there had been a concentrated effort to undermine and undo his magnificient achievements as president. His enemies attacked him personally, I added, because they could not defeat him politically.

"In my heart, I am certain that history will bring out the truth, that Bill Clinton was one of the greatest presidents our country has ever been fortunate enough to have. He brought about one of the greatest economic revivals in American history. He generated nineteen million new jobs, and succeeded in balancing a budget nearly destroyed by his predecessors, leaving surpluses that could have benefited Social Security and Medicare for years to come.

"Because of his college tuition credits, ten percent more young people were able to attend college. Each of these gains by itself might not be earth-shattering, but together they add up to momentous progress, and all of this was going on while Bill was undergoing the impeachment process! What Republican or Democrat could have done as well?"

Hillary left my office with her head lowered, as if she didn't want me to look into her eyes.

December 31, 2013

Hillary went on with her story at our next session. "Early in 1999, I made an effort to rescue myself from the Lewinsky affair. Tired of the continued conflict of White House living and also, I must admit, of riding on Bill's coattails, I decided to run for the U.S. Senate seat in New York held by Senator Daniel Patrick Moynihan, who was retiring. I knit together a coalition of urban minority groups, Giuliani Democrats, and white voters from upstate I was told was impossible to bring together. That just goes to show that you shouldn't listen to anyone but yourself."

"I agree, Hillary," I said. "That you listen to yourself is what makes you a leader."

She smiled. "We bought the house in Chappaqua to establish residency in New York, and in November 2000, I was thrilled to be elected to the U.S. Senate. It was a job I loved from the very first day.

"Bill retired after leaving the presidency on January twentieth, opened an office in Harlem, and began to write his autobiography. *My Life* was published in 2004 and became a bestseller. He made a lot of money—more than me for a change—Bill received an advance of $10 million, while I only got $8 million for *my* autobiography! It was the first time in Bill's chaotic life that he made a great deal of income, not that he hadn't always deserved more. To our great pleasure, his presidential library opened in November 2004 on the Little Rock River front. We were thrilled to have a whole library devoted to his presidency.

"Bill then traveled extensively around the world, particularly in Africa and Asia, where he began efforts to import medicine to fight the AIDS epidemic. In 2005, President George W. Bush appointed Bill and the elder President Bush to direct humanitarian relief efforts for the victims of a tsunami that killed more than 200,000 people along the coasts of the Indian Ocean in late December 2004. In 2010, Bill and George W. Bush created the Clinton Bush Haiti Fund to assist the people of Haiti after an earthquake there in January. Can you believe that a Republican ex-president and a Democratic former president could work so well together?

"After I became a senator, even the Republicans whom I expected to greet me with crucifixes and garlic learned we could work together and grudgingly began to respect me. My constituency apparently did as well. In the 2000 election, New York City's firefighters supported my Republican rival for the Senate seat. Six years later, when I ran for re-election, the firefighters publicly endorsed me before any Republican threw his or her hat into the ring.

"Although I was sworn in as a U.S. Senator on January 1, 2001, I remained the First Lady until January twentieth. I served simultaneously for twenty days as a member of one branch of government while married to the leader of another branch, another historical first I recorded. I got a little dizzy jumping from one position to the other and was relieved it was only for twenty days. The first year, while working to understand my new state and position, I assumed the low public profile typical of most freshmen Senators.

"I was thrilled to be re-elected in 2006, winning more than sixty-seven percent of the popular vote in New York State. As of November 2007, I enjoyed a sixty percent job approval rating. In February of 2008, *The Washington Post* reported that I was among the top ten senators for securing federal funds for my home state, generating more than $342 million in earmarks for New York. In the Senate, I became a staunch opponent of the Iraq War.

"Although I voted in 2002 in favor of the initial invasion," she explained, "knowing what I know now, I would never have voted for it. I later cast votes against the war, including against a troop surge and in favor of calls to withdraw troops."

"Oh?" I said, lifting my head. I was not completely convinced.

She continued without picking up on my skepticism. Either she hadn't noticed, which I doubt, or she didn't care. "I added a wide variety of causes that were important to me in the Senate, like expanding access to family planning and contraceptives and supporting unwanted pregnancy prevention through education. I quickly leapt in when the media revealed that a popular video game contained explicit sex scenes, which disgusted me. I have nothing against sex, but portraying it before the eyes of children? Come on!

"Although Bill sometimes calls me a prude, he couldn't stop me from co-sponsoring the Family Entertainment Protection Act, which called for stricter rating guidelines and better enforcement of existing guidelines. In March 2007, I introduced the Count Every Vote Act in the Senate, which required that voter-verified paper copies of electronic votes be used as the standard in a recount. The bill also tightened guidelines on electronic voting machine security.

"During my time in the Senate, I served on several major committees. Among others, I was a member of the Senate Armed Services Committee; the Senate Committee on Environment and Public Works; the Senate Committee on Health, Labor, and Pensions; and as a tribute to my departed parents, helped create the Senate Special Committee on Aging.

"I introduced 377 bills between January 2001 and August 2008. Of these, 323 died in committee, earning me a rating of 'extremely poor' in relationship to my peers—not surprising when you consider how much the Republicans hate me. Ten of these bills were enacted into law, and I also co-sponsored 1,858 other bills.

"In the Senate, I voted along Democratic Party lines 97 percent or so of the time. After the ghastly terrorist attacks of September eleventh, I felt proud that I initiated a fund of $21.4 billion to assist in clean-up and recovery, to provide health tracking for volunteers at Ground Zero, and to create grants for new development.

"In 2005, I issued two studies that examined the disbursement of federal homeland security funds to local communities and first responders. I made a point of visiting American troops in Afghanistan and Iraq during the war in those two nations. The soldiers made such a fuss over me that I felt like a rock star.

"In public and in my Senate work, I also became a national advocate for improving veterans' health benefits. As a champion of New York state, I led a bipartisan effort to bring broadband access to rural communities, co-sponsored the 21st Century Nanotechnology Research and Development Act, included language in the Energy Bill to provide tax-exempt bonding authority for environmentally conscious construction projects, and introduced an amendment calling for funding of new job creation to repair, renovate, and modernize public schools. I won an extension of unemployment insurance, which passed on the first day of the 108th Congress.

"I was a vocal opponent of the Bush Administration's tax cuts. I instigated many changes that will improve the lives of New Yorkers forever. I don't think the constituents of New York made a mistake when they elected me," she said shyly, "or re-elected me."

"My memoir, *Living History*, was published in 2003 and sold over three million copies worldwide; it was eventually translated into many foreign languages, including Chinese. At last I felt like a real writer, a profession I had always wanted to follow. Unfortunately, it sold fewer copies than Bill's book, a fact that he never misses the opportunity to remind me of. I always answer, 'I'm not finished yet, Bill Clinton! I'll write another book that will sell better than yours!'

"When Bill required immediate heart surgery in October of 2004, I was terribly upset and canceled my public schedule to stay with him. I sat beside him and held his hand for twenty-four hours. The thought of my losing him was agonizing. I found myself thinking, 'If he dies, I will go with him.' I found out by his bedside that his life and well-being were more important to me than my career. Who says I'm not a good wife?"

I nodded. I thought she was a wonderful wife.

January 3, 2014

"Happy New Year, Doctor!" she said to begin the new hour.

When I responded, "Thank you, Hillary. A very happy New Year to you, too," she said glumly, "Well, let's get on with things, shall we? I've never been one to waste any time."

She paused, and then hesitantly asked, "Then what *do* you think, Doctor? Do you believe Bill's actions were as inexcusable as I do?"

I gave her question much thought before responding, as I knew it was the most important issue of her analysis and that the outcome of her treatment depended upon my answer. I also knew that I could give her no false reassurances, because all analytic treatment must be based upon the truth. I thought deeply for a few moments about what I had learned of disorders like Bill Clinton's during my many years of training and practice.

When I finally felt ready to answer, I said, "My reaction may surprise you, but I will speak only the truth, so I will tell you exactly what I think. I'm sorry for the almost intolerable pain Bill's behavior has caused you and your daughter and deeply sympathize with you on what he has put you through. Nobody should have to experience such an ordeal, but sordid as the situation sounds, I don't agree with you that it is completely a moral issue. Nor do I think the responsibility is all Bill's. He is an addict, who turns to the objects of his addiction when he is distressed. Everyone has his or her own way of dealing with unbearable stress. Some withdraw completely, others turn to alcohol or drugs, while still others abuse their wives or children.

"Bill turns to extramarital affairs to self-medicate himself. I don't think anyone could have stood up to the terrible, unceasing accusations made against him and not broken down in some way. I doubt whether I could have. What is remarkable is not that Bill regressed, but that he was able to carry out the duties of the office of the president as well as he did under the horrendous pressure he was forced to live under for so many years. I, for one, am forever grateful for his accomplishments and wish our country was in the condition today that it was when Bill left office. I hope future generations of Americans will remember the good condition he left the country in and that the affair of Monica Lewinsky will slide into the obscurity it deserves."

I paused, and looking directly into her widely opened eyes, said, "What I also believe is this: If Bill hadn't been persecuted so intensively from the moment he took office, he would not have needed his addiction as badly. He probably could have controlled his impulses, and there would have been no Monica Lewinsky."

Hillary's eyes glistened over, and she looked at me with appreciation. "Thank you, Doctor," she said when she was able to speak. "You are the only person who makes any sense about Bill's behavior, the only one who really feels for him. Everybody else is so busy condemning him that nobody before you has asked why he did such a foolish thing. Are you saying that he had no choice but to rescue himself from the vicious assaults in the only way he knew how?"

I nodded.

"I am sure you are right, and I am grateful," she continued. "I've always said the Republicans were out to get him and to ruin his presidency. They almost succeeded. I can see now that the affair was really a regression to his earlier way of handling problems."

I nodded, pleased that despite her pain and humiliation, she was able to see the other side of the coin.

She paused and then said tearfully, "As I understand it, you believe that Bill is essentially a good man who was in over his head because of the unceasingly brutal attacks of the opposition, in addition to his personal losses."

I nodded again.

"I can understand the affair with Monica now," she said. "But this new woman in Chappaqua is more than I can bear. Why do you think he needs a new lover now when things are going so well?"

"Hillary, things are going well for *you*. Can you imagine what it must feel like to leave the office of the President of the United States in disgrace and to become a private citizen? After being president, where else can he go but down? All this while watching his wife becoming more and more popular and important. For such a narcissistic man, there can be no worse an ordeal. He is seeking self-medication again and needs your compassion."

She thought deeply about what I had said, and with tears running down her cheeks responded, "In light of your opinion, Doctor, which really echoes my deepest feelings, I think I'll be able to find it in my heart to forgive him."

I heaved a deep sigh of relief.

January 6, 2014

"It will be good to start today by talking about Chelsea. I can't wait to tell you about my dear daughter, Doctor. She's unquestionably the most important person in my and Bill's life," she said enthusiastically. I couldn't wait either, as I was anxious to hear about their relationship and the kind of mother Hillary was.

"Since very early in our marriage," she continued, "we had been trying hard to become parents. Our lack of success almost demolished me—I never felt I could be a complete woman without having a child. To me, it was the worst failure of my life, and every month when 'the curse' arrived, I felt a deep despair. Things didn't look very promising. In the summer of 1979, as a last resort, we scheduled an appointment with a famous fertility specialist in San Francisco, to take place after we returned from a short vacation in Bermuda. Immediately after our return and before our appointment with the specialist, a miracle of miracles happened. I discovered I was pregnant!

"Bill and I attended Lamaze classes together to prepare for natural childbirth. The other members of the class took it in stride that their classmates were the governor of Arkansas and his wife. What was important to them was their pregnancies. Bill and I are both heavy readers, so we poured over Barry Brazelton's handbook on parenting, talked about my pregnancy night and day to each other and whoever else we could corner, sought advice from our friends who had children and even from some who didn't, and barraged doctors, nurses, and midwives with questions until they ducked into closets when they saw us coming. I discovered Bill talking aloud one day and was amused to hear him asking questions of our cat.

"On February 27, 1980, fifteen minutes after Bill came home from a governors' conference in Washington, and three weeks before my due date, my water broke. Bill swore I was waiting for him to come home. I've never seen him so flustered. You'd think he was the one having the baby. I, of course, was calm. Unfortunately, that didn't last too long. When we got to the hospital, we were told that Chelsea would be a breech birth and would have to be delivered by a Caesarian section. There would be no natural childbirth for me.

"I screamed at the doctor, wondering and worrying if my baby was in any trouble. The doctor tried to reassure me, but I wasn't convinced until I held Chelsea in my arms and counted ten tiny pink fingers and ten tiny pink toes.

"Although a nurse blocked his way into the delivery room, Bill would not accept her dictum. He told her she'd be making a big mistake if she didn't let him in there. When she protested that Bill might faint at the sight of my blood, he answered that she was wrong, and he insisted on seeing his daughter born.

"Never mind that Bill was the governor of Arkansas. He is a big man with a booming voice. When Bill is in an uproar, they don't even know I'm around! The nurse didn't hear my weak protest at his exclusion. Eventually, Bill was allowed inside the delivery room to hold my hand, and the hospital changed its policy after that for fathers who wanted to help their babies be born.

"Because of the Lamaze classes, Bill knew what to expect and how to help me by holding my hand, rubbing my back, doing breathing exercises with me, and putting ice on my tongue when I was thirsty. He went through every contraction with me, and even screamed when I screamed. I must say I am still a little resentful that he saw more of the birth than I did—the doctors put up a screen to block my view of the cutting and bleeding.

"It's not entirely fair—I went through all the pain of childbirth, and Bill was the one to watch the process! That was fine with him. I've never seen him so happy as when the nurse handed our six-pound baby to him and he cuddled her to his breast. It was the greatest thing that ever happened to him. While I was in the recovery room, Bill couldn't put the baby down. He carried her around to show her off to his mother, friends he had invited, and members of the hospital staff. He sang to her, talked to her, and crooned to her. As he told me later, he never wanted that night to end.

"As for me, I glowed from the miracle of child birth. 'I have a perfect child. I have a perfect child' were the words that kept running through my mind. What can be more wonderful than to create another human being?

"We had chosen her name on our Christmas vacation in London in 1978, after we heard Judy Collins sing 'Chelsea Morning.' We both loved the song, and Bill said with delight, 'If we ever have a daughter, let's call her Chelsea,' because that's where we were walking when we first heard the song.' So Chelsea she was from that moment on."

"We'll have to stop now, Hillary," I said. "We'll continue with Chelsea next time."

"Stop now?" she exclaimed angrily. "Just when I'm getting into the best part! What good are you? You're not an analyst; you're a warden. Right when I'm really getting into things, you lock me out!"

I was sorry about that, but out she went, like all my other patients from the time I first started my practice.

January 8, 2014

Hillary came in for her session and seemed to have forgotten she had left angry with me the last time.

"I guess you know by now, Doctor, that I am the world's worst worrier, so I was anxious for months after Chelsea was born. I was concerned that I wouldn't be a good mother—some aspects of mothering did not come easily to me. For instance, I had a lot of trouble nursing her. Our friend, Carolyn Staley, paid a visit to the three of us shortly after Chelsea arrived. Carolyn was an opera singer, and wrote a song she sang to celebrate Chelsea's birth. It was written mostly about the awe of giving birth to a child. I totally agreed with that part of the song. It was one of the subsequent lines that gave me trouble. She had written, 'We may not be worthy, but we'll try to be wise.' Instead of feeling grateful to Carolyn for her creativity on our behalf, I felt greatly insulted that she thought I was unworthy to be a mother. Such is the sensitivity of the brand new mother!"

I smiled. Hillary had brought back memories of my own state of mind after bearing a child. I told her she was not alone, that it was true for many women, and that I, for one, had experienced similar ultra-sensitivity after giving birth. Hillary loved hearing that her "shrink" felt the same way, and said it made her feel better about her own unchecked flow of tears at that time.

January 10, 2014

"Once home, we hired a series of babysitters who were available around the clock. We never knew when we would be called away on important business. We tried to devote as much time to Chelsea as possible, as did our parents and friends, as did members of the governor's staff. I vowed to do everything I could for her and to put her above everything else in my life. My mother had done that for me, and I will be eternally grateful.

"Chelsea was a precocious little girl from the moment she opened her big blue eyes and took me in. I could almost see her thinking, 'Is *that* my mother?' I'm not sure it was a compliment. She began speaking at age two, and yelled, 'Where's my mommy? I want my mommy!'

"During the terrible time after Bill lost the election for governor, Chelsea was the one spot of sunshine in our lives. Virginia, Bill's mother, and Chelsea adored each other, so we spent a lot of time at her house. It was there she learned to walk and talk and taught Bill a lesson he has never forgotten. He was holding her one day while watching a basketball game on TV.

"'Da,' she called out softly. *No answer from Bill.* 'Da da!' she cried out more forcefully. *Still no answer from Bill.* Then Chelsea resorted to more drastic means. She grabbed him by the nose and chomped down on it with her four teeth. He yelped, and I watched with alarm as his nose swelled rapidly. I don't believe it has ever gone back to its original size. Check out his photos and see for yourself!

"Very little took precedence over our sweet child. When my career called for frequent flights between Little Rock and Washington, Chelsea waited up for me to come home. Bill would practice the piano and do homework with her. From the beginning, I instructed my staff that my late afternoons and evenings were to be kept as free as possible to spend with Chelsea. I didn't leave the Governor's House during those hours unless I absolutely had to.

"When I was home later on, she and I sat around the family kitchen table piled up with her books and did her homework together. When I needed to be out of town, she would fax me her assignments, and I would answer her questions—by return fax. We had many discussions together—at the dinner table, while driving her to school, while playing Scrabble and other games with her, when cheering her on from the bleachers at her soccer games, and when watching movies with her, especially her favorites, *Snow White and the Seven Dwarfs* and *High Noon.*

"Bill and I were determined that if we could help it, our beloved child would not suffer because of our political careers. Often when I was away and dead tired and had retired to my hotel room at night and needed nothing so much as to collapse on my bed, I would force myself to listen without interruption to Chelsea's stream-of-consciousness account of her day over the phone. If my eyes would shut occasionally, I doubt if Chelsea noticed. When I woke up, she would still be talking."

January 13, 2014

"During all the uproar about Bill's infidelities, real and imagined, we were sure that sooner or later Chelsea, who was old enough at age six to read well and watch TV, would hear nasty things about her father. So we decided to teach her a role-playing game to try to prepare her for the harsh truths of the political world. I told her that for us to remain in our beautiful house and near all her friends and school, her daddy had to run for governor again and that his opponents would be saying terrible things about him.

"She couldn't believe anyone could say anything bad about her daddy. We explained to her that there were mean people in the world who would say these awful things. We played different roles to practice how Chelsea could react. Bill pretended to be one of those mean people we told her about and said some nasty things about himself, and Chelsea's part was to tell people how wonderful her father was and how they should all vote for him.

"The tears were literally bathing Chelsea's cheeks, and I felt bad for what we were putting her through. 'Why would anyone want to say such mean things about my daddy?' she kept asking.

"I still don't know the answer to that one, but we went on repeating 'the game' over and over again until I could see her gaining mastery over her feelings and even to enjoy the role playing. I hoped we had neutralized the awful words that soon would surface about Bill, and felt good that we had taught Chelsea the kind of emotional desensitization I had learned at my mother's knee many years ago using the image of a carpenter's level as a tool.

"Sure enough, shortly after we had played 'our game,' the newspapers began battering Bill again. Going through the checkout line at a supermarket, I almost gagged to see the lurid newspaper headlines about him. But I swallowed my nausea and said to Chelsea, who was also reading the headlines, 'This is just what we expected in a political campaign, isn't it, Chelsea?'

"She said, 'Yes, Mommy, but I don't have to read it, and when I hear anybody say bad things about my daddy on TV, I can just turn it off!'"

January 15, 2014

"When Chelsea was six years old, we took her on a trip to England with us," Hillary said. "She wanted very badly to meet Queen Elizabeth and Princess Diana, but in those days that wasn't so easy to arrange. So we took her to an exhibit showcasing the history of all of the kings and queens of Great Britain. She studied it carefully for close to an hour, and then said it looked like being a queen or king would be a very hard job. Now I wonder, where in the world could she have gotten that idea?

"While Bill was president, we took a trip to try to straighten out his relationship with Russian President Boris Yeltsin. The Yeltsins hosted a state dinner for us, and Chelsea joined us for the entertainment after dinner. The next morning, our long motorcade left the Kremlin. Somehow, with all the excitement, nobody noticed that Chelsea, her caretaker, and Secret Service agent weren't with us.

"As the last car of the motorcade pulled out, the Secret Service realized what had happened. An agent rushed up to an old white van nearby and commandeered it. Wouldn't you know, the driver didn't understand English or was hard of hearing, and kept saying, 'Eh, what? Eh, what?' The agent had to repeat the story over and over before it made any sense to the Russian. Then he pushed the Americans into the van, jumped into it himself, and raced past the barricades to the airport, but the problem wasn't over yet. Russian security refused to let them enter. They recognized Chelsea but couldn't believe we had actually left her behind. Neither could I!

"While they sorted out the confusion, Chelsea's party grabbed her and their bags and made a mad dash for the airplane. I didn't discover until I saw them walking up the stairs to the plane that my daughter had been missing. I yelled out, 'Oh my God! We almost lost Chelsea! Can you believe we almost lost my Chelsea? I swear I'll never let go of her again!' and hugged her for the rest of the trip.

"We loved Chelsea so much that even in my forty-ninth year, we talked of having another child. I told a startled *Time* reporter that we were thinking of a brother or sister for Chelsea. He looked at me incredulously and wondered if we were planning on having that child naturally. I explained it would be a pleasant surprise but that we might even adopt a child, though it would have to be after the 1996 presidential re-election campaign. As I watched the shocked reporter stagger away, I laughed out loud and thought what a long way I had come since my prissy early years.

"Adolescence is a difficult period, but an adolescent's life at the White House is even harder. I particularly sympathized with Eleanor Roosevelt, who had a terrible time with motherhood. All her children ended up leading somewhat troubled lives. Eleanor once said that she was so busy disciplining her children that she had no time to show them any affection. I had to watch out that I didn't become a mother like her, because I was the designated disciplinarian, while Bill was always warm and loving to Chelsea, captivating her with his far-ranging discussions, vast knowledge, and interesting stories.

"In my bad moments, I am resentful that he had all the fun and left the discipline to me. You know, good cop, bad cop? Good parent, bad parent. Guess which one of the Clintons was the bad cop? I didn't force Chelsea to go out in the ice and snow to locate a lost toothpaste cap, but picking up spilled popcorn on a White House floor was a milder example of the same sort of thinking. I didn't want to come across as a monster to my daughter, so I was very relieved when Bruce Lindsey, Bill's chief personal aide, told some of my friends I was a warm and tender mother.

"Chelsea was a perfectly normal teenager, and as such her behavior was not always to my liking. When she was sixteen years old, she and I were going to march in a parade. Chelsea walked down the White House stairs covered, not coincidentally, I'm sure, with a full-length coat. As we were leaving, I asked to see her outfit. She opened her coat and, to my shock, saw she was wearing a miniskirt that stopped at the middle of her thighs. Unfortunately, it was too late for her to change clothes, and being a teenager, she probably would have refused anyhow.

"I'll never forget her striding down the middle of the procession without her coat, with the eyes of the media fastened upon her. Some of the reporters clapped loudly as she sailed by. So much for trying to keep her out of the public eye! Chelsea just waved and smiled without embarrassment and appeared happy and confident. I wasn't. I kept imagining the headlines that would erupt, 'Hillary Lets Chelsea Walk Half Naked In Parade.' Luckily, they didn't. When I complained to Bill about *his* daughter, he just laughed and said, 'Come off it, Miss Priss!'

"I won't repeat my response."

January 17, 2014

"Nothing was more important to me than that Chelsea lead as normal a life as possible in the White House. In Little Rock, she had gone to a public school, and could do everything the other kids did. But obviously, that was not possible as a president's daughter. Chelsea was not thrilled being trailed and shadowed by Secret Service men twenty-four hours a day.

"Even Socks, her cat, had to be kept on a leash when they went outside. I tried to have Chelsea walk a thin line between taking part in normal activities and staying out of danger from possible mental cases.

"*Who could I ask?* I thought. *Who could possibly know?* Then I thought of Jackie Kennedy Onassis. I had great admiration for the way she had brought up her children in the White House, so I decided to ask her for advice.

"Jackie and I were alike in many ways. We both were reserved women, with a shameless sense of humor lurking right underneath the surface. Jackie was notoriously witty, and I was known among friends for being a wicked mimic. We both idolized accomplished men of intelligence and wit. Not incongruous to our growing friendship, we each had knowingly married womanizers who became president.

"As soon as she herself picked up the phone when I called, Jackie insisted I come to lunch at her elegant Fifth Avenue apartment. I was dropped off at her home by the Secret Service men, and Jackie greeted me at the door of the fifteenth floor elevator. I found her taller, slimmer, and more beautiful than in her photographs. As always, she was impeccably dressed, in beige and gray silk pants and matching blouse. She was just as glamorous at age sixty-three as she had been as our First Lady.

"I was delighted to find her home warm and comfortable, overflowing with books, paintings, and works of art, rather than one designed to demonstrate the latest in society decor. I was immediately stuck dumb in her presence. 'She is truly America's queen,' I thought anxiously. 'I am just a little girl from Illinois by way of New Haven and Little Rock. How can I ever hope to follow in her footsteps?'

"With her brilliant intuition, however, she sensed my discomfort and put me at ease right away. She seemed to know immediately what I had come to talk about, and started in on her years as First Lady, when she had found herself confused and her job undefined. 'There is no book of rules,' I remember her saying, 'on how to be a First Lady. You have to make them up yourself. It's not easy. If you're under twenty-five, you are an indifferent Generation X-er; if you're over 40, you're a selfish Baby Boomer; if you're a liberal, you're a bleeding heart; and if you're a conservative, you have no heart at all.'

"'Yes, I added, 'and if you're a Democratic president from Arkansas, you're every one of those things, depending on what day it is.' Jackie laughed, and said she understood what I meant.

"Her erudite refurbishment of the White House served to define her role for herself, as well as of the Kennedy presidency, and greatly contributed to the myth of Camelot. I wondered how I would define the role of First Lady for myself. I doubted very much if I could equal the brilliant, highly original role Jackie carved out for herself as First Lady.

"We had lunch at a table in the corner of her living room overlooking the gorgeous trees of Central Park and the Metropolitan Museum of Art, and discussed how to keep Chelsea shielded from the media, who otherwise would hound her. Jackie told me what she had done to protect Caroline and John and said that providing a normal life for Chelsea would be my number one priority. She warned me that we would have to allow Chelsea to grow up and even to make mistakes, all the while shielding her from the constant presence of reporters. She said her own children were lucky to have been surrounded by cousins and children of friends and that it would be harder for Chelsea, who was an only child.

"She said I had to protect her and keep her surrounded by family and friends, but that it wasn't a good idea to spoil her. I had to smile at that remark. Being my father's daughter, it didn't seem too likely that I would spoil Chelsea. 'Maybe I should have Jackie talk to Bill,' I thought. She warned me about the women who would try to get their children to be friends with Chelsea simply to get into my good graces.

"I told Jackie how grateful I was that she had created a dining area upstairs at the White House and that we were converting the butler's pantry into a small kitchen where we could relax in a less formal manner than in the usual presidential dining room. She wholeheartedly agreed. I told her it was hard to maintain a normal life for a child who lives in a fish bowl. She graciously said she had heard Chelsea was adjusting beautifully and that I should keep doing what I had been doing. I felt a rush of warmth for my new friend. On parting, we gave each other a big, friendly hug, and kept in touch by phone for years to come. She remained a help and an inspiration for me until her death."

January 20, 2014

"When Chelsea was fifteen and developing into a delightful young woman, we took our first extended trip abroad without the president. He had asked me to make a twelve-day official visit to South Asia because he wanted to oversee the development of good relations with India after their forty-year policy of non-alignment with the United States and ties with Russia during the Cold War. The State Department approved of our visit, seeing it as a way to highlight the administration's commitment to the region, and I wanted to extend my passionate crusade to improve the rights of women.

"The trip was a treat for both Chelsea and me. She was excited about seeing a brand new part of the world. I knew it would add to my pleasure to see the new world through her fresh young eyes. My own had become jaded after years of Washington politics. We landed in Islamabad, Pakistan after a plane trip of seventeen hours.

"As you know, the press and I have never been bosom friends. To my surprise, that changed a little on our trip. Like Jackie Kennedy with her children, I had always tried to protect Chelsea from publicity to keep her life as normal as possible. Everything that happened on airplanes or in hotels was always strictly off limits to them, as was anything she did or said on her own. But in India, it was difficult to keep the media away from Chelsea. We shared many of the same moments—government dinners, visits to historical places of interest, and meeting celebrities.

"For the first time in Chelsea's life, the press was able to see her up close, and they were most impressed with her poise and fortitude and how very special she is. They watched her gently help weigh undernourished babies, so fragile they winced at the slightest touch. They saw her as a confident, sophisticated adult dining with the prime minister. They noted her brilliant questions and her insightful remarks.

"Many of the reporters begged me to allow them to quote her.

Finally, when visiting the Taj Mahal, I had to give in. Her remark was so wise I thought I would have to let the world hear it. She said, and the journalists quoted, 'When I was little, this was the embodiment of the fairy tale palace for me. I would see pictures of it and dream I was a princess. Now that I am here, it is just as spectacular as I had dreamed.'

"How could I not let the world know how wonderful Chelsea was?"

I knew exactly what she meant. Even today, I still brag about my grown children to anyone I can corner.

January 22, 2014

"During that same trip, Chelsea came to me with a peculiar look on her face," Hillary continued as if there had been no time at all between sessions.

"I asked if anything was wrong.

"She said it wasn't so much wrong as strange. A Secret Service agent had told her that the hotel emptied the swimming pool and filled it with bottled water just for us. I laughed and suggested they were joking. But it seems the Secret Service agent hadn't been joking. The next day, Chelsea came back to me with a smirk and told me the Indians had paved a dirt road because we were planning to walk down it.

"'Oh, Jackie,' I thought, 'could I use your advice today! How do I keep Chelsea unspoiled when they pave a road so she doesn't have to walk in the mud?' It didn't help when we took a long walk in the hills above the city, and hordes of people waiting for us at the roadside applauded as we passed by. I thought, 'I'll just have to hope that Chelsea's upbringing will keep her level-headed.'"

January 24, 2014

"We returned from Asia just in time to get Chelsea in school. She was now fifteen, and behaving more and more like a teenager every day. I remembered what Jackie had told me about Caroline as a teenager: 'She knows everything. I know nothing.' I knew precisely what Jackie meant. A little voice inside of me told me to be happy that Chelsea was behaving normally for her age, but a bigger voice shouted, 'What happened to my nice little girl who always did what her mother asked? Where is she? I miss her!'

"She kept testing her independence, which I must say was made particularly difficult for an adolescent girl because she was followed every minute by Secret Service agents, to say nothing of a very loving, overprotective mother. Finally, she stomped her foot and said, 'I want to ride with the other girls, and not be driven around like a freak in a car driven by Secret Service agents!' Sometimes teenagers are right. Hard as it was for me, I saw her point and gave in.

"As with other girls her age, Chelsea's life revolved around her friends, school, church, and ballet. Chelsea loved ballet, and every day after school, she took lessons for several hours at the Washington School of Ballet. At that time, she wanted to be a professional dancer, but I didn't tell her that her chances for success, especially as a president's daughter, were not so great. I figured that every girl wants to be an actress, dancer, or singer when she grows up, and Chelsea eventually would outgrow that ambition. Thank goodness I was right.

"I'm no Harry Truman, who bawled out the music critic who dared to criticize Margaret Truman's singing, although Bill might have been. I'm happy I didn't have to tussle with the two of them over it, the way Jackie did with John, Jr. when he wanted to be an actor. After ballet class, Chelsea came home to tackle the mountains of homework assigned to high school juniors already facing the college application process. With all my educational experience, I thought I could be a great help to her in applying to colleges.

"But do you think she wanted my assistance in filling out her applications? No. She made it extremely clear that she was old enough to take care of her own business and that I should get off her neck! I am embarrassed to tell you, Doctor, that I went to bed and cried myself to sleep. After passing several nights like this, I decided that Chelsea had a right to be her own person and I resolved to do as she wished. And I followed through, at least most of the time.

"It was hard to believe, but Chelsea was now sixteen. To my dismay, she wanted to learn how to drive. Even worse, Bill was going to teach her. The Secret Service didn't ordinarily allow Bill to drive, which I thought was a good thing. He has a garbage collector mind which stores up so much information that at any given moment, he might not see where he is going. But since neither he nor Chelsea paid any attention to my fears, he insisted on doing his paternal duty, and inveigled the Secret Service into lending him a car at Camp David.

"Her first driving lesson focused on backing up and parallel parking. I went to bed with my head under the covers. After the lesson, I asked how it went. Chelsea merely said that her dad had learned a lot. I looked them both over carefully. Chelsea appeared exhilarated, but Bill looked a little nauseated!"

January 27, 2014

"Shortly after she learned to drive," Hillary began, "I came upon Chelsea and a group of her friends discussing where they would apply to college. 'What, already?' I thought. 'It seems only a little while ago that I was holding her on my lap and we were reading *The Cat in the Hat* together. I'd give anything to have those times back again. Unfortunately, she was then as tall as I was, and it would have been a bit difficult to hold her in my lap. Despite my pain at the thought of her leaving home, I resolved to hide my feelings with the hope that she would choose a nearby college and we could at least spend weekends together.

"Sidwell Friends School holds a College Night every year in which they have qualified speakers discuss various colleges and the application process. Bill and I went with Chelsea to see what we could learn. On driving back to the White House, Chelsea seemed deep in thought. Finally, she declared that she'd like to go to Stanford. Forgetting the advice in all the books I had read on how to be a good mother, I shouted, 'Stanford? Are you crazy? That's three thousand miles away. We would never get to see you!'

"Bill, wise man that he sometimes is, pressed my arm and told her she could go to any college that would admit her. Of course, I realized he was right. I was not ready for her to leave me, but I knew I would be glad for her if she were admitted to the college of her choice. I gritted my teeth and determined to spend as much time with her before then as she would let me.

"Speaking of Chelsea's adolescent rebelliousness, I had to laugh when I read in the newspapers that she was to be given an award by the National Hispanic Health Foundation (NHHF) at its annual awards gala in New York. According to a press release, Chelsea was due praise for 'motivating and informing young adults, especially Latinas, to be independent and make healthy decisions for themselves.'

'Independent' is not exactly the word I would choose to describe my teenager's sometimes snotty behavior.

"I had been reading stories about the traumas experienced by parents whose children left home for college. One mother snuck back on campus to squeeze in one last look at her son, only to find herself slinking around the hallway of his dorm like a spy in a B-movie. Then there was the father who couldn't sleep at night because he was worried that his son wasn't getting enough sleep. Sounds like Bill. One crazy mother couldn't bear to erase any phone messages from her absent daughter until her system was so cluttered that it wouldn't work anymore, so she missed hearing from her daughter when she really wanted to talk. Worst of all were the parents who sobbed every time they walked by the empty room their kids once used to play music loud enough to break their eardrums. I'm not that bad, although Bill might tell you a different story.

"I got a lot of comfort from such stories because misery loves company, and I really dreaded the moment Bill and I would have to say goodbye to Chelsea at Stanford. I'm the person who cried when she went off to kindergarten. Oh, I know that good parents should feel great at their children's achievements and full of excitement about the wonderful life that lies before them. That's how I felt at my mature moments, but unfortunately, most of the time I wondered why I let her skip third grade.

"I sympathized with the other mothers suffering from premature separation anxiety during a month of intense preparation for a hallowed Sidwell Friends tradition: The Mother-Daughter Show. Mothers of Sidwell seniors participate in an evening of comic sketches poking fun at their graduating daughters. I joined several mothers of Chelsea's friends in a series of skits in which each of us played the part of our respective daughters. I did a lot of pirouetting like a ballerina and talking endlessly on the phone about plans to go out. The audience howled. In the opening scene, we mothers draped ourselves in sheets like togas and sang, 'I Believe I Can Fly.' I wouldn't be surprised if Chelsea could. She can do everything else. Despite my stage fright, I was able to find my inner ham, but fortunately for both me and Chelsea, my voice was drowned out by more musical mothers during the opening number.

"Chelsea's high school graduation was much like many others I have attended, with one major difference: The President of the United States spoke. Bill made me cry when he asked the graduates to realize that their parents might seem a little sad or even act a bit strange. He said, and I remember this clearly, 'You see, we are remembering your first day of school and all the triumphs and failures that occurred between then and now. Although we have raised you for this moment and are very proud of you, we long to hold you on our laps one more time as we did when you were little and read you *Madeline* or *The Little Engine That Could*.' He wiped away a tear, and so did I and every other parent at the ceremony.

"All too soon after Chelsea's graduation, it was time for all us parents to depart the kids' new campus and for the kids to rearrange their rooms and possessions as they really would like them. After weeks of imagining our parting, I had steeled myself for this moment and was almost ready to leave Stanford. Not Bill, though. He suddenly seemed filled with anxiety about leaving Chelsea.

"As far as Chelsea was concerned, she was more than ready for us to depart. Because Stanford starts much later in the fall than most schools, she already had heard from many of her fellow students about the excitement and miseries of college life, and couldn't wait to start. I tried to keep her from seeing the woe-begone look in her parents' eyes.

"I hoped we had given her the really important things a child needs to do well at college, and that she had her own conscience firmly locked inside her," Hillary continued. "Like most mothers, I was really concerned about whether she'd make good friends who would like her for herself and not for who her parents were, if she'd like her classes, and if she'd eat the right foods.

"Unlike every other mother, however, I worried about the security and privacy that went along with being the president's daughter. Bill and I trusted Chelsea to take care of herself on her own. She always has been a level-headed and well-controlled person. But the nuts of the world are not so predictable, and we wouldn't be able to shield her from them as we did while she lived with us."

January 29, 2014

"Speaking of the nuts in the world," Hillary said, picking up where she left off in the previous session, "that was a problem that bothered me more after Princess Diana's death and my resulting concern about her sons. Neither Chelsea nor William and Harry chose their parents. I thought that, like all young people, they should be permitted space and privacy. These children, like all others, deserved to pursue their educations and emotional development without the pressure of living under the eyes of the world. Unfortunately, Prince Charles did not seem to be able to fill the bill, nor did the queen and her Prince Consort. I can only hope that Diana gave her boys enough emotionally to guide them on the rocky path to adulthood.

"I will be everlastingly grateful that Chelsea was spared intrusive media attention during our White House years. Once I made it clear to the press that Bill and I were deeply committed to protecting Chelsea's privacy and would go to great lengths to enforce it, they avoided stalking her most of the time or bothering her with unwelcome attention outside of public events she participated in because of her father's presidency.

"The media's sensitivity and feelings of responsibility for Chelsea's welfare helped her a lot, and allowed her to grow up as normally as possible in the White House. They permitted her to be a regular teenager, free to pursue her studies and interests without journalists gawking at her night and day. That's as it was for Caroline and John Kennedy, and exactly the way it should have been. I'm happy Jackie was around long enough to see it.

"That's also how it should have been for William, Harry, or the child of any public figure. They must be left in peace to mature, away from the intense glare of the public eye, and that's how I'd hoped it would remain for Chelsea as she embarked on her college years.

"I prayed that she and her friends would be able to spend their next four years learning, finding out what was important to them in life, and moving toward fulfilling their dreams. Then I could return to worrying about everything else at Stanford, like the color of her sheets.

"When Chelsea was interviewed on *The Rachael Ray Show* in October 2013, I was shocked to learn some things about my daughter that I had never dreamt of. She had her first necking party in the basement of the White House—the White House!—at some point during Bill's presidency, with an unknown guy who later become her boyfriend.

"And here I thought I'd taken such good care of her, making sure she was always carefully supervised. I guess she just wasn't a Miss Priss like her mother at that age. It must be the Bill Clinton in her. Jackie, where was your advice about such matters?"

January 31, 2014

"In the fall of 1997, Chelsea became a student at Stanford, and chose History as her major," Hillary told me.

"Not surprising when you think that she had helped to make history, and conceivably would do it more in the future. The week before she registered, I published an open letter in my syndicated column warning journalists to leave my daughter alone. Chelsea arrived at Stanford in a motorcade with Bill and me, Secret Service men, and almost two hundred and fifty journalists. For her security, bullet-proof glass was installed in her dorm windows, and cameras were placed in nearby hallways. In addition, Secret Service men dressed as students lived in her dorm. To my satisfaction, with the exception of an occasional, infuriating tabloid story about her, Chelsea's four Stanford years remained largely hidden from the public.

"She graduated in 2001 with highest honors and a B.A. in History. The topic of her 150-page senior thesis was the 1998 Good Friday Agreement in Northern Ireland. She knows more than I do about it, and I was Secretary of State!

"In July 2001, Bill issued a statement that, later that year, Chelsea would attend University College, where he had studied politics between 1968 and 1970 on a Rhodes Scholarship. Chelsea did not apply for one. We felt that such a scholarship should be awarded to a needy child. Lord Butler of Brockwell, the Master of University College, said, 'Chelsea Clinton's record at Stanford shows that she is a very well-qualified and able student. The college is also pleased to extend its link with the Clinton family.' Upon the suggestion of British and American advisors, the university heightened security measures, and students were ordered not to discuss Chelsea with the media.

"Arriving at University College shortly after 9/11, Chelsea was attracted to other American students who were feeling as she did about the traumatic after-effects of the attack. She told *Talk* magazine she ran into anti-American feeling every day. She was expecting to seek out non-Americans as friends but instead looked for support among fellow Americans.

"Chelsea was heavily criticized for her comments in the press and by the students' newspaper, *Oxford Student,* which angered the university by attacking Chelsea in an editorial. In contrast, many people who met her described her as charming, poised, and unaffected, which she is, and unless she hid her feelings from me, which is unlike Chelsea, she seemed to be adjusting well to life overseas. During her Oxford years, I was surprised to see Chelsea adopting a sophisticated look, helped by our family friend Donatella Versace, whose fashion shows Chelsea never missed. Geordie Greig, the editor of *Tatler Magazine,* ranked her fifth on his 2002 'Top 10 Girls' list.

"In 2003, I was thrilled when Chelsea was awarded a Masters of Philosophy in International Relations. Following her graduation, she returned to the United States, where she began working toward a D.Phil. in International Relations from the University of Oxford, doing her doctoral work at Columbia University. I always said I had a smart kid! In the spring of 2010, Chelsea completed a Master of Public Health degree at Columbia's Mailman School of Public Health and began teaching graduate classes there in 2012."

February 3, 2014

"Now for Chelsea's work life," Hillary said. "I can't wait to tell you what she's been up to. In 2010, my brilliant daughter began serving as Assistant Vice Provost for the Global Network University of New York University, working on international recruitment strategies. She also was the co-founder of the Of Many Institute for Multifaith Leadership at NYU and served as its co-chair. In 2012, she was given an award from the Temple of Understanding for her 'work in advancing a new model of integrating interfaith and cross-cultural education into campus life,' together with Imam Khalid Latif and Rabbi Yehuda Sarna.

"In 2003, Chelsea was hired by the consulting firm McKinsey & Company in New York, and in the fall of 2006, changed jobs to work for Avenue Capital Group. She was appointed co-chairperson for a fundraising venture by the Clinton Foundation, and at her young age is already on the board of directors of the School of American Ballet. Leave it to my Chelsea to get what she wants, one way or another. If she couldn't be a ballerina herself, she does the next best thing by participating in the lives of young dancers."

"Certainly an admirable idea," I said.

"Agreed. NBC announced in November 2011 that they had hired Chelsea as a special correspondent. She was to report feature stories about 'Making a Difference' for *NBC Nightly News* and *Rock Center*. It was a three-month contract that permitted her to continue working for the Clinton Foundation and to remain at Columbia. Although she received some critical reviews for her work, her NBC contract was renewed.

"In December 2007, my dear Chelsea, on her own initiative, began campaigning in Iowa in support of my bid for the Democratic presidential nomination. She spoke largely on college campuses across the country. By early April 2008, she had appeared at one hundred colleges to speak on my behalf. What a daughter I have! Most girls desert their mothers when they begin to go about their own lives, but not Chelsea. She continues to show her love for me in her actions. I suppose she takes after me in that respect. I stuck by my mother to the bitter end and was happy to return her love for me when she grew to need it.

"When I read about all the problems people have with their children, I thank God I have Chelsea for a daughter and wish everybody could be as lucky as Bill and me. But then, is it really luck? I like to think I have had some role in helping her become the wonderful person she is.

"While Chelsea was campaigning, she answered audience questions but refused to give interviews or respond to press questions. Philippe Reines, my press secretary, always stepped in when the media attempted to barge in on Chelsea. He did a good job, and I was grateful. When MSNBC's ignoramus of a reporter David Shuster called Chelsea's activities on my behalf 'being pimped out,' Reines violently objected. Shuster subsequently apologized on-air and was suspended for two weeks. I am completely in favor of free speech, but I suspect I would turn my head away if David Shuster were being gagged!

"The first time she was asked about how I handled the Lewinsky scandal at a campaign stop, Chelsea responded with her mother's tart tongue that it was none of their business. As she became a more experienced campaigner, she toned down her responses and deflected questions on such issues with comments like, 'If that's what you want to say, then that's what you should say. But there are other people who are interested in important things like healthcare and economics.' Smart girl, my Chelsea! Or did I mention that before?

"At the 2008 Democratic National Convention, to my great delight, Chelsea called me 'my hero and my mother' and introduced me with a long video tribute. She then returned to New York City and her private life."

February 4, 2014

"Now for the best part. On July 31, 2010, Chelsea and an investment banker named Marc Mezvinsky were married in an interfaith ceremony in Rhinebeck, New York. The wedding was held at Astor Courts, an estate overlooking the Hudson River, which at that time was the home of one of my supporters, Kathleen Hammer, once a producer at Oxygen Media, and Arthur Seelbinder, a developer and businessman. Although I was terrified of losing her, I liked Marc, and was happy for both of them.

"Marc was born December 15, 1977, to former Pennsylvania Democratic Congresswoman Marjorie Margolies-Mezvinsky and former Iowa Democratic Congressman Edward Mezvinsky. Marc was raised in the Conservative Jewish tradition. We and the older Mezvinskys were friends in the 1990s, and our children met on a Renaissance Weekend retreat in Hilton Head, South Carolina. They first were reported to be a couple in 2005 and became engaged over the Thanksgiving weekend in 2009.

"Before her marriage to Marc, Chelsea's love life, such as it was, had been tabloid fodder, much to the chagrin of Bill and me. Her first reported boyfriend was Matthew Pierce, whom she met at Stanford, but the two split in 1998, reportedly due to the emotional toll of Bill's sex scandal with Monica Lewinksy. Chelsea was later linked to fellow Stanford student Jeremy Kane, who even interned for Bill in the White House, and Chelsea was later romanced by Ian Klaus at Oxford. She finally settled down with Marc, and the world (and her mother!) immediately wanted to know when a Clinton grandbaby would appear on the scene.

"When asked by the ever-present press, Chelsea answered that she hoped that would be in the not-too-distant future, but at the time, she and her husband were both working very hard, adding that they were focusing on getting to a place where they could make a child their top priority. I could only answer with the Jewish word, *alevei*, meaning 'it should only happen to me,' a word I learned from the Mezvinskys. Hey there, Doc, I'm getting to be as Jewish as my daughter and future grandchild!

"Chelsea and Marc live in an elegant condo that cost $10.5 million near Madison Square Park in Manhattan. Incidentally, Chelsea's in-laws must have been thrilled when I was awarded a Lifetime Achievement Award from the American Jewish Congress, though my father surely turned over in his grave. I hope somehow he learns about it. It would serve him right!"

February 5, 2014

"Writing my book, *It Takes a Village*, showed me there were sometimes other things in the world besides mother-daughter relationships and helped me a lot with the loss of Chelsea from my daily life. My book tours offered exciting moments that often made me forget about Chelsea for a few hours at a time. Dozens of people showed up at my book signings wearing Hillary Fan Club t-shirts. There were hundreds of chapters all over the country whose members seemed to sense when I needed a boost.

"They would send out their troops to greet me with smiles, hand waving, and homemade signs. It made me feel great, although my hand always hurt so much from all the handshaking and book-signing that I had to retreat to my hotel room at night and soak it in Epsom Salts. It took away the pain until the next day, when the process repeated itself. I might mention it didn't detract at all from my improved spirits that people lined up around the block at many bookstores to buy an inscribed copy of my book, which made me a lot of money. So there, Bill Clinton! You're not the only one whose readers line up for hours outside bookstores to buy an autographed book.

"Chelsea became heavily involved in the work of the Clinton Global Initiative, and it was at one of these meetings where it became evident to me that Marc seemed to be madly in love with Chelsea. He couldn't keep his eyes off her as she stepped out in a bold orange dress during the closing plenary session of the Initiative in New York. He was 37, and once described Chelsea as 'the yin to his yang.' He sat alongside her during the final day of the Clinton Global Initiative's annual meeting in New York, flashing her adoring looks.

"The couple was joined in the audience by Bill and me. I modeled my new shorter hairstyle and an eye-catching mint green pant suit. Despite unfounded reports by the media that their marriage was on the rocks, Chelsea and Marc explained in an interview with *Vogue* last year that they were more in love than ever and gearing up to start a family 'in a couple of years.' Their appearance together appeared to confirm these feelings.

"Marc beamed as he sat alongside Chelsea, and she looked equally happy with life. They both were all smiles. She wore her long blonde hair straight, and accessorized her pretty sleeveless dress with a pair of nude heels. Like mother, like daughter; we struck matching poses as we stood on the stage at the Clinton Global Initiative. It was said that we also selected equally loud outfits. Oh, Bob Dylan, you had it right about being stoned.

"I think Marc and Chelsea are a perfect match; they seem to fit together like Bill and me, although I pray to God without the philandering! Towards the end of the Clinton Global Initiative closing session, Chelsea went up on the stage with us to address the crowds. She spoke beautifully, and I was so proud!

"The annual CGI meeting provides a platform for Bill, Chelsea, and me to announce a series of financial commitments from corporations, nongovernmental organizations, and philanthropists to the Foundation so we can help solve intractable problems around the globe. Created in 2001, the Foundation allows Bill to tackle problems across continents and shore up his legacy. It now serves as a home base for me, too, as I consider running for president in 2016. It also could become a launching pad for Chelsea, should she live out her heritage and become a political person like her parents. What began with one man's drive to help people everywhere quickly morphed into a foundation full of people of great passion and great gifts.

"CGI's four-day annual meeting illuminates how we, the Clintons, have moved on from the White House to establish a worldwide clearinghouse in which overwhelming problems like AIDS prevention, nutrition, female equality, and low income existence are examined with an eye to finding solutions. In a testament to our continuing ability to convene big names, the ballroom is always bursting with former

Clinton administration officials, CEOs, and corporate executives, as well as celebrities.

"As my slob of a husband searched for his notes backstage, Bono kept the crowd entertained with an impromptu Clinton impression, complete with a Southern drawl. The crowd howled. Even Bill thought it was funny and laughed loudly. I laughed to be polite. In smaller sessions, actor Sean Penn talked about his development work in Haiti, and the lovely actress Kate Hudson promoted leadership roles for women.

"I spoke about how I, through the Foundation, would lead an effort to evaluate the progress made by women around the globe in advance of the twentieth anniversary of my remarks at the U.N. women's conference in Beijing. As First Lady at the 1995 conference, I had made the much quoted remark that 'human rights are women's rights, and women's rights are human rights.' It's one of the best things I've ever said, and is still resounding around the world. Chelsea left her husband in the audience as she joined me on stage. Voicing both of our thoughts, I delighted when she spoke about a CGI commitment to stop the poaching of African elephants.

"During a session on Wednesday, I announced three new commitments to help women around the globe, including a $1.5 billion effort over the next five years to help businesses owned by women. Financial partners include Coca-Cola, Wal-Mart, and Exxon Mobil. Our family has been raising money to build the Foundation's endowment, holding recent fundraisers in New York's Hamptons and Washington. A benefit concert in London was planned for the fall, along with events in Washington and Miami.

"Bill was forced to defend his Foundation in August after media reports of infighting among staff and questions over the organization's financial management. Tell me, Doctor, why, oh why, do they continue to persecute us? Surely we've paid the price of whatever sinfulness we may have indulged in. The Foundation disclosed that an outside firm conducted an audit in 2011 that recommended a stronger management staff and a more independent board. We tried to give it to them, but I suspect they'll continue to try to throttle us as long as we Clintons are in politics.

"Republicans have already indicated that the Foundation's work will be fair game if I run for president in 2016. The Republican National Committee has already cited 'mismanagement and conflicts of interest' within the Foundation and said it showed 'how the Clintons operate and is part of the baggage tied to me.' So what else is new?"

February 6, 2014

Hillary happily returned to our next session to brag some more about her daughter Chelsea and her husband Marc, and especially the big event at which they got married.

"For some reason I don't understand, fewer famous people attended the wedding than I expected. It's strange, because I am very good about attending weddings of the famous and near-famous. Recognizable faces included acting couple Ted Danson and Mary Steenburgen, former Secretary of State Madeleine Albright, the incredibly wealthy Warren Buffett, and former Democratic National Committee chairman Terry McAuliffe. I was upset that Oprah Winfrey, Steven Spielberg, and Barbra Streisand all failed to show up. Don't they like me?" she asked wistfully.

I quickly informed her that they must certainly like her, for she is very likable, but they probably were kept from attending the wedding by long-standing engagements, but I didn't think she believed me.

"I wish I weren't so sensitive," she said, continuing the same thread. "I felt every no-show and every non-RSVP to the wedding as if an arrow had been shot through me. And I wasn't even the one getting married! Why do you think my feelings are so easily bruised, Doctor?"

"I think you were very hurt each time your father was critical of you. No matter how well you did, there was always something he said about how you could've done better. And here you are now, giving a spectacular wedding for your daughter, and apparently it still isn't good enough for some people to attend."

She smiled and said, "You're right. That is exactly the way it feels when someone turns down my invitation—it's just like how I felt when I pleaded for a compliment from my father and he refused to give it to me."

"Good that you know that, Hillary. And it's their loss, not yours. Perhaps in the future, when someone rebuffs you, you can tell yourself,

'I am not a little girl anymore." She nodded thoughtfully and returned to discussing Chelsea's wedding.

"The road to the exclusive estate was blocked off for the uninvited, and a no-fly zone imposed," she continued. "Guests were prevented from bringing any device that texted, tweeted, took photos, or sent any kind of description anywhere. To my consternation, a few sneaky guests got away with taking photographs, which they proceeded to sell to tabloids for what I'm sure was a pile of money. I should have been more careful who we invited!

"The wedding, which was called the social event of the year, included dinner and dancing for 400 guests. The people I invited who didn't come don't know what they missed. They will never see anything like it again. The mansion where it took place dates back to 1902 and boasts an indoor tennis court and white marble swimming pool. The wedding ceremony was inside a premium windowed tent lit by chandeliers. The inside of the tent was transformed into a fairyland. The ceiling and walls were draped in silks, its support poles blossomed with flowers, with tables covered in gray-blue cloth and arrangements of pink, blue and lavender hydrangeas and roses. Not bad for the daughter of a little girl from Pine Ridge, Illinois!

"Although Chelsea is a vegetarian, the guests dined on locally raised grass-fed beef (short ribs) or grilled Atlantic char, risotto, salad, and dinner rolls, catered by the St. Regis Hotel in New York. All the bread served was gluten-free, in deference to the bride's allergies. The eleven-tier chocolate cake, which was created by La Tulipe Desserts in Mt. Kisco, NY, cost $11,000 and was all that a wedding cake can be. It certainly was not modest. At $11,000, it couldn't be. Can you believe it?

"The parsimonious father in me cried out, 'How can you waste all that money? Whole families in India can live a year on much less than that!' I answered, 'Shut up, Papa! She is only going to get married once.' Fortunately, he was not around to smack my butt.

"Neither I nor anyone present will ever forget Bill's toast to the bride. Perhaps his most quoted line addressed the battle of the sexes; because Chelsea had been taught by her mother to voice her opinions, Bill, who was not known for being meek, said he had 'been outnumbered in his household by women. Now, with a son-in-law, 'the playing field is being evened. I have someone else on my side.' He added, 'My daughter is happy. I like and admire my future son-in-law, so I couldn't be happier.' I didn't believe him. I suspect he is secretly very jealous of Marc.

"The new couple performed a choreographed tango routine to the Etta James classic 'At Last.' They danced so graciously and brilliantly, I was ready to burst with pride.

"Bill helped to mastermind the nuptials to a limited degree. Though he told Ryan Seacrest in March that his role was limited 'to walking Chelsea down the aisle and paying the bills,' he informed NBC on April 19 that his daughter had decided to allow him to tap his world-leader expertise by being made part of the decision-making process. Still, Bill made sure to keep the focus on the bride."

February 7, 2014

"Only a few members of Chelsea's inner circle had seen her engagement present until she flashed her huge diamond ring at the opening night of *Promises, Promises* on Broadway," Hillary began. "The media, of course, published photos of the future bride on crutches. My dear daughter had broken her heel, and insisted she had no idea how it happened. Chelsea is a very honest person, but that one is hard to believe. Leave it to Bill Clinton's daughter to mess things up! Fortunately, she was expected to recover in time for her wedding.

"Before the wedding, I was asked if it would be a religious ceremony. I said the answer was complicated. I'm a Methodist, Bill is Southern Baptist, and to complicate matters further, Marc is Jewish. The couple had a range of choices, including conversion or a melding of both traditions into one ceremony. After all, the year before, Chelsea attended Yom Kippur services with Marc in New York.

"It turned out that duties at the ceremony were divided between Yale University's Jewish chaplain, James Ponet, and Reverend William Shillady of the Park Avenue Methodist Church in New York. At one point, after a breeze flipped a page in Shillady's service book, Chelsea helped him remember his next line. After they exchanged vows and rings, friends and relatives read the customary Jewish Seven Blessings. Chelsea and Mark stood under an arch of twigs, vines, and flowers.

"One of their friends read a 1943 poem by Leo Marks called 'The Life That I Have,' which I love. Here is the first verse:

The life that I have
Is all that I have
And the life that I have
Is yours.

"I cried, along with everyone else.

"Security proved to be a problem right from the start. Two Norwegian journalists were arrested and charged with trespassing for snapping photos at the estate's gate. To my great satisfaction, as a means of keeping out the paparazzi, Federal authorities ordered the closing of airspace over the area the entire weekend. I really appreciate it when the government steps in to help me out, rather than the other way around.

"After their marriage, Chelsea and Marc took up residence in New York City's Gramercy Park neighborhood, and in March 2013 they purchased that expensive condominium in the Flatiron District of Manhattan. If only Bill and I had been so rich at their age! I don't feel that rich even now. We probably aren't. I'm only a little bit jealous."

February 8, 2014

"To return to the Foundation, Democrats call attacks on it just a typical assault upon the Clintons and say the charitable work we do speaks for itself," Hillary said "The Foundation said this week that it had helped more than five million people with AIDS receive medication in seventy countries, its agriculture work in Africa had helped 4,300 farmers feed 30,000 people, and its work led to the planting of 4.5 million trees in Rwanda and Malawi. I think that is a pretty wonderful record, despite what the Republicans may say about it.

"Everything and anything available, and even some charges that are fabricated, will be used against us, but if the Foundation's work is the biggest complaint they can dig up about me—that my family has helped save lots of lives around the world—I'll take it.

"The Foundation's future could well rest in the hands of my dear Chelsea, who has traveled far and wide on its behalf and, despite her youth, serves extremely well as vice chair. She recently presided over a panel on non-communicable diseases and announced several philanthropic commitments, including efforts to provide clean drinking water and promote the health of women and children in Latin America. Following right in my footsteps! How proud can a mother be?

"Chelsea has hinted that politics could be in her future. With Bill and I as parents, it wouldn't surprise me. Who could have had a better preparation? She heard politics discussed every day from the moment she was born. When she was only two years old, she had already shared the podium with Bill and me as we campaigned throughout Arkansas for Bill's gubernatorial race. In an interview with CNN from Rwanda, she said she was leading a public life intentionally and that she might consider entering politics if she thought she could make a difference.

"If I don't win the presidency, maybe my daughter will do it for me. I hope I'm around to see it! If not, my mother and I will shine down on her from Heaven. If politics are then anything like they are today, Chelsea will need all the help she can get."

February 10, 2014

"Today, Doctor, I want to tell you about what were probably the most wonderful years of my life," Hillary said.

I had been listening to sad stories all day long about deaths, illnesses, and rejected lovers. I felt weighted down by them. I looked at Hillary with pleasure, thinking what a great relief it would be to hear about happy occasions for a change. I said, "That will be good to hear, Hillary. Tell me about them."

She said, "Toward the end of Bill's final term, I woke up one morning to find myself thinking, 'I am weary of riding on Bill's coattails. I am as smart as he is, and practically ran the presidency with him. Why don't I resurrect Hillary Rodham, who was a natural-born leader, and run for office myself? I mulled over the idea for a while until early in 1999, when it occurred to me that I could run for the U.S. Senate seat in New York to be vacated by Daniel Patrick Moynihan and possibly win. The more I thought about it, the more plausible it seemed, so I decided to discuss it with my best friend and advisor, Bill. I asked him what he would think about me starting a career of my own by running for senator of New York after we left the White House.

"One of the nicest things about Bill as a husband is that he always encourages me in whatever I want to do. If I said I wanted to go lion hunting on Mount Everest, he'd say, 'Let's hop on a plane tomorrow.' When I asked him what he thought about my running for New York senator, he said he thought it was a great idea and that we'd win by a landslide.

"I thought, 'What do you mean, *we*?' But I said thanks and that I appreciated his support. So we quickly bought a beautiful house in Chappaqua, New York, to establish our New York residency. I ran for the office in November 2000, and as usual found that Bill was right. His political instincts are unsurpassed. I did win by a landslide and served as a United States Senator from New York for eight years, from

January 3, 2001 to January 21, 2009. I was happy as a lark, and indeed found myself singing in the shower most days. I had found my calling at last. I was 60 years old. It takes some of us a little longer to find our calling."

February 11, 2014

February 11 is my birthday. To my surprise, I received two dozen gorgeous long-stemmed roses. *How lovely! I haven't received any flowers since my husband died. Who could have sent them?*

I opened the little card that accompanied the roses, and almost fell over when I read, "Happy, Happy Birthday, from Hillary. I'm happy you were born." I was very touched. What a thoughtful woman!

"Thank you so much for the flowers, Hillary," I said as she came in for our session. "But you shouldn't have done that. Patients aren't supposed to give presents to their analysts."

"I only follow the rules when I agree with them," she quipped with a smile.

"How did you know it was my birthday?"

"Oh, I have my ways," she said, fluttering her lashes. "Enough of that, or you'll know all my secrets," she said, and began to talk further about her time in the Senate.

"My quest for the Senate was met with some skepticism, but I was able to win over voters. After I became a senator, even the Republicans whom I expected to hate me learned we could work together and, grudgingly, began to respect me.

"The first year, while working to understand my new state and my new position, I tried to maintain a low public profile while building relationships with senators from both parties. I also wanted to avoid the media circus I'd experienced as First Lady. I joined religious senators by becoming a regular participant in the Senate Prayer Group, which I found most soothing in the midst of the hustle and bustle of the Senate.

"I was thrilled to be re-elected in 2006. As of November 2007, I enjoyed a 60 percent job approval rating.

"Perhaps my most important achievement," she said, "was one that very few people know about." She examined her fingernails.

"Sometimes when you do something especially good for people, you feel shy talking about it."

I smiled. "I know what you mean, Hillary."

"After the horror of the September 11, 2001 attacks,' she continued, "I rushed to the aid of New Yorkers by obtaining funding for their recovery efforts and for additional security improvements in the state. New York's senior senator, Charles Schumer, and I quietly secured $21.4 billion in funding for the World Trade Center site's redevelopment. I also took a leading role in investigating the health issues faced by 9/11 first responders, and supported improving health benefits for veterans."

I nodded. She was right to feel proud about her actions, and she was also right that many people, including yours truly, had not known about her efforts.

"Although I have taken a lot of flak for this, maybe even yours," she said, "I strongly supported the 2001 U.S. military action in Afghanistan, saying that it was a chance to combat terrorism while improving the lives of Afghan women who suffered under the Taliban government. I still think I was right."

I decided to remain quiet about my stance on U.S. military action in Afghanistan.

"Similarly, although some people denounced me as a hawk, I voted in favor of the October 2002 Iraq War Resolution, which authorized President George W. Bush to use military force against Iraq, should such action be required to enforce a United Nations Security Council Resolution, *after* pursuing all possible diplomatic efforts. I also believe strongly that the United Nations must remain, at all costs, the guardian of the world's security, or we will have a repetition of what happened to the League of Nations after World War 1. I always thought it was a dreadful mistake that the Congress kept us out of the League. At the time—and I emphasize that key qualification—I thought that authorizing military force against Iraq was justified."

Again, I remained quiet, thinking she had a right to her own beliefs, although I didn't happen to agree. Hillary didn't seem to notice.

"In accordance with my belief that the middle class deserves some relief in contrast to the millionaires of the country, I voted against the two major tax cut packages championed by President Bush. At the 2000 Democratic National Convention, I had called for maintaining a budget surplus to bring down the national debt for your children and mine.

"At a fundraiser in 2004, I told a crowd of financial donors, 'Many of you are well enough off that the tax cuts may have helped you, but for America to get back on track, we're probably going to cut that short. We're going to have to take things away from you on behalf of the common good.' I probably made myself a lot of enemies with that speech, but I have to vote for what I believe in—in this case, the common good."

Here I agreed with her, but also remained quiet. It really wasn't her business what my politics were.

"In line with my interest in education," she said, "I led a bipartisan effort to bring broadband access to rural communities, and co-sponsored the 21st Century Nanotechnology Research and Development Act. To my great pleasure, continuing the work on education I had done in Arkansas, I introduced an amendment that funds job creation to repair, renovate, and modernize public schools.

"This one you may find hard to believe, Doctor. I still do. In 2005, I was joined by former House Speaker Gingrich—imagine me and Newt working together! He once led the Republican opposition to my husband's administration. But we both backed a proposal for incremental universal health care. That was one proposal I particularly loved! I also worked with Bill Frist, the Republican Senate Majority Leader, in support of modernizing medical records with computer technology to reduce human errors, such as misreading prescriptions. I joined Frist in working for the bill when I found out that a little girl had died after being given the wrong prescription. I vowed to do all I could to keep another such tragedy from happening.

"I voted against the confirmation of John Roberts as Chief Justice of the United States. I did not believe he had been clear and specific enough in his views for me to vote for him. In committee, I also joined with about half of the Democratic senators in opposing the nomination of Samuel Alito to the United States Supreme Court, and subsequently against his confirmation along with almost all Democratic members of the Senate. On the Senate floor, I said Alito would roll back on progress made. Again, I am happy I followed my Methodist conscience, even though it made me more enemies.

"I voted twice against the Federal Marriage Amendment that sought to prohibit same-sex marriage. I did so because of my belief that all people should have the right to love whomever they please, so long as they are not hurting anyone. I wouldn't want the government to tell me who I could or could not marry, and I wanted the same privilege for everybody," she said vehemently.

"If the Republicans were unhappy about my record, I am delighted to tell you that, among my New York constituents, I enjoyed excellent approval ratings for my job as Senator, reaching an all-time high in December 2006 of seventy-four percent approving and twenty-four percent disapproving. I made a speech to New Yorkers in which I thanked them for the eight years of joy they gave me from a job I love, working on issues I deeply cared about. I wasn't the only one in tears. Everywhere I looked, I saw people blowing their noses."

She looked up at me and said, "Not a bad record, eh, Doc?"

"No," I answered with a feeling that came from deep inside me. "I am profoundly moved to hear of your magnificent contributions to the people of our state. You should know that I am honored to be your analyst."

February 12, 2014

To my surprise, Hillary called today and asked for an extra session. Knowing she wouldn't have asked if it weren't important to her, I stayed past my usual quitting time to see her.

"What's wrong, Hillary?" I asked, concerned about her pained expression.

"I want to tell you about the worst thing that ever happened to me. This is very hard for me to talk about, but I've found out here that I'd better do it right away while I have the impulse or I'll never be able to."

"You did the right thing," I said.

She remained silent until she regained control of herself and then said, "As you well know, I ran for president of the United States and lost. There I was, two steps away from the White House, and Barack Obama had to come in at the last minute and ruin everything for me. I don't think I'll ever recover from the shock.

"I had dreamed of becoming the first woman president of the United States since I was a little girl and had secretly begun preparing for my potential candidacy since early 2003. On January 20, 2007, on my website, I announced the formation of a presidential exploratory committee for the United States presidential election of 2008, stating elatedly, 'I'm in, and I'm in to win!' I exalted in the millions of hurrahs from all over the country.

"No woman before me had ever been nominated by a major party for President of the United States. When Bill became president in 1993, a blind trust was established in our name; in April 2007, we obliterated the trust as I began the presidential race. Later statements revealed that our combined worth as a couple was now over $50 million, and that we had earned over $100 million since 2000, with most of it coming from Bill's book and speaking engagements. Imagine, after me supporting him for years, it was Bill who finally made us a fortune!

"To my delight, I led all candidates for the Democratic presidential nomination in opinion polls throughout the first half of 2007. Most polls placed Senator Barack Obama and former Senator John Edwards of North Carolina as my closest competitors, but I wasn't too worried. I am someone who's used to winning every competition I enter. Obama and I both set records for early fund raising, trading the money lead each quarter. By September 2007, polls in the first six states holding Democratic primaries showed that I was the leader in all of them, which kept up my good spirits. By the following month, national polls showed me far ahead of all Democratic competitors. It sure looked like I was about to become the first woman president of the United States!

"But somewhat to my surprise, that didn't last too long. I soon began to worry that things were shifting toward Obama. Unfortunately, at the end of October, I fell ill while I was debating him, and performed quite badly. I think that was the beginning of my downfall. Obama's oratorical abilities, along with his message of change, began to resonate with Democrats more than my record of experience. For a while more, we ran neck and neck, especially in the polls for the early primary states of Iowa, New Hampshire, and South Carolina. But by December, I began to lose my lead in some polls, and consequently started to lose my sense of well-being, both political and otherwise.

"In early 2008, I came in a bad third in the Iowa Democratic caucus, behind both Obama and Edwards. In the next few days, all polls predicted a victory for Obama in the New Hampshire primary. But I pulled off a surprise win there on January 8, narrowly defeating him, which made me feel better. I believe I did better because I was seen more sympathetically there, especially by women, after my eyes filled with tears and my voice cracked while answering a voter's question about starving children in Africa. I wanted to yell out, 'See, I'm not Sister Frigidaire after all!'

"The nature of the contest, however, changed drastically in the next few days. Several remarks by Bill and I about Martin Luther King,

Jr. were mistakenly interpreted by the media as pigeon-holing Obama as a racially-oriented candidate and otherwise minimizing his overall political accomplishments. Imagine anyone believing that Bill and I would make a racially-oriented comment given our long history of standing for racial tolerance! Never mind the truth. The damage was done. As a result, I lost much of my support among African Americans.

"My campaign had counted on winning the nomination by Super Tuesday, and we were unprepared for a prolonged financial effort. When our Internet fundraising began to lag, I lent my own money to the campaign. You must know from that how important winning the presidency was to me. After all, I am my father's daughter, and we know what a penny pincher he was.

"There was also continuous squabbling within the campaign staff. Thinking that was causing the problem, I made several top-level personnel changes. It didn't help. Starting in February 2008, Obama won the next eleven caucuses and primaries across the country, often by large margins, and took a considerable delegate lead. He did particularly well in primaries where African American voters, or younger, college-educated voters, or more affluent voters were heavily represented among primary voters.

"I did better in primaries where Hispanics or older, non-college-educated, or working-class white voters predominated. Some Democratic Party leaders expressed concern that the drawn-out campaign between the two of us could damage the winner in the general election contest against the Republicans' presumptive nominee, John McCain. Fortunately for the Democratic Party, if not for me, it didn't.

"In late March, I had to admit as untrue my repeated campaign statements about having been under hostile fire from snipers during a 1996 visit to U.S. troops at Tuzla Air Base in Bosnia and Herzegovina. That attracted considerable media attention and risked undermining my credibility and claims of foreign policy expertise. I didn't mean to lie about it. Sometimes, I get carried away by my imagination. Snipers *were* shooting nearby, and I was terrified that I would be hit. From the fear of being shot at, it was a short step to feeling that snipers had fired at me. Try and explain that to the press!

"On April twenty-second, I won the Pennsylvania primary, and was elated at the possibility that I could still win the nomination. But my exuberance didn't last long. On May sixth, my very slight win in Indiana, along with a large loss in North Carolina, ended any realistic chance I had of gaining my party's nod. My mother wouldn't let me be a quitter, so I resolved to stay on through the remaining primaries. Because of her teaching, I could accept losing, but not quitting. Despite Obama's lead, I won some of the remaining contests, and indeed, if you look only at the last three months of the campaign, I finished with more state wins, more votes, and more delegates than Obama, but was unable to overcome his initial delegate advantage.

"After the final primaries on June 3, 2008, Obama had enough delegates to become the nominee. In a speech before my supporters on June seventh, I tearfully ended my campaign as my mother cried in the wings. Even though I was broken-hearted, I enthusiastically endorsed Obama, saying something like, 'The way to continue our fight now to accomplish the goals for which we stand is to take our energy, our passion, our strength, and do all we can to help elect Barack Obama.' We had each received over seventeen million votes during the nomination process, both of us breaking the previous record. You'd think being a record-setter would make me happy, but it didn't. I'm a poor loser, even if I try to disguise it.

"I gave a passionate speech supporting Obama at the 2008 Democratic National Convention and campaigned frequently for him in the fall of 2008, which concluded with his victory over McCain in the general election on November fourth. My campaign ended up severely in debt; we owed millions of dollars to outside supporters. I wrote off the $13 million that I had personally lent the campaign. My father would have been horrified. Fortunately for my peace of mind, the rest of the campaign debt was finally paid off by the beginning of 2013."

We were silent for a few moments. Then I said sadly, "I'm so sorry you lost the election, Hillary."

"So am I," she answered.

February 14, 2014

"Look what Bill gave me for Valentine's Day," she said, rushing in and thrusting out her hand to show me a beautiful diamond ring.

"He didn't have enough money to buy me one when we got engaged and is making up for it now. Better late than never, I always say!"

"It's beautiful, Hillary," I said. It really was. "I hope it brings you lots of pleasure."

"I'm sure it will, even though I'm not much for wearing jewelry. Well, onto important things," she said, only half seriously. "After I lost the election to Obama," she said, "I was distraught. Nothing Bill, Chelsea, my mother, or close friends could say helped. 'I'm a failure,' I thought.

"But guess who made me feel better? None other than my arch-rival, Barack Obama, by offering me the position of Secretary of State! I've always liked Barack, and his generous proposal made me feel a little guilty about all the nasty things I'd said about him during the campaign. I suspect he didn't take my put-downs personally, but understood they were just political rhetoric. Not many people I know would be able to put aside hurt feelings and appoint their former competitor to the second most important position in the United States government. On thinking about it, I doubt if I would have appointed him Secretary of State, or indeed, anything at all, if I had won the election."

"Maybe not, Hillary," I said. "But I admire your ability to tell the truth, even when it isn't particularly flattering to you."

She considered my remark, then said, "Thank you, Doctor. I'm glad you think so. Some people just call me blunt. I'm very open about what I think, and am not reluctant to say what's on my mind. If some people want to interpret that the wrong way, I can't help it. But I'm not always doing myself a service when I run off at the mouth. As a private person, I could do that, and lived to regret it when Bill or a dear friend got mad at me.

"But every time I opened my mouth as Secretary of State, it was America speaking. Every word I said was carefully examined, weighed, and assigned significance. People tried to read between the lines, below them, above them, and even look for meaning in every comma and space. It got a bit tiresome, and I sometimes found myself longing for the days when I could get away with saying whatever I felt like." She added, "I'm not a stupid woman. I know I should butter up the press, that it annoys people when I change my hairdos. I know I should behave as if I don't have any opinions, but I'm just not going to. I'm able to compromise, I have compromised; I gave up my name and bought contact lenses. But I refuse to pretend to be somebody I'm not!"

I smiled. That is Hillary at the most Hillary.

"Within a week after the presidential election," she continued, "the President-elect called me and spoke about the possibility of my serving as U.S. Secretary of State. I remember our conversation well since I was flabbergasted when he repeated, 'I want you to be my Secretary of State.' I said, 'Oh, no, you don't! Please, there are so many other people in the United States who could do the job better than me!' He answered, 'I don't think so.'

"During our run for the presidency, Obama had criticized my foreign policy credentials, and the idea of him appointing me as Secretary of State was so unexpected I told one of my aides, 'Not in a million years.' But despite our primary battles, the political differences between us never were very great and we developed a respect for one another that allowed me to campaign for him without reservations in the general election.

"To tell the truth, even though I was honored, I didn't want to take him up on his offer. I liked being a New York senator. I wasn't finished with my work there and didn't want to leave the job. There didn't seem much opportunity for Senate advancement, however. While the Senate leadership had discussed possible leadership positions or other promotions with me, nothing definite had been offered. Prospects of my ever becoming Senate Majority Leader looked mighty slim. That didn't look good to me. My philosophy of life is that it's a see-saw: If you don't go up, you go down.

"I also was concerned about Bill's role if I accepted the job. I was honest with Obama about my fears. I also was concerned that Bill's post-presidential activities might violate conflict of interest rules for cabinet members. There already was considerable speculation in the press about the effect that taking the position would have on my political career and any possible future presidential aspirations, and I hadn't even decided if I would take the job yet. *Why are they so worried about it?* I thought: *Why don't they just go about their own business?*"

I considered her query. "That's a good question."

"As Obama and I continued talking, I began thinking that if I had won and called him, I would have wanted him to say yes. You know, I'm a pretty old-fashioned girl; that's just who I am. So if your president asks you to serve, naturally you say yes. My friend Capricia Marshall, then serving as Chief of Protocol of the United States, had known me since my White House days. She confirmed my rationale, saying that, in the past, when I'd been asked to serve, I'd served.

"After swallowing my pride, I accepted the offer. After eight years of the Bush administration, America was at a crossroads. It was being shunned by many countries. I planned to make the U.S. a desirable partner again as I searched out new areas of power and extended the boundaries of twenty-first century diplomacy.

"As a condition of my accepting the offered nomination, Bill agreed to a number of restrictions on the fundraising activities of his pride and joy, the Clinton Presidential Center and the Clinton Global Initiative. In essence, he agreed not to have those two entities solicit funds from foreign governments likely to deal with me as Secretary of State. He consented for my sake, and for the country's.

"I love that man!" she said, her eyes all aglow. "I can always count on him to stand behind me. I also suspected Barack was just being nice, and really didn't expect me to accept. It seems I was wrong about that.

"So with trepidation in my heart and wobbly knees, I accepted. He sounded as if he had expected me to take the job all along. He certainly is one cool cucumber! If, God forbid, there ever were an atomic attack on the United States, I would want him to be at the helm. Well, I am happy I accepted the job. Even though it almost killed me, it was perhaps the greatest experience of my life—even better than being a U.S. Senator. So, if you can stand hearing about my tenure as Secretary of State without being bored to death, Doctor, I would like to tell you about it. I'll try to be as brief as possible. At this point, it's only of interest to historians . . . and no doubt Republicans."

"On the contrary, Hillary," I said, though politics have never been my area of greatest interest. "I would like very much to hear about your tenure."

Hillary is pretty shrewd. She looked at me skeptically but continued anyway. I felt sorry for her and regretted that I had not been more interested in politics—I could have served her better if I had. I resolved to read the newspapers more thoroughly in the future. That shouldn't be too difficult, I realized, because I would be reading about one of my patients.

That is one of the things I like most about my work; each patient brings me a different view of the world, like the changing refractions of a diamond when it is turned.

Regardless of my limited political knowledge and interest, Hillary needed to finish telling me the story of her life.

February 17, 2014

"At the State Department, I was preceded in office by Condoleezza Rice, who is not my favorite person, and I was succeeded by John Kerry. I was only the third woman in our entire history to hold the position. I was also the only former First Lady of the United States to become a member of the United States Cabinet. Not a bad record for a girl who never could do anything well enough to please her father! What would you have to say about that today, Poppa? I know. You'd say, 'You shoulda made president!'

"Confirmation hearings before the Senate Foreign Relations Committee began on January 13, 2009, a week before the Obama inauguration. I remember some of what I said during the hearings. 'I believe the best way to advance America's interests in reducing global threats and taking advantage of worldwide opportunities is to design and implement global solutions. We must use what has been called 'smart power,' the full range of tools at our disposal—diplomatic, military, economic, political, legal, and cultural—picking the right tool or combination of tools for each situation. With smart power, diplomacy will be the vanguard of our foreign policy.'

"Despite my gut-felt aversion to war, I was at the forefront of the U.S. response to the Arab Spring, the revolutionary wave of demonstrations and non-violent and violent protests in the Arab world that began in December 2010. Later, I pushed for military intervention in Libya, because I believed that early military engagement might prevent a holocaust later on. Unfortunately, it didn't, although I am happy to say that it helped to oust the vile Libyan dictator Moammar Gaddafi in 2011.

"As Gaddafi's forces gained momentum and threatened to massacre innocent citizens in early 2011, influential Obama advisors, including then U.N. Ambassador Susan Rice and national security aides Ben Rhodes and Samantha Power, argued for air strikes. Even with public opinion running more than 2-1 against them, I joined the interventionists. My philosophy has always been that diplomacy, development, and defense are only effective if used together. Kind of like Theodore Roosevelt's maxim, 'Speak softly and carry a big stick.'

"There was something strange about how all of a sudden, the people of Tunisia, Syria, Egypt, and Yemen all started revolutions at the same time. People are always asking me what got into them. I answer that all of this had been boiling under the surface for a long time. No one had predicted that there would be so many simultaneous explosions, but there had been warnings for years that the region was highly unstable. Poverty, dictators, population explosions, and severe unemployment make for an explosive combination. The United States was not planning a comprehensive strategic approach to the Arab Spring, but dealt separately with each country's distinct situation."

February 19, 2014

"I need to talk to you about one of the most terrible experiences of my life," she began, looking distraught. "As you must know, on September 11, 2012, a heavily armed group of between 125 and 150 gunmen attacked the American diplomatic mission at Benghazi in Libya, killing U.S. Ambassador J. Christopher Stevens and another diplomat. The date of 9/11 certainly was not a coincidence.

"Several hours later, in the early morning of the next day, a second group launched an attack on a different compound about one mile away, killing two other embassy security personnel. Ten others were injured in the assaults, which were strongly condemned by the governments of Libya, the United States, and many other countries throughout the world. Stevens was a dear friend," she said, wiping away a tear. "It broke my heart when I heard about his death. I haven't recovered yet. I doubt if I ever will.

"Stevens was a much admired diplomat, loved and respected by men and women on both sides of the political gulf. Personable and humble, he was a brilliant practitioner of personal diplomacy. They don't make them like him much anymore. He was the rare kind of diplomat who achieved agreements and cooperation through interpersonal relationships and was known to have accomplished more over cups of coffee in the marketplace than ever could have been gained in reams of paper or thousands of emails.

"A vicious report by the Senate Intelligence Committee wrapped up their investigation with the conclusion that the attack that killed the four Americans in Benghazi could have been prevented, and it blamed the State Department for its failure to bolster security after receiving warnings about a security crisis in the city. The inquiry placed at least part of the blame on Stevens himself. General Carter Ham, the commander of the United States Africa Command at the time, said that he had called Stevens to ask if the embassy in Tripoli needed additional military personnel for use in Benghazi, but Stevens advised Ham that it didn't.

"A short time later, General Ham repeated the offer at a meeting in Germany, and Stevens again declined. I myself had sent Stevens to Benghazi as a special envoy, which makes the incident even more painful to me. What I can't fathom is why a man as intelligent as Stevens would do such a foolhardy thing as to turn down Ham's offer. If anyone told me I was in danger, I would want all the protection I could get. I don't like to say anything unkind about so remarkable and beloved man who is not around to defend himself, but I'll tell you, Doctor Dale, that Stevens' pigheadedness has caused me a lot of political trouble, and, sadly, it cost him his life.

"At various times between September eleventh and seventeenth, eight other diplomatic embassies in the Middle East, Asia, and Europe were attacked by spontaneous outbursts that some officials believed was in reaction to an inflammatory video, *Innocence of Muslims*, an American-made movie denigrating Islam's Prophet Muhammad. It originally was thought that the Benghazi attack developed out of a similar unplanned protest. But further investigations by the U.S. State Department and the House of Representatives committees on Armed Services, Foreign Affairs, Intelligence, the Judiciary, and Oversight and Government Reform concluded that there was no such outburst and the attack was premeditated and carried out by Islamist militants.

"I received a lot of flak for urging military engagement in Libya, and I would hate my tenure as Secretary of State to be judged solely on that. I was clearly wrong, but my heart was in the right place. I was trying to avert a humanitarian disaster, and though that was averted, and the dictator removed, the country remains highly unstable.

"In contrast to my own sense of guilt, I was happy to hear what David Brooks, a *New York Times* columnist and PBS and NPR commentator, had to say about the attack. According to him, it was purely an operational matter. He said the Secretary of State wouldn't be involved in something low-level like this; I'd be responsible for larger policy issues. Brooks is right, but the Republicans are trying to get all the mileage they can out of the attack. Nevertheless, I believe with all my heart that my push for military intervention in Libya was the greatest mistake of my political life. As I prepared to step down from the post, feeling that I had done a good job as Secretary of State, I was attacked, in an interrogation reminiscent of the Spanish Inquisition, by Republicans in both the House and the Senate over what went wrong in Benghazi.

"A Senate intelligence committee report distributed the blame among the State Department and intelligence agencies for not preventing the attacks. The two party report revealed more than a dozen facts about the assaults. It said that the State Department failed to increase security at its diplomatic mission despite warnings, and blamed intelligence agencies for not sharing information about the CIA outpost with the U.S. military. Although the Republicans never stop badgering me about the attack, as if I had personally thrown the bombs or shot the rifles, they don't need to. If they want me to feel bad, they should know that I chastise myself all the time about it. The Benghazi situation continues to haunt me. I suppose it will as long as I live. Four dead men, all of them fine servants of the government. I will never forgive myself.

"I take full responsibility for what happened in Benghazi. I still insist that the Obama administration did not intentionally mislead the American public when it indicated that the attack grew out of the protest over the anti-Islam film. I believe the hatred the film engendered contributed to the violence of the assaults. I also pointed out that, before the attack, I was not shown requests for additional security at the U.S. diplomatic mission in Benghazi.

"To my relief, not everybody in the Congress blamed the catastrophe on the State Department and me. Senator Dianne Feinstein of California, the top Democrat on the Senate Intelligence Committee, criticized critics who said that the panel's report on Benghazi placed blame on me. The day following her panel's release of a lengthy review of the Benghazi attacks, some Republicans pointed out that my name was not even mentioned in the fifty-eight pages of findings that members of both sides of the intelligence panel signed. Feinstein wanted to clear the record, condemning the use of the report for political purposes.

"I love you, Dianne Feinstein! Because of people like you and David Brooks, I can sleep a little better at night."

February 21, 2014

"Greetings, Doctor," Hillary said with a smile that lit up her face.

I thought, *What a difference her smile makes! She looks twenty years younger.*

"Well, enough of Benghazi, at least for a while," she began. "To change the topic, in 2010, I introduced a major management change at the State Department—the Quadrennial Diplomacy and Development Review process—in an effort to make our programs and our allocation of resources more in line with our major goals. The QDDR is a State Department study to be done every four years to analyze the short, medium, and long-term blueprint for the United States' diplomatic and developmental efforts abroad. It sought to plan on a longer basis than the usual year-to-year appropriations and to bring together diplomacy and development plans under one aegis.

"It also sought to correlate the department's missions with its capacities and identify its shortcomings. We completed the first such review toward the end of 2010. I am pleased that, through the QDDR, I could help our country plan ahead for a better world for women and all humankind.

"I was also the first Secretary of State to use social media to get our message out to the world. For some people, it's nice to be first. For me, it's essential."

"I was the most widely traveled Secretary of State in U.S. history. And oh, my bones still feel it!"

She began to giggle.

I said, "What's so funny, Hillary?"

"I was thinking of a trip I took to China, and that made me recall once saying to Bill, 'We shouldn't argue so much. As the Chinese say, 'When you are in the same boat, you need to cross the river peacefully together.'

"Bill said, 'I can always swim.'

We both doubled up in laughter and got nothing more accomplished the rest of that session.

February 24, 2014

Our next session, Hillary came in sounding more serious than she had at the end of our last one.

Good, I thought. I was beginning to worry that we were enjoying ourselves too much at the expense of her analysis.

"Obama's choice of me for Secretary of State was seen as part of his plan to put together a 'team of rivals' in his administration," she said, "following in the footsteps of Abraham Lincoln. The philosophy of rivals working successfully together also has been found useful in war, as when Generals George Marshall and Dwight Eisenhower functioned well together when launching the Allied invasion of German-occupied Western Europe during World War II. The technique also has been used in business, by such notables as Indra Nooyi, who kept on her top rival for CEO at Pepsi Co. So Barack and I were treading in giant footsteps.

"During the Obama Administration's transition period after the election, I found my passage to my new job to be difficult, possibly because I had never even dreamt of being Secretary of State or any other Cabinet secretary, for that matter. Then, to add to my difficulties in the early days of my tenure, there was considerable jockeying for department jobs among those in 'Hillaryland,' my longtime circle of advisors and staff aides, as well as other staff members who had worked with me in the past.

"Unfortunately, there were more applicants than there were jobs, so I had to turn down some people I would have liked very much to have worked under me. Barack gave me more freedom to choose my staff than he did any other cabinet member. In other ways, too, he treated me with greater respect than any other person in the cabinet. Did he feel guilty that he had taken the election away from me? Or is it possible that he just admires me?

"Much as I did at the beginning of my Senate career, I kept a low profile during my early months as Secretary of State. I worked hard to familiarize myself with the history of the department. Unlike some members of the cabinet, not to mention any names, I don't believe in speaking up until I know what I am talking about. To help me 'feel my oats,' I spoke with all the living former secretaries, and especially with my close friend, Madeleine Albright, who was of incalculable help. Incidentally, I just found out something fascinating about Madeleine; she plays the drums! I wish I did. I can't even whistle in tune. Maybe in the next lifetime."

February 27, 2014

"I spent most of my first days as Secretary of State on the phone, calling dozens of international leaders who were breathlessly awaiting a new American foreign policy. We had a lot of damage to repair. I didn't mention that the Bush administration was responsible, but everybody knew that. I did state that not all past policies would be repealed, and in particular I thought it essential that the six-party talks over the North Korean nuclear weapons program continue.

"During my first speech to State Department employees, I reemphasized my views when I said (cleverly, I think, if I must say so myself), 'There are three legs to the stool of American foreign policy: defense, diplomacy, and development. We are responsible for two of the three legs. And we will make clear as we proceed that diplomacy and development are not only necessary tools in achieving the long-term goals of the United States, but that robust diplomacy and effective economic development are the best tools in the long run for securing America's place in the world.

"Around that time, I also visited the United States Agency for International Development, where I met the employees and told them they would be getting extra funds and attention during the new administration. I am happy to say they applauded my speech.

"I kept a low profile when it was a necessity for diplomatic reasons, but from the beginning maintained a close working relationship with the president, particularly in foreign policy decisions.

"My first one hundred days saw me learning my new trade and gaining skills as a member of the cabinet. To everyone's surprise but mine, I found it easy being a team player subordinate to President Obama. I had learned how to play that role as the wife of Bill Clinton. Nevertheless, I was an international celebrity with a much higher profile than most secretaries of state. My background as an elected official was helpful in that it gave me insight into the needs and fears of the elected representatives of other countries.

"By the summer of 2009, there was a lot of discussion in the media about the level of influence I had in the Obama administration, with every kind of speculation imaginable. What did they think? That I was trying to be a co-president again? Someone even suggested we were lovers! I don't think that would have gone over very well with Michelle. Actually, Barack and I are two very different kinds of people, despite the fact that we usually agreed on policy. I didn't care for his lofty speeches, and I believe my bluntness made him uncomfortable. I never became a member of his trusted inner circle, although he always had the greatest respect for me and generally took my advice.

"Although we learned to work well together, we never became buddies, but over the last two years of my tenure, he listened more closely to me. If I weren't in the room when a foreign policy issue was being discussed, he would say he wanted to get my take on it. I, in turn, grew more confident in my position, and voiced my views and offered advice more often. I added my pragmatic views to his more theoretical ones, and believe that my voice was given more weight.

"I reevaluated my role as Secretary of State in a prominent mid-July speech to the Council on Foreign Relations, in which I said something like, 'We cannot be afraid or unwilling to engage. Our focus on diplomacy and development is not an alternative to our national security arsenal. The United States still has the largest military establishment in the world, a bigger one than the next three largest combined. But military might is no longer enough to protect us, especially when budgets are being cut. Our country has to reinvent its diplomacy.' I'm afraid that this kind of thinking began to give me the reputation of being a hawk, but that's not what I meant to imply. I merely wanted to follow Theodore Roosevelt's advice about speaking softly and carrying a big stick."

February 28, 2014

"In connection with the Quadrennial Diplomacy and Development Review I instituted at State, you will not be surprised to learn, Doctor, that an important goal of the review process was my lifetime goal of empowering the female population in developing countries around the world. To show you how central female empowerment was to the first QDDR report, it mentioned women and girls 133 times! By making my goals in this area part of official policy, my co-workers and I hoped that my work for the empowerment of women would last long after my term in office ended, as well as shatter the glass ceiling characteristic of business in the United States.

"In September, I spoke of the Global Hunger and Food Security Initiative at the yearly meeting of Bill's Global Initiative. The goal of the drive was to battle hunger everywhere on an organized basis as an essential part of our foreign policy, rather than simply distributing food as shortages occurred.

"I myself am not fussy about when I eat, and can make due with grabbing a sandwich or a banana until there is a break in my schedule for a meal. I don't need to eat at a set time and can put up with the rumbles of my stomach without being too miserable. But that is nothing like true hunger. If you have ever been hungry, really hungry, you know how painful and all-consuming it is. When it takes over, nothing else matters. Have *you* ever been that hungry, Doctor?"

I shook my head. She said, "I thought not. Neither have I. We are among the luckier ones on earth. Food security is not just about food. It concerns all security: economic security, environmental security, even national security. Massive hunger is a threat to the stability of governments, societies, and borders. The Global Initiative sought to develop agricultural economies, fight malnourishment, increase productivity, expand trade, and encourage creative thinking in developing nations. I said that women should be placed at the center of the effort, because, believe it or not, we constitute a majority of the world's farmers. No mother should have to see her child crying from hunger.

"What a great job I had! It was a 24/7 position that filled every one of my thoughts, despite its effects on every part of my aching body. Who said, 'If you love your work, you'll never have to work again'? Those are my sentiments exactly. I never felt I was working because I loved my job so much, and I would have stayed on forever if only my body had held up.

"During that time, I never had to think about whether the president and I were making the same foreign policy judgments, and I gave absolutely no thought then to ever running for the presidency again. While some friends and advisers thought I was only saying that to focus attention on my then-current role and that I might change my mind about running for president in 2016, others understood that I was content with the direction my life and career had taken and no longer had presidential ambitions. That was pretty much the way I felt, but I wasn't surprised when nobody believed me."

I smiled. I hadn't believed her either.

March 3, 2014

"By the close of 2009, twenty-five countries had appointed women to be ambassadors to the United States, the highest number ever. This was dubbed the 'Hillary Effect' by some observers. I'm proud to think that may be true. Amelia Matos Sumbana, the Mozambique Ambassador to the United States, said I was so visible as Secretary of State that I made it easy for other countries' leaders to appoint female officials.

"It's true that two other recent U.S. Secretaries of State, Madeleine Albright and Condoleeza Rice, were women, but my international fame from my days as First Lady of the United States made my impact the greatest of the group.

"But at home, all was not rosy. In testimony in February 2010 before the Senate Appropriations Subcommittee on State, Foreign Operations, and Related Programs, I sounded off again about the tortoise-paced Senate confirmations of President Obama's nominations to diplomatic positions, some of which were delayed for political reasons and deliberately held back by Republican senators. I insisted that the problem badly hurt America's overseas image. It became more and more difficult for me to explain to significant countries why we had not confirmed an ambassador for them to interact with. Do you think that deterred the Senate Republicans from frustrating me at every turn?

"By this time, I was exhausted from my extensive travels and battles around the world, and was aware every time I looked in the mirror that the struggles of being Secretary of State had aged me by at least ten years. Check out my photos, Doctor, and you will see that I'm not exaggerating. I am not a vain woman, but who likes to age ten years in four? In 2009, and again in 2010 and 2011, I informed President Obama that I was committed to serving out my full term as secretary, but would not serve a second term should he be reelected. As General William Tecumseh Sherman said after the Civil War when the whole country was pressuring him to run for president of the United States, 'I will not run. If elected, I will not serve.' Obama was not happy about my decision, but nothing he said could convince me to change my mind. If he had, I'd probably be dead by now."

"You did the right thing, Hillary," I said. "If you were dead, who would the Republicans torment?"

She cackled.

March 7, 2014

"In February 2009," Hillary began, "I made my first trip as secretary to Asia, visiting China, South Korea, Indonesia, and Japan on what I called a 'listening tour,' which helped me lay out my future path as Secretary of State. My plans revolved around what people told me they would like me to accomplish. I continued to travel extensively during those first months in office, often finding the locals as excited as I was about my goals to improve the lives of women everywhere.

"It was wonderful to listen to so many different kinds of voices. Everywhere I went, I met a person or saw something new to me that opened up my heart and mind and expanded my understanding of humankind. As a result, the world will always be a larger place for me. What I learned on my 'listening tour' made me part of who I am today.

"In March, while attending the NATO foreign ministers meeting in Brussels, I brought up the idea of including Iran in a conference on Afghanistan, and suggested that that conference be held at the end of the month in the Netherlands. It didn't work out, but I still think it would have been a good idea.

"A media event with Russian Foreign Minister Sergei Lavrov was designed to illustrate that the U.S. was pressing the 'reset button' in our somewhat troubled relationship with Russia, but things went a bit amiss as a result of an incorrect translation. It seems that the word we Americans chose, 'peregruzka,' meant 'overloaded' or 'overcharged' rather than 'reset.' Put me in an embarrassing position.

"During March 2009, I won an internal debate with Vice President Joe Biden about sending an additional 20,000 troops to Afghanistan. I said yes. He said no. Good ole' Joe! He and I are old competitors from way back, and it felt great to win an argument with him. Of course, I also felt it was the right thing to do."

March 19, 2014

I was sick for a bit, which explains the gap between the date of the last session and today's.

Hillary began with, "In January 2010, I cut short my trip to the Asia-Pacific regions to check out the destructive effects of the earthquake in Haiti and to meet with President René Préval. I also wanted to evaluate relief efforts and help to evacuate Americans stranded there. Everyone was working hard to restore the country to its former condition. I also had a special interest in Haiti going back decades to our delayed honeymoon there. Bill was the United Nations Special Envoy to Haiti. I cried when I visited a beach where we'd had a particularly lovely time, only to find it reduced to a huge pile of ashes.

"As a Baby Boomer, I've been fascinated for a long time by the different ways various countries make use of the Internet, some for the benefit of their citizens and some, unfortunately, in a manner that does not benefit humankind. In a major speech on January 21, 2010, speaking for the U.S., I said we wanted a single Internet where everyone has equal access to knowledge and that, even in authoritarian countries, people, because of Internet access, were discovering new facts about their governments and attempting to make them more accountable. I also drew analogies between the Iron Curtain and the free and unfree Internet.

"My speech, which followed a controversy about Google's changed policy toward Chinese censorship, apparently marked a split between authoritarian capitalism and the Western model of free capitalism and Internet access.

"Chinese officials protested strongly, saying my remarks were 'harmful to Sino-American relations,' and insisted that U.S. officials 'respect the truth.' Some foreign policy observers thought I had been too provocative. Fortunately, the White House stood behind me, and demanded that China provide better answers about the recent Chinese cyber-attack against Google. My speech scored a bull's eye among diplomats. It was the first time a senior American official had expressed a vision in which the Internet was a key element of American foreign policy.

"In February 2010, I made my first visit as Secretary to Latin America. I toured Uruguay, Chile, Brazil, Costa Rica, Guatemala, and Argentina. My first stop was Buenos Aires, where I talked to Argentine President Cristina Fernández de Kirchner. We discussed Falkland Islands sovereignty and the issue of oil in the Falklands. I said we wanted to see Argentina and the U.K. resolve the issues between them in a peaceful and productive manner.

"I offered to help facilitate such discussions but did not agree to an Argentinian request that I mediate such talks. I figured I had enough troubles. Within twelve hours of my remarks, Downing Street also emphatically rejected the role, saying they welcomed my support in keeping diplomatic channels open, but that there was no need for direct involvement from the U.S.

"I then went on to Santiago, Chile to witness the after-effects of the disastrous 2010 Chile earthquake and to bring some equipment to aid the inhabitants in their recovery efforts."

March 21, 2014

"In April 2010, there was a rush of gossip that I would be nominated to the U.S. Supreme Court to fill the vacancy left by Justice John Paul Stevens' retirement, including a recommendation from ranking Senate Judiciary Committee member Orrin Hatch. I was flattered but made peace with the idea that any such nomination would be quashed by President Obama, who soon announced he thought I was doing an excellent job and wanted me to remain as Secretary of State.

"I was happy to hear that he thought so. A State Department spokesperson bore out the president's statement when he said that I loved my present job and wasn't looking for a new one. He was right, but sometimes I look back and think wistfully, 'Just imagine, I could have been a member of the Supreme Court! My mother would have been so proud!' And serving on the High Court would have been so much less physically taxing than being Secretary of State."

I said, "Well, I for one am glad you stayed put."

"By the middle of 2010, the president and I had developed a smooth, untroubled working relationship. I had proven myself a team player inside the administration and made certain that neither Bill nor I ever upstaged the President. In turn, he usually accepted my viewpoints and in some cases even adopted my more hawkish approaches. I met with him weekly but did not have the intimate, daily relationship that some of my predecessors had with their presidents, such as Condoleezza Rice with George W. Bush (I always suspected she was in love with him), James Baker with George H. W. Bush, or Henry Kissinger with Richard Nixon.

March 24, 2014

"During an early June 2010 visit—" she began.

As soon as she mentioned "June 2010," I found myself so absorbed with the question of how she remembered all those dates that I thought I better stop and ask her, so I could turn my full attention to her again.

"Sorry to interrupt you, Hillary," I said, "but I was wondering how you remember all those dates."

"Everybody always asks me that," she said, smiling. "First of all, I have an excellent memory. People are sometimes surprised when I remember their names and the names of their children. Also, I make a great effort to remember things. I am an orderly, organized person, and it helps me keep things straight in my head if I know the dates when events occurred. And I must confess, sometimes when I know what I want to talk about with you in a session, I check on the date ahead of time so you'll think I'm smart," she said with a shy smile. "But then you remember every detail, too, Doctor. You often quote back to me what I told you, that so and so said this or that, even months later. I guess we recall what is important to us," she said.

I remembered Theodore Reik's book, *Listening with the Third Ear*. I agreed with Hillary's conclusion and was able once more to listen to her with all three of my ears.

She picked up where she had stopped. "During an early June 2010 visit to Colombia, Ecuador, and Peru, I had to deal with questions at every stop about Arizona's widely controversial immigration law, which had damaged the United States' image in Latin America. The Support Our Law Enforcement and Safe Neighborhoods Act (introduced as Arizona Senate Bill 1070) was a legislative act in the U.S. state of Arizona that was the broadest and strictest anti-illegal immigration measure in recent U.S. history.

"The bill stated that U.S. federal law requires all aliens over the age of fourteen who remain in the United States for longer than thirty days to register with the government. Violations of this law—namely, if an alien was found to be in Arizona without the required documents— would be considered both a federal and a state misdemeanor. It required that state law enforcement officers determine an individual's immigration status during a 'lawful stop, detention, or arrest,' when there was reasonable suspicion that the individual was an illegal immigrant. Critics of the law said that it encouraged racial profiling, while supporters said the law itself barred the use of race as the only basis for investigating someone's immigration status. There were protests opposing the law in more than seventy U.S. cities. Nevertheless, polling found the law to have widespread popular support.

"On April 30, 2010"—she looked at me and smiled, apparently about remembering the date—"the Arizona legislature passed, and Governor Brewer signed, a bill which modified the act signed a week earlier, with the amended text saying that 'prosecutors would not investigate complaints based on race, color, or national origin.' The new text also stated that police could only investigate immigration status incident to a 'lawful stop, detention, or arrest.' In the United States, opponents and supporters of the bill roughly followed party lines, with most Democrats opposing the bill and most Republicans supporting it. Guess which version I supported?

"When answering a question from local television reporters in Quito, I said that President Obama was opposed to the law, and that the Justice Department, under his direction, was planning to bring a lawsuit against it. This was the first public declaration that the Justice Department intended to act against the law. One month later, the case became official as *The United States of America vs. Arizona*.

"In August 2010, I included the dispute over that law in a report to the Office of the United Nations High Commissioner for Human Rights, citing it as an example to other countries of how difficult issues can be resolved under the law.

"In July of 2010, I visited Pakistan for the second time as Secretary, bringing with me a large United States economic assistance package as well as a U.S.-led bilateral trade agreement between Pakistan and Afghanistan. That was one time I had no doubt I was a welcomed guest." She laughed. "While there, I had an amusing conversation with the governor of Punjab, Salmaan Taseer, who loved cracking jokes. He said, 'Mrs. Clinton, I'd like you to know that when I was in London [where I was planning to travel], I used to throw rocks at the American Embassy in Grosvenor Square. 'Don't worry about it, Mr. Governor,' I said without missing a beat. 'So did I.'"

We both laughed hysterically.

March 26, 2014

"I then flew to Afghanistan for the Kabul Conference," she said, returning to her travels as Secretary of State, "during which time Afghan President Hamid Karzai vowed to initiate reforms in exchange for a continued Western commitment. I told them that the U.S. had no intention of abandoning our promise of achieving a stable, secure, and peaceful Afghanistan. Too many countries had suffered far too many losses for us to pull out prematurely.

"I then went on to Seoul and the Korean Demilitarized Zone, where Defense Secretary Robert Gates and I met with South Korean Foreign Minister Yu Myung-hwan and Minister of National Defense Kim Tae-young to commemorate the sixtieth anniversary of the Korean War. I said there that the U.S. in remaining in Korea for decades had led to a successful result, which also might be applicable to Afghanistan. Finally, I went to Hanoi, Vietnam for the ASEAN Regional Forum, wrapping up what *The New York Times* termed 'a grueling trip that amounted to a tour of American wars, past and present.'

"*Grueling* is hardly the word! *Killing* would more accurately describe what I went through. I got home and dissolved into my bed for a week. My body clock was stuck in limbo. Not all of me had returned to the United States; some of me remained stuck in the airplane. When my secretary came into the bedroom and said, 'You have an important phone call,' I answered, 'Tell them I died.' The statement wasn't too far wrong.

March 28, 2014

"In a well-publicized September 2010 speech before the Council on Foreign Relations, I emphasized the primacy of United States power and involvement in the world, declaring the present time a 'great new American moment.' Referring to many actions during my tenure as Secretary of State, from reviving the Middle East talks to U.S. aid following the 2010 Pakistan floods, I said that after years of uncertainty and war, the United States was leading the world in this new century.

"With Democrats facing the possibility of great losses in the 2010 midterm elections and President Obama sinking fast in opinion polls, there was chatter in Washington that I would take over as Obama's vice-presidential running mate in 2012 to add to his electoral appeal. Do you think I am more appealing than Joe Biden, Doctor?"

I smiled but didn't answer.

Hillary didn't like it when I resorted to the psychoanalyst's privilege of remaining quiet. She huffed and continued. "Some versions of this gossip had Vice President Biden replacing me as Secretary of State. Don't people have anything more important to do than gossip? When the idea of job-swapping was mentioned to me, I just smiled and shook my head. A couple of months later, President Obama shot down the idea for good, saying the notion was 'completely unfounded' and that we were both doing excellent work at the jobs we had. That's all I need, to be vice president! I wouldn't take that job for a bucket of gold. As if it isn't wearing enough to be Secretary of State!

"In the summer of 2010, the stalled peace processes in the Israeli–Palestinian conflict were revived when both countries finally agreed to talk to each other. While President Obama was the orchestrator of the movement, I had gone through months of sweet-talking the concerned parties just to get them to the table, and convinced the reluctant Palestinians by arranging support for direct talks with Egypt and Jordan. Speaking in September at a State Department meeting between Prime Minister Benjamin Netanyahu of Israel and President Mahmoud Abbas of the Palestinian Authority, I reminded them that, from experience, we knew it would be difficult.

"My role in the back-and-forth was to take over from George Mitchell, U.S. Special Envoy for Middle East Peace, when discussions threatened to break down. The talks were generally given little chance to succeed, and I faced the history of many such past failures, including Bill's near-miss at the 2000 Camp David Summit. Nevertheless, my prominent role in these sessions catapulted me further into the international spotlight and affected my legacy as Secretary."

"How so?" I asked.

"As if I hadn't traveled far enough already, in October I embarked with shaking knees on a seven-nation tour of Asia and Oceania. The Minister of Foreign Affairs for New Zealand, Murray McCully, and I met in New Zealand and signed the Wellington Declaration to commemorate the close ties between our nations and to establish the framework of a new United States-New Zealand strategic partnership. Our agreement healed the long stalled diplomatic and military relationship between New Zealand and the United States.

"The signing took place twenty-five years after the United States, in the wake of the USS Buchanan incident, suspended ANZUS treaty obligations with New Zealand. We had requested a visit to their country by the USS Buchanan, to test out the nuclear-free policy of New Zealand. The United States refused to confirm whether the Buchanan was nuclear-armed, and the New Zealand government denied the Buchanan entry. As a result, we broke off diplomatic relations with them, and that lasted for twenty-five years! I was delighted to have an old breach healed. In my opinion, this is international diplomacy at its best.

March 31, 2014

"Unfortunately, when things are going well is when disaster is most likely to strike. In October 2010, WikiLeaks, an international online organization which publishes secret information and news leaks, released a set of almost 400,000 documents about Iraq and Afghanistan called the 'Iraq War Logs.' Among other things, they exposed the extent of failures in Afghanistan and a higher number of civilian casualties than had been revealed. The group wanted to expose the black inner-machinations of the Afghan government, and promised that the State Department would be the next target. I'm usually a good sleeper, but for a month I couldn't sleep, worrying about what they would reveal.

"Sure enough, in late November, WikiLeaks released confidential State Department cables, selections of which were then published by major newspapers around the world. The organization had gotten hold of 250,000 official documents and worked with international media to spread its treasure on front pages all over the globe. WikiLeaks planned to release the leaks during the Thanksgiving weekend.

"I was in Chappaqua with my family for Thanksgiving, and Chelsea requested I not take any phone calls during the holiday. Crisis or not, I had to agree. I made up for it on Friday, though. I was constantly on the phone. I walked around with my earpiece on my right ear, calling officials in Germany, Great Britain, France, Saudi Arabia, the United Arab Emirates, China, Afghanistan, and Canada to alert them to the coming disclosures and to ask for their indulgence. I had to repeat the same things over and over until it was coming out of my ears.

"We didn't know yet which classified matters of each country would be revealed. Beyond the hurt feelings of world leaders, I worried that confidential sources could be identified. Even worse, it was necessary to inform certain leaders that their names had to be removed from the documents, or their lives would be in danger. I took my responsibility very seriously and believed that the best way to soften the blow was to use my charm and ask for their understanding.

"The leak of the cables led to a crisis in the State Department, as blunt statements and pronouncements of U.S. and foreign diplomats became public. I led the damage control effort for the U.S. abroad and also sought to bolster the morale of shocked Foreign Service officers. Some foreign leaders accepted the frank language of the cables. For example, the Canadian foreign minister, Lawrence Cannon, told me not to worry because apparently what they had said about me was much worse than what we'd said about him.

"I harshly criticized WikiLeaks, saying something like, 'Let's be clear about these leaks: They are not just an attack on America's foreign policy interests. They are a violation of the international community— its conversations, alliances, and negotiations that safeguard global security.' The State Department went into immediate 'war room' mode to deal with the effects of the disclosures and implemented measures to try to prevent another such leak from happening in the future.

"The WikiLeaks disclosures sent the whole world into a panic, as everyone, including me, frantically sought to find out what the United States really thought of them. People in every country did a quick index scan. Which country came out the most favorably? Which one got the most mentions? How were they portrayed? How did friends or enemies come across? Every country kept score. The WikiLeaks cables were turning into an international gossip column, with a lot of juicy details about the habits of foreign leaders. I must say I read them with interest, along with the rest of the world.

"The cables disclosed the web of connections our government had established around the world over the span of decades. The gap between what the United States said it was doing and what we actually did was surprisingly small. The biggest disparity was what foreign leaders told their people publicly and what they said in private. I soon found out that a few of the cables released by WikiLeaks directly concerned me.

"For example, I was horrified to discover that directions to members of the Foreign Service had gone out in 2009 under my name to gather details on foreign diplomats, including officials of the United Nations and U.S. allies. These included Internet and intranet usernames, email addresses, web site URLs useful for identification, credit card numbers, frequent flier account numbers, work schedules, and other biographical information in a process known as the National Humint Collection Directive.

"State Department spokesman Philip Crowley said I had not drafted the directive and that the Secretary of State's name was regularly attached to the bottom of cables originating in Washington, and it was unclear whether I had actually seen them. The material in the cables was actually written by the CIA before being sent out under my name, because the CIA cannot directly instruct State Department personnel. The disclosed cables went back to 2008, when they were sent out under Condoleezza Rice's name during her tenure as Secretary of State. The practice of the U.S. and the State Department gathering intelligence on the U.N. or on friendly nations was not new, but the types of information requested went far beyond past practice and was not the kind of data diplomats would be expected to gather.

"For months to come, every time the administration made a comment about an issue, I found myself comparing it to statements Julian Assange had released about it. Despite all the fuss, nothing important really was disclosed. The cables were of the lowest classification, and none were top secret. There were no indications that coups were being planned or that various countries had amassed secret supplies of weapons no one had ever heard of. I continued to make calls about WikiLeaks until the next spring, which brought a new set of problems.

"Thomas Monson, an American religious leader and author, wrote as follows—let me just read this: 'The principles of living greatly include the capacity to face trouble with courage, disappointment with cheerfulness, and trial with humility.'

"I'm working on it, Mr. Monson! Being Secretary of State gave me plenty of opportunities to practice."

April 2, 2014

"On December first, soon after the Wikileaks fiasco, I flew to Astana, Kazakhstan for a summit of the Organization for Security and Cooperation in Europe. There I met with fifty leaders who were subjects of embarrassing comments in the leaks, including the President of Kazakhstan, Nursultan Nazarbayev. A Kazakh official said that during such encounters, I 'kept my face' and didn't run away from difficult questions. I emphasized that the leaked cables did not reflect official U.S. policy but rather were just instances of individual diplomats giving unfiltered feedback to Washington about what they saw happening in other countries. The situation led some leaders to turn against me my strong remarks about Internet freedom earlier in the year.

"The OSCE summit also featured a meeting between Ban Ki-moon, Secretary-General of the United Nations, and me. In the attempt to repair the tension caused by the Humint spying revelations, I expressed regret to Ban for the leaks, but did not make a direct apology, because I didn't believe I had done anything wrong. A U.N. statement said Ban thanked me for the clarification and concern about the difficulties the leaks had caused.

"About this same time, our dear friend Richard Holbrooke became seriously ill. He first fell ill during a meeting with me, and I was terrified. I sensed that he was in irrevocable danger, but hoped I was wrong. I wasn't. He died shortly after. I'm proud that I was a good friend to his wife Kati before, during, and after Richard's illness and death. I sat by his bedside with Kati and held her hand while Richard was dying. I hope someone does the same for me when Bill dies.

"After his death on December thirteenth, I presided over a spontaneous gathering of forty senior State Department personnel and aides at George Washington University Hospital, where we grieved together. At a memorial service for him a few days later, Bill and I praised Holbrooke's work. I said, 'Everything we have accomplished in

Afghanistan and Pakistan is largely because of Richard.' Unfortunately, that was not completely true. Holbrooke had developed poor relations with the White House during his time as our special envoy to Afghanistan and Pakistan, and my vision of him forging a successful agreement with Afghanistan modeled on his Dayton Accords (the peace agreement that ended the war in Bosnia, and was signed at the Wright-Patterson Air Force Base outside Dayton, Ohio) proved unrealistic. But I guess I can be forgiven (hear that, Dad?) for wanting to say only nice things about a person at his memorial."

I nodded and said how pleased I was that she was learning to forgive herself. "You really are making progress, Hillary!"

"I know I am," she said.

April 4, 2014

"On December 22, 2010," she began, "I returned to the floor of the Senate during the lame duck session of the 111th Congress to witness the ratification, by a 71–26 margin, of the New START (Strategic Arms Reduction Treaty). I had spent several days glued to the phone, calling wavering senators and badgering them into giving us their support. The New START is a nuclear arms reduction treaty between the United States and the Russian Federation.

"Under the terms of the treaty, the number of strategic nuclear missile launchers was reduced by half. A new inspection and verification regime was established, although it did not limit the number of stockpiled, operationally inactive nuclear warheads, which remained in the high thousands in both Russian and American inventories. Still, it was a good start. If I did nothing else as Secretary of State, I earned my stripes on the ratification of the New START treaty."

I stared in awe at Hillary. Here is this unremarkable looking woman, and she is telling me that she may have made possible the continuation of life on earth. How many analysts have patients as essential to life? I know how Hillary felt. If I helped only this one patient in a long lifetime of practice, I had "earned my stripes" as a psychoanalyst.

"As the year closed, I was pleased to be named again by Americans in a Gallup poll as the woman around the world they most admired," she continued. "It was my ninth win in a row and fifteenth overall." She smiled and added, "Do you think I am narcissistic, Doctor? I do so like to be admired!"

"No, I don't," I answered, being only partially truthful. "You have earned every word of praise you receive, and then some."

"Good!" she answered. "I don't want you to think I'm a narcissist, even if I am."

April 7, 2014

In our next session, Hillary, as usual, seamlessly picked up our discussion without any help from me. "I began the year 2011 in Brazil attending the Inauguration of Dilma Rousseff. President Obama sent me to represent the U.S. Rousseff was the first woman to rule her country. Brazil is way ahead of the United States in that respect. Maybe we'll catch up one of these days."

I waited for Hillary to make some remark about the possibility of her serving as president of the United States, but she remained stubbornly silent. Like everyone else, I was curious. And like everyone else, I would have to wait. I once made the mistake of asking her if she was going to run. She answered, "I wish I knew!"

"In mid-January, I packed my bags again and dragged myself to the Middle East, visiting Yemen, Oman, The United Arab Emirates, and Qatar," she continued. "Speaking in unusually blunt language at a conference in Doha, I criticized the failure of Arab governments to move more rapidly towards reform, saying that in too many places, the foundation was weak. The new Middle East I pictured had a firmer ground so it could take root and grow. The Arabs weren't exactly delighted with my observations.

"My visit to Yemen, the first such visit by a Secretary of State in twenty years, found me stressing the dangers of terrorism in that country. To my delight, an impromptu tour around the walled old city of Sana'a found me cheered by onlooking schoolchildren. Nothing is as sweet as the love of little children. They made me miss my little Chelsea—who isn't so little these days—even more than usual.

"When the 2011 Egyptian protests began, I was in the forefront of the administration's response. My public statement on January twenty-fifth that the government of President Hosni Mubarak was stable and 'looking for ways to respond to the legitimate needs and interests of the Egyptian people' was criticized in the media for being lukewarm and behind the times, although others agreed that the U.S. must not be out front in undermining the government of a long-term ally.

"I must have been in a critical mood, and thought, 'If I got worried every time somebody said something critical about me, I would be incapacitated. My skin seems to be getting a little thicker.' The next day, I attacked the Egyptian government's blocking of social media sites. By the end of January, President Obama put me in charge of sorting out the administration's confused response to new developments in Egypt.

"During the frenetic day of January 30, I made appearances on all five Sunday morning talk shows—the so-called "full Ginsburg," as it were. I stated publicly, for the first time, the United States' view that there needed to be an 'orderly transition' to a 'democratic participatory government' and a 'peaceful transformation to real democracy' in Egypt.

"I soon found myself en-route to Haiti to mark the anniversary of its terrible earthquake, engaging on both flights in conference calls regarding Egypt. Whew, Doctor! I get tired just telling you all this! Are you sick of listening to it yet?"

"No," I said, shaking my head. It was an honest reply. "I find it fascinating, and feel privileged to be an observer of your trip through history. I am learning a lot from you."

She turned her face to the wall. I suspected she was trying to hide her tears.

April 9, 2014

"The Egyptian protests became the most critical foreign policy crisis in the Obama administration," she went on, "and the president increasingly came to rely upon me for advice. I had known President Mubarak for twenty years and had formed a close relationship with Egyptian First Lady Suzanne Mubarak by supporting her work on human rights.

"When Mubarak responded violently to the protests in early February, I strongly condemned such actions, especially those against journalists covering the events, and urged Egyptian Vice President Omar Suleiman to conduct an official investigation to hold accountable those responsible for the uprising.

"When Frank Wisner, sent by President Obama to Egypt, baldly stated that Mubarak's departure should be delayed to accommodate an orderly transition to another government, I rebuked him, although I must say I felt somewhat the same way. Mubarak finally stepped down on February 11 as the protests developed into the 2011 Egyptian Revolution. I told the Egyptians that the U.S. understood their country still had much work to do and difficult times ahead. In mid-March, I visited Egypt and promised support for an Egyptian move towards democracy but made sure to avoid specific promises of U.S. aid.

"President Obama was unhappy with U.S. intelligence agencies because of their failure to foresee the 2010 to 2011 Tunisian uprising and the downfall of Zine El Abidine Ben Ali as well as the Egyptian protests. Reacting to criticism that the State Department had failed to anticipate developments in Egypt, I defended the U.S. in an interview on Al-Arabiya, and then soothed ruffled feathers by saying, 'I don't think anybody could have predicted when this all started that we'd be sitting here together talking about the end of the Mubarak presidency.'

"Reflecting not only on the situation in Tunisia and Egypt but also on the 2011 Yemeni protests and the 2011 Jordanian protests, I said at a February meeting of the Quartet on the Middle East that the status quo was not satisfactory. I added that while the transition to democracy could be chaotic, and free elections had to be accompanied by free speech, a free judiciary, and the rule of law to be effective, in the end free people govern themselves the best.

Traditional U.S. foreign policy had sided with rulers who suppressed internal dissent but provided stability and supported U.S. goals in the region. When the monarchy's response to the 2011 Bahraini protests turned to force and bloodshed, I urged a return to the path of reform, saying that violence against the protesters was totally unacceptable. I said that we wanted to see human rights protected and to see reform take place.

"At the same time, I said that the U.S. could not dictate outcomes. As Bahrain continued to erupt in episodes of violence against protesters, I remember saying, 'Our goal is a credible political process that can address the legitimate aspirations of all the people of Bahrain. Violence is not and cannot be the answer. A political process is.'

Hillary turned to look at me and said, "Are you getting groggy from all this information, Doctor? I know it is not always interesting to non-political people."

Hillary's question put me in a bit of a dilemma. I firmly believed in telling the truth to patients and everyone else whenever possible. Yet I didn't want to discourage Hillary from speaking her mind. I remembered a conversation I'd had a long time ago with my training analyst, Dr. Theodore Reik, when I told him I was bored with a long story a patient was telling me. He said, "Being bored is the price you have to pay while you are waiting for the good stuff to surface."

Bearing in mind Dr. Reik's comment, I said, "Of course I'm not groggy, Hillary. I always want to hear what you are thinking about." A little white lie? Yes. Necessary? That, too, although I must say I was surprised that Hillary, with her extraordinary B.S. detector skills, hadn't picked up on my subterfuge. Or maybe she had and just decided to ignore it. One can never be sure with Hillary Clinton.

"The 2011 Libyan civil war began in mid-February," she began, "then intensified into armed conflict. When the rebels scored some military successes in early March 2011, I expressed my opinion to President Obama that Gaddafi had to go without any further delay. As Gaddafi conducted counterattacks against the rebels, I initially was reluctant, as Obama had been, to impose a Libyan no-fly zone. As the prospects of a Gaddafi victory and possible bloodbath expanded, I traveled to Europe and North Africa and found support for military intervention increasing among European and Arab leaders, and so I changed my mind and encouraged the President to back U.N. action to impose the no-fly zone and authorize other necessary military actions.

"The United Nations Security Council approved a no-fly zone in March. The resolution included provisions for further actions to prevent attacks on civilian targets. I helped gain the financial and political support of several Arab countries, in particular convincing Qatar, the United Arab Emirates, and Jordan that a no-fly zone would not be sufficient and that air-to-ground attacks would be necessary. In regard to whether the U.S. should send arms to the anti-Gaddafi forces, I said that this would be permissible under the resolution, but no decision had been made yet on doing so."

April 14, 2014

"U.S. policy towards turmoil in the Middle East countries involved backing some regimes and supporting protesters against others," she went on. "By then I had logged 465,000 miles in my Boeing 757, more than any other Secretary of State had done in a comparable period of time, and had visited seventy-nine countries. *Time* magazine wrote that my endurance was legendary and that I would still be going at the end of long work days even as my staff members were conking out. The key was my ability to fall asleep on demand, at any time and place, for power naps."

Wow! I thought. *She can go to sleep whenever she wants to. I wish I could. I'll have to ask her how she does it.*

"I also saw the potential political changes in the Middle East as an opportunity for an even more fundamental change to take place in the world," she went on, "the empowerment of women, something *Newsweek* magazine saw as my major interest in life. I remarked about this in countries like Egypt. 'If a country doesn't recognize minority rights and human rights, including women's rights, they will not have the stability and prosperity that is possible.'

"In Yemen, I spoke poignantly of President Nujood Ali and her campaign against forced marriage at a young age. I can't imagine my dear Chelsea or me being forced to marry a stranger at age twelve or younger. I'd kill the guy!

"On the subject of women and girls, I was even more expansive. I said that their rights were the unfinished business of the twenty-first century. I also maintained that the well-being of women in other countries has a direct influence on American self-interest. This is a big deal for American values and for American foreign policy and our interests, but it is also important for our security. Where women are dehumanized and powerless, we are more likely to see extremism that leads to security challenges for us all. A lot of the work I did in the State

Department on women's or human-rights issues was not just because I cared passionately about the subject, which I do, but because I see it as a way of increasing security to fulfill American interests.

"In the midst of all this turmoil, which also included my pledging government support to Japan in the wake of the devastating 2011 Tohoku earthquake and tsunami, I said in a mid-March interview with CNN's Wolf Blitzer that I had no interest in becoming a two-term Secretary of State, a one-term Secretary of Defense, a vice president, or a candidate for president again. I stressed how deeply I cared for my current position because it was the best job I could ever have.

"But I was weary from constant traveling, still not part of Obama's intimate inner circle, and looking forward to a time of less stress, along with the opportunity to work for, write about, and teach on international women's rights."

April 18, 2014

"I was among those in the White House Situation Room who received hour-to-hour briefings on the May 2011 mission to kill Osama bin Laden. In early 2011, the CIA believed it had discovered his hiding place, and the White House held a final discussion on April twenty-eighth to decide whether to go ahead with a raid to kill him, and if so, how to do it.

"I supported the idea of sending in Navy SEALs, thinking that the U.S. could not afford to ignore a chance that might never come again, and the assassination of bin Laden was so important that it outweighed any risks. I believed with all my heart that we owed it to the victims of 9/11 to get rid of that S.O.B. once and for all. I was thrilled when the U.S. fulfilled its mission at his hideout in Abbottabad, Pakistan in early May.

"There was subsequent criticism from various Americans that Pakistan had let bin Laden hide almost in plain sight for years. Not wanting any more trouble with Pakistan, I praised its past record of helping the U.S. hunt down terrorists. Our alliance with Pakistan, after all, had contributed to our efforts to dismantle al Qaeda.

"I then played an important role in the administration's decision not to publish photographs of the dead bin Laden, reporting that U.S. allies in the Middle East did not favor doing so. I agreed with Secretary Gates that such a release might cause an anti-U.S. backlash overseas. As usual in such circumstances, there was some talk that bin Laden was not really dead, because no one had ever seen a photograph of his dead body, but in my opinion, that was ridiculous. We had enough proof of his death from people who saw his body.

"A June 2011 trip to Africa found me consoling my friend and longtime aide Huma Abedin after the sexting scandal involving her husband Anthony Weiner broke out. I knew exactly how she felt. The world is not kind to women. I also emphatically denied reports that I wanted to become the next president of the World Bank, which needed a successor to Robert Zoellick after the end of his term in mid-2012. Of course, nobody believed me. Can you tell me, Doctor, why nobody ever believes me?"

I smiled and shook my head.

She continued anyway. "In July, sounding more confident than I felt, I assured China and other foreign governments that the ongoing U.S. debt ceiling crisis would not drive our country into sovereign default, a prediction that turned out to be correct when the Budget Control Act of 2011 was passed and signed at the very last minute. Whew! We really were lucky that time! I shudder to think what would have happened to our country if we had gone into default. But who knows what the next crisis will bring?

"I spent much of that summer trying unsuccessfully to persuade the Palestinian National Authority to drop its efforts to become a full member of the United Nations at the September 2011 General Assembly meeting. By September 2012, with their application stalled because of the Security Council members' inability to make a unanimous recommendation, the Palestine Authority sought an upgrade from 'observer entity' to 'non-member observer state.'

"Their request was put to a vote in the General Assembly on November 29. In addition to granting Palestine 'non-member observer state' status, the resolution asked the Security Council to consider the application submitted in September 2011 by the State of Palestine for admission to full membership in the United Nations, which was predicated on the two-state solution that contemplated pre-1967 borders.

"General Assembly Resolution 6719 was passed on November, 29, 2012 in a 138-9 vote, upgrading Palestine to non-member observer state status in the United Nations. This change was described by *The Independent* as 'de facto recognition of the sovereign state of Palestine.'

"The vote was a historic moment for Palestine and a tremendous diplomatic setback for Israel and the United States. Palestine's new position in the UN allowed the Palestinian Authority to enter into treaties and deal directly with UN agencies. It permitted Palestine to claim legal rights over its territorial waters and air space. It also gave Palestinians the right to sue in the International Court of Justice for control of the territory they believe is rightfully theirs and allowed them the right to bring war-crimes charges against Israel in the International Criminal Court. I was dismayed at the passage of the resolution, and believe it was a drastic error that will delay the course of peace for many years. To be more graphic about it, every time I think of the vote, I feel like throwing up!

"I continued to receive high poll numbers, with a September 2011 *Bloomberg News* poll earning me a sixty-four percent favorable rating, the highest of any political figure in the nation. A third of those polled said I would have made a better president than Obama, an observation I heartily agree with, but when asked what the likelihood was that I would stage a campaign against the president, I answered, 'Below zero.' I believed that one of the great things about being Secretary of State was that I could remain above politics and retain my dignity. After my dreadful experiences with the media at the White House, I was not interested in being pulled back into a mud-slinging contest. Of course, things were to change significantly later on, but I didn't know that at the time."

I wondered, *Does she mean she will run for president in 2016?* But I knew better than to ask.

"After Obama's historic October 2011 announcement that the withdrawal of U.S. troops from Iraq would be completed by the end of the year," she went on, "I vigorously defended the decision. I said that despite the absence of military forces, the U.S. was committed to strengthening Iraq's democracy. I also praised the effectiveness of Obama's foreign policy in general, and as proof, pointed to the death of Muammar Gaddafi, which ended the Libyan intervention. This statement essentially avoided criticism from those running for the 2012 Republican presidential nomination. In October 2011, I visited Tripoli and, in private, was somewhat guarded about Libya's future following the rebel success. A video of my exclaiming 'Wow!' upon first reading on my BlackBerry of Gaddafi's capture was widely circulated. I added, 'We came, we saw, he died.'"

April 21, 21014

Hillary entered my counseling room crying and wiped away the tears pouring down her cheeks. Alarmed, I wondered what was the matter. Practically all of my patients cried, but somehow I was more concerned when Hillary did. She didn't cry lightly.

She said in a choked up voice, "I was thinking what I would talk to you about today and remembered, to my great sorrow, that my mother, Dorothy Rodham, died in Washington on November 1, 2011. I canceled a planned trip to the United Kingdom and Turkey to be with her on her deathbed."

She stopped and was quiet for a few moments, which seemed an eternity to me. Then she said with shaking voice, "At the end, I squeezed her hand and told her I loved her. She squeezed my hand gently in return and said, 'I love you, too, Hillary, more than anyone in the world.' Then she closed her eyes for the last time. I was completely broken up and unable to work for weeks. As you know, Doctor, I loved my mother deeply and knew I had to pull myself together for the sake of Chelsea and my country, but I couldn't imagine how I would be able to function without my mother watching me from behind the curtain. She was always there for me, no matter how terrible the problem; talking things out with her always made me feel better. She was my best friend, my teacher, my mentor, my adviser. Losing my mother was the worst loss of my life.

"Bill asked if it was enough that, since I believed in an afterlife, I would see my mother again someday. It wasn't. Nothing was enough. But somehow, probably because of the strength she had given me, I was able to draw upon forces I hadn't known I had, and little by little, rejoined the world."

She shut her eyes and opened them to proceed with less emotional topics. I could see her leveling her "carpenter's tool."

"When the 2011 to 2012 Russian protests began in late 2011 in response to the Russian election results, I was very blunt about their need for democratic processes. I said the Russian people deserved the right to be heard and to have their votes counted. I added that Russian voters deserved a thorough investigation of possible electoral fraud. In return, Russian Prime Minister Vladimir Putin publicly criticized me, accusing the U.S. of financially backing Russian protesters and precipitating protests. When Putin won the Russian presidential election in March 2012, some officials in the State Department wanted me to denounce Russian politics again but were overruled by the White House. Despite Putin's attack on me, I thought it would help to cease all the bomb-throwing and to state simply. 'The election had a clear winner, and we are ready to work with President-elect Putin.'

"In early December of 2011, I made the first visit to Burma by a U.S. Secretary of State since John Foster Dulles stopped there in 1955. I sought to support the 2011 Burmese democratic reforms and met with Burmese leaders as well as the opposition leader Aung San Suu Kyi. Because Suu Kyi and I had kept in touch with each other over the years, it felt like I was visiting a friend I hadn't seen for years, even though it was our first actual meeting.

"I'll tell you more about that next session. The relationship between us is very important to me, and deserves time of its own.

"Naturally, my outreach to Burma attracted criticism, with Congresswoman Ileana Ros-Lehtinen saying it sent the wrong message to Burmese military thugs. Others said my visit combined idealism and statesmanship in trying to keep Burma out of the direct Chinese sphere of influence. I had to overcome opposition from the White House and Pentagon, as well as from Senate minority leader Mitch McConnell, to make the trip. I personally appealed to Obama and won his approval. I think it is hard for him to say no to me. Probably to the formidable Michelle, too.

"When asked if I thought the Burmese regime would follow up on reform pledges, I said I couldn't predict what was going to happen, but I thought it important that the U.S. support democratic reform. I added (cleverly, I think), 'This is a first date, not a marriage, and like all first dates, nobody can predict where it will lead.'

"I also continued to address rights concerns, in this case those of gay people, in a December 2011 speech before the United Nations Human Rights Council. I said the U.S. would advocate for gay rights abroad. 'Gay rights are human rights,' I said spontaneously, in a statement that became famous, and 'It should never be a crime to be gay.' This, of course, drew vicious criticism.

"At the end of the year, I was named again by Americans in Gallup's most admired man and woman poll as the woman around the world they most admired. It was the tenth time in a row that I had been so honored and my sixteenth overall. If they keep this up, I may have to believe them."

April 23, 2014

"Before we get started today, Doctor, I wanted to share some very exciting news with you," Hillary began.

"Go ahead," I responded.

"We just announced publicly that Chelsea is pregnant! I'm going to be a grandmother!" She beamed.

"Congratulations, Hillary!" I said, truly happy for her. "You must be very excited."

"Yes, of course! I can't wait for that baby to come into the world!" She smiled and continued more seriously, "Well let's get back to business, shall we?"

I nodded.

"On January 26, 2012 in a State Department town hall meeting, I informed the world of my need to come down from 'the high wire of American politics after twenty exhausting years of balancing myself on it.' I remember I said, 'I have made it clear that I will stay on until the president nominates someone else for the position and the transition can occur. It has been an extraordinary personal experience and honor. But I really need to have my own time back. I just want to be my own person, and maybe find out more who that is.'

"Why did you really leave the post, Hillary?" I asked.

She answered, "I felt I had done my part to make the world a better place to live, and enough is enough, even for me. I had visited a hundred and twelve countries during my tenure, the most of any other Secretary of State in U.S. history. I was simply worn out, and needed some time to be with my family and perhaps write another book."

She looked at me in alarm. "Are you critical of my decision, Doctor? Do you think I shouldn't have quit?"

"I am not your father. I think you should do whatever makes you happy."

She looked at me and smiled.

"As the brutal Syrian civil war intensified, the U.S. proposed a UN Security Council resolution that urged Syrian President Bashar al-Assad to resign and permit the formation of a unity government. Russia and China refused to endorse the resolution, an action I called a travesty. I then called for friends of a democratic Syria group to band together, as nations, to promote a peaceful and democratic solution to the controversy. As a result of my efforts, the Friends of Syria was formed.

"At the first meeting of the group in Tunis, I again criticized the actions of Russia and China as contemptible and predicted that the Assad regime would meet its end via a military coup. During the summer of 2012, I repeated my criticism. Then CIA Director David Petraeus and I developed a plan to send arms to and perform training of selected groups of Syrian rebels.

"Unfortunately, because he was loath to become involved in the Syrian situation in the middle of an election year, President Obama rejected the idea.

"At a keynote speech before the International Crisis Group, I connected my thinking on women's empowerment with that of peacemaking, saying the innumerable connections women have with communities keep us more concerned about the quality of life issues that blossom in peacetime. Women also identify more than men with minority groups, because we are discriminated against ourselves and know how it feels. I said that women have so much talent that it was time for us to take our rightful place next to men. I added that I believe empowerment of women will cascade, as people become more and more aware that it leads to economic growth."

April 25, 2014

"My trip to China in late April and early May of 2012 put me smack in the middle of a drama starring the blind Chinese dissident, Chen Guangcheng," she continued. "Sightless since a childhood illness, Chen grew up in a village of five hundred and attended school for the first time at age seventeen. Chen became interested in law. He audited classes and became a self-trained attorney who developed a career as a 'barefoot lawyer' defending peasants in cases of forced abortions under the country's one-child policy, corruption, and pollution. Although he spoke very little English and I no Chinese at all, we were kindred souls in our interests.

"His best-known cause was exposing the ghastly practice of forced abortions and sterilizations in his native Shandong Province. Chinese authorities first arrested this valiant activist in 2005 after he filed a class-action lawsuit for women who had undergone forced abortions and sterilizations as part of China's one-child policy. Chen's efforts enraged local officials and led to nearly seven years of imprisonment. Incredible! It made me appreciate living in the United States even more, where we have freedom of speech!

"After his release, he and his wife and two children were confined to their home for nineteen months. He compared his experience with the government to the 'collision between an egg and a stone.' I presume Chen felt like the egg. In his character, he was more like the stone.

"One night in April 2012, he slipped past his guards and climbed over the wall of his farm house, breaking his ankle but continuing on. How he managed to do so with a broken ankle, not to mention his blindness, I'll never know. I'm sure I couldn't do it with two eyes and two intact feet. With the help of friends, he reached Beijing, where he appealed to the American Embassy for shelter. It happened I was then on my way to Beijing for talks, and both the U.S. and Chinese governments were eager to keep the negotiations from failing. Chen asked permission to stay in China and be guaranteed safety. After a deal for that fell through, he requested and was given a seat on my plane when I flew back to the U.S., along with his wife and children. After Chen made it to this country, he was appointed a visiting fellow at NYU's law school.

"After my departure, I personally negotiated with senior Chinese diplomat Dai Bingguo to have Chen's deal put back in place. Despite an environment that had, as one aide said, 'exploded into an absolute circus,' I somehow was able to find a path for the United States that kept China from losing face. I'm a pretty good diplomat, Doctor, don't you think?"

I smiled. *What am I going to say? No?*

"After the high-level al Qaeda official Abu Yahya al-Libi was killed in June 2012 during a U.S. drone attack in Pakistan," she continued, "I defended the action, saying we would always maintain our right to use force against such terrorist groups. We were complying with the laws of war and were taking great precautions against the loss of innocent life. Beginning with my 2009 trip to Pakistan, I had faced many questions about U.S. drone strikes, which I usually refused to answer. Unknown to the media, I was one of the leading proponents of expanding the strikes when the safety of Americans was involved. In 2011, I even sided with the U.S. Ambassador to Pakistan, Cameron Munter, when he requested more control over the U.S. 'kill list' selections for that country."

"What exactly is a *kill list*?" I asked Hillary.

She looked surprised that I didn't know. "President Obama is the leader of a top-secret procedure designed to designate terrorists to be killed or captured," she answered. "In my opinion, using it will protect the United States from another 9/11 attack."

I swallowed and didn't know what to think. I am a psychoanalyst, not a politician. My job is to help people, not destroy them. I loathed the idea of a "kill list," but on the other hand, Hillary might be right that a record of enemies who wish to do us harm serves to shield our country. To my surprise, Hillary, the world's best B.S. detector according to her husband, didn't pick up on my ambivalence, and proceeded with the story of her tenure as Secretary of State.

"In June of 2012, I arrived in Riga, Latvia, the 100th country I had visited during my term of office. This was a touchstone for me. The previous record among Secretaries of State had been held by Madeleine Albright, who managed to visit 96 nations. I was happy to rack up four more country visits than Madeleine—I do love recording such firsts!

"Similarly, in July 2012, I became the first U.S. Secretary of State to visit Laos since John Foster Dulles set foot on the soil there in 1955. I also held talks with Prime Minister Thongsing Thammavong and Foreign Minister Thongloun Sisoulith in Vientiane, where we concentrated on economic matters and the sad after-effects of the Vietnam War. We had bombed Laos viciously during the war, and unexploded bombs and land mines were still a menace to the Laotian people. I was horrified to learn this, and determined to do all we could to help remove all remaining traces of the bombs. How awful that we live in a world where such actions are necessary!"

"I agree with you one hundred percent, Hillary," I said. "How wonderful that you were doing something about it!"

April 28, 2014

"In July 2012, I visited Egypt for the first time since Mohammed Morsi became its democratically elected president," she began. "As I arrived in the country, my convoy was met by protesting mobs. Shoes, tomatoes, and bottles of water were hurled at us, although I lucked out that nothing hit either me or my car. Protesters also embarrassed me by chanting 'Monica, Monica,' referring of course to the Lewinsky scandal. They behaved as though that whole mess was my fault. I was also accused of secretly aligning the U.S. with the Muslim Brotherhood.

"The Muslim Brotherhood? The United States? They've got to be kidding!

"On September fourteenth, remains of the Americans killed in Benghazi were returned to the U.S. The president and I attended the ceremony, where a young woman with covered head, and with eyes haunted by sadness, held up a handwritten sign saying, 'Thugs and killers don't represent Benghazi or Islam.' When I saw that, I was very upset. Our government's preparation for the Benghazi assault, as well as explanations of what happened afterward, blew up into a big political issue in the U.S., particularly because of the ongoing presidential election.

"Unfortunately, the State Department had listed embassy security as a major choice for cutbacks in its budget report. On September twentieth, I gave detailed testimony to the U.S. Senate, for which I was severely criticized by several Republican attendees, of course. They were furious at President Obama's consistent refusal to inform them directly about the circumstances of the Benghazi attack, only to find his comments published the next day in *The New York Times*. I guess I would be mad about that, too, if it happened to me. To make everybody happy, I arranged for the formation of an Accountability Review Board panel to investigate the attack, to determine what the State Department did right and did wrong.

"On October fifteenth, I announced to the media that I was at fault for the deaths of the officials; I said, 'I take full responsibility for the deaths. I'm in charge of the State Department's people all over the world, and the blame is on my shoulders. I take the attack to heart and am flooded with guilt about it. I promise to get to the bottom of the catastrophe, and to do everything possible to prevent it from happening again.'"

"I meant every word of it, Doctor," she added tearfully. "It was one of the worst experiences of my life. Everybody thinks I'm so tough. They have no idea that I spent many nights crying myself to sleep over it.

"Barack Obama was re-elected as president on November 6, 2012. I had told him before that I would stay on the job until my successor was chosen. Despite my insistence that I was not interested, speculations about me as a possible candidate in the 2016 presidential election kept growing. A poll taken in Iowa, the first state in the nomination process, showed that in a hypothetical 2016 contest, I would have fifty-eight percent support, with Vice President Biden coming in second at seventeen percent. What! Do they think I'd go through all that again? Not on your life!"

I looked at her skeptically. "You don't believe me?" she said.

I smiled and said, "If you say so. In here, the customer is always right."

She blinked and let it go. "In November, I traveled to Jerusalem, the West Bank, and Cairo, and met with Benjamin Netanyahu, Mahmoud Abbas, and Mohamed Morsi in a combined attempt to end the 2012 Gaza conflict. On November 21st, Egyptian Foreign Minister Mohamed Kamel Amr and I announced that a cease-fire agreement had been reached between Israel and Hamas in Gaza. Who was it who said when it looks like something is too good to be true, usually it is? The 2012 Egyptian protests against Morsi broke out soon after. When I was asked by the media how long I thought it would take for peace to come about between Israel and Gaza, I answered that it was unfortunate we didn't have any magic wands to wave."

I just loved her sense of humor.

April 30, 2014

"A personal catastrophe happened to me in mid-December," she said. "I somehow picked up a stomach virus during a trip to Europe, became very dehydrated, and fainted. As I fell, I banged my head and suffered a mild concussion. As a result, I had to call off an appearance at Congressional hearings about Benghazi. A few conservative figures, including Congressman Allen West and former U.N. Ambassador John Bolton, accused me of cooking up an illness to avoid testifying before Congress. I was furious!

"Fortunately, a State Department spokesperson said their accusations were 'completely false.' Even Senator Lindsey Graham, a Republican, denounced the allegations. Do West and Bolton think I actually would lie about something so easy to check up on? I am a very honest person, as those who know me well can attest to. If I were to betray my Methodist conscience and tell a falsehood, it would have to be about something much more important than a concocted illness.

"The Pickering-Mullen Accountability Review Board report about the Benghazi attack was released and publicized on December 19. It strongly criticized State Department officials for ignoring requests for security upgrades, and for failing to adopt safer surveillance. It openly attacked the Bureau of Diplomatic Security and the Bureau of Near Eastern Affairs, and berated leadership at senior levels within two bureaus of the State Department. According to the report, the security measures for Benghazi were completely inadequate to deal with the attack. After the release of the report, four State Department officials were fired from their positions. I was lucky the document did not criticize more senior officials in the department, including yours truly.

"My good friend Pickering (at least he is now) said they placed the blame at a lower level, where the decision-making actually took place in this instance. I was temporarily off the hook, at least everybody's hook but my own. I wrote in a letter to Congress that I accepted the conclusions of the Pickering-Mullen report, and had formed a State Department task force to carry out the sixty changes recommended by the investigation. The Deputy Secretary of State, William Burns, and the Deputy Secretary of State for Management and Resources, Thomas Nides, testified for me before two Congressional committees on December 20. I myself planned to testify in January, when I expected to complete my recovery from my fall.

"Although I was not yet well enough to attend the December 21 public announcement of John Kerry's nomination to succeed me, President Obama described me there as being 'in good spirits.' He also praised Kerry as being of the 'highest caliber.' *Hmm.* Do you think the president meant higher than me?

"I intended to return to work on December thirty-first, but the day before that, I had to be admitted to New York Presbyterian Hospital after my doctor discovered that the concussion had caused a blood clot to form. That New Year's Eve, he announced that the clot was behind my ear, near my brain. I prayed to God, my mother, my father, and anyone else who was listening. Someone must have heard me. After being treated with anticoagulants, I was told that I had not suffered any neurological damage and was expected to make a full recovery. I was thrilled, of course, and like Blanche Dubois said, 'Sometimes, there's God so suddenly!'

"I was released from the hospital on January second and returned to work at the State Department on the seventh. To my delight, co-workers welcomed me back with a standing ovation and a joke gift of a football helmet featuring the department's seal. I also received a football jersey with 112 on it—the number of countries I had visited during my tenure. The illness, however, put an end to my days of traveling on the job.

"Finally, on January twenty-third, I gave more than five hours of testimony about the Benghazi affair at hearings of the Senate Foreign Relations Committee and the House Foreign Affairs Committee. It was a heart wrenching ordeal I wouldn't go through again for all the tea in China! I said in a trembling voice that it wasn't just about policy for me; it was a personal trauma that had broken my heart. President Obama and I had huddled close to each other at Andrews, hoping, I guess, to draw strength from the other's presence, as the Marines solemnly carried the flag-draped caskets of the victims, one by one, off the plane. As each casket passed me, my spirits catapulted downward another degree. By the time the last one passed, I would gladly have joined them.

"I put my arms around the mothers and fathers, sisters and brothers, sons and daughters of the victims, and we cried together. I again accepted formal responsibility for the departmental security lapses that led to the deaths but did not admit any personal blame for them. Although I wished with all my heart that I had been able to prevent the attack, I never believed in my gut that it was my fault. I said I felt responsible for all the State Department employees, but that I never saw the request concerning Benghazi. I hadn't approved or rejected it. I did acknowledge that I had agreed to keep the Benghazi consulate open after an earlier report that its security had deteriorated, but had assumed the security personnel responsible would take care of the matter.

"Senator Ron Johnson, a Tea Party Republican, persisted in asking me whether UN Ambassador Susan Rice had misled the public after the attacks. His interrogation made me furious. In a raised voice, I answered with something like, 'With all due respect, Senator (which is more than he deserved), the fact is that we have four dead Americans. We don't know at this point whether the attack was caused by a protest or if some guys out for a walk one night decided they'd kill some Americans for fun. What difference does it make? The Americans are dead, and nothing we can do will bring them back to life again. It is our job to figure out what happened and to do everything we can to prevent such a catastrophe from ever happening again.'

I was also attacked by other Republicans. Representative Jeff Duncan accused me of 'national security malpractice,' and Senator Rand Paul said the president should have dismissed me from my job for having failed to read security-related cables coming into the State Department. I answered, 'There are over a million cables that come into the State Department, Senator Paul. Could you have read over a million cables?' He had the good grace not to answer. My arch-rival Senator John McCain said that while it was nice to see me in good health, he wasn't satisfied with my answers.

"During my testimony, I also addressed the opposition in Mali and Northern Africa. Mali was considered a model African democracy until the military seized power in March 2012, and the north fell under al Qaeda control. I said, 'This has opened a new security challenge for the U.S. We cannot allow northern Mali to become a safe haven for terrorists. Perhaps because of my interventions, presidential polls in August 2013 contributed to the return of civilian rule."

May 2, 2014

"*60 Minutes* aired an interview with me and President Obama on January twenty-seventh. It was the president's first broadcast with a member of his administration. In it, he enthusiastically praised my performance. I remember what he said well: 'Hillary will go down in history as one of the finest Secretary of States the United States has ever had.' He made me feel so good I almost forgave him for winning the presidency instead of me.

"He said the relationship between us was very comfortable, and that getting past our 2008 primary campaign battles had not been difficult. When asked about my health, I said, 'I still have some effects from falling on my head and having the blood clot. But the doctors tell me that will recede. And so I'm looking forward to returning to work.' I didn't mention the times I was up all night worrying about whether I would fully recover, and if so, when.

"Two days later, I held my fifty-ninth global town hall meeting of my tenure, and my last. It made me a little sad."

I said, "A *little* sad, Hillary?"

"Okay, maybe a lot sad," she conceded, "Also on that day, the Senate Foreign Relations Committee unanimously approved Senator Kerry's nomination, and the full Senate confirmed him by a 94–3 vote. In my final public speech, on January thirty-first, before the Council on Foreign Relations, I reopened the theme of 'smart power.'

"I suggested that a new structure was needed for developing relationships in the changing world. I added something like, 'We are truly the essential nation. That is not an empty slogan or boast, but merely recognizes our decisive role and the enormous responsibilities we face in the continued development of humankind. That's why the conservatives are dead wrong. It is why the United States will remain the leader in this century, even as we move ahead in new and possibly unknown ways.'

"My final day as secretary was February 1, 2013, when I met with President Obama to hand him my letter of resignation. We hugged each other and cried a little. 'We have been through a lot together,' he said, 'and the United States and the world are better for it.' I later gave farewell remarks at a meeting of employees at the State Department headquarters.

"Well, that's pretty much what my tenure as Secretary of State was like, Doctor. I'd like to evaluate for you, as well as for myself, how I did. Maybe we can decide together what kind of Secretary of State I really was. Will you help me do that, Doctor?"

I nodded, overwhelmed with the enormity of the task she was assigning me. I only hoped I would understand what she was talking about.

When I could speak, I said, "I am not a politician, Hillary. As you are surely aware by now, I am not even particularly knowledgeable about politics. What I *can* do is give you the most honest opinion I am capable of."

She smiled, and said, "That's all anybody can ask. Let's start tomorrow."

I answered, "Of course."

I didn't sleep too well that night.

May 5, 2014

Hillary came in shivering and said, "Brrrrrr! It's freezing outside. Don't you have any heat in this place? You're just like my father— always trying to save a few pennies."

I got up and adjusted the thermostat.

"I was only kidding," she said. "You really aren't at all like him, thank goodness! What do you call it? Transference?"

I nodded, pleased that she had recognized the phenomenon.

She then picked up the thread where we had stopped the session before. "While my tenure as Secretary of State by and large is well thought of," she began thoughtfully, "certain unfriendly observers insist that there was no significant diplomatic breakthrough during it nor improvement on major issues such as those made by Dean Acheson, George Marshall, and Henry Kissinger. I disagree. It is true that the insoluble conflicts existing when I entered office, such as those in Pakistan and Iran, Arab-Israeli relations, and North Korea, had not disappeared when I left.

"But, in my opinion, the conditions of the political world during my tenure were far too complicated to allow breakthroughs such as the Marshall Plan or Nixon's trip to China. What I suspect is that many of my contributions in smart power will take much longer to evaluate, and my reputation will be enhanced as time goes by. In other words, I believe that my success is less tangible but longer lasting.

"Brookings Institute analyst Michael O'Hanlon said I was more 'solid than spectacular' in that few victories were actually achieved during my time in office. If so, I don't think being 'solid' is such a bad thing, do you? It is better than being called mediocre. Some other people disagreed with O'Hanlon. For example, Eric Schmidt argued that I was 'perhaps the most significant Secretary of State since Acheson.' All agreed about my celebrity. And one unnamed official called me a global rock star."

"A rock star! Me?" Hillary said, laughing. "Can you believe it? Do I look like Michael Jackson? Frankly, Doctor, sometimes I don't understand why I'm so popular with so many people. Underneath all the claptrap, most of the time I still feel like the drab girl nobody gave a second look at until Bill Clinton came along."

"Why do *you* think you are so popular, Hillary?"

"I've been thinking about that, and believe it is because I have their interests at heart. People know when it is real and not put on. But I wonder even more why I'm so *un*popular with a lot of men. I decided that it is nothing personal, that I represent major change to them. Sometimes I think it isn't really me they hate at all, but that I represent the woman boss they are embarrassed to work under, the wife who went back to school and makes more money than they do, and the daughter they wish weren't so independent."

"Well put," I said.

She smiled and continued, "The conflicts between me and Barack Obama that many observers predicted never came to pass. A writer for *The New York Times Magazine* wrote that we led the 'least discordant national security team in decades.' That's pretty good, don't you think, for two people who had fought so hard for the same position? "Not many people I know have the capacity to make friends with their successful rivals. Most of us are too jealous and vengeful."

She was pleased. I was glad she didn't ask me if I were one of those people. I wouldn't have known how to answer.

"Nevertheless," Hillary continued, "there were limitations to the amount of influence I had. Much of the handling of the Middle East, Iran, and Iraq during my tenure was done by the White House or the Pentagon. Obama likes to control his own affairs of state as much as possible. Some people—and I won't mention any names—might even call him a 'control freak.'

"On other issues, policy making was locked inside the White House among the president's inner circle of advisors. They must have thrown away the key. The circle never included me. You'd think the highest office in the land would be above such things, but it isn't. The glass ceiling still exists in Washington, Doctor, as it does in the business world, although I'm proud to say that I put a few cracks in it.

"Obama and I also had some important differences of opinion. Unfortunately for Syria, I failed to persuade him to arm and train Syrian rebels in 2012 but overcame his initial opposition to my visiting Burma in 2011. The trip turned out brilliantly, if I may say so, and I made one of the best friends of my life, Aung San Suu Kyi. She is very important to me. My original idea of handling key trouble spots through special envoys under my aegis fell apart. I did edge out the U.S. Commerce Department, however, by having the State Department take a lead role in pitching sales on behalf of U.S. companies. I believe the commercial aspects of diplomacy and the promotion of international trade are vital to America.

"My background as an elected politician showed in my talent for dealing with people, my ability to remember personal connections that people (they don't know I carefully memorize their names before every meeting), in visiting staffs of the State Department offices overseas, and in understanding the problems of elected foreign leaders. It sometimes worked out to my detriment, however, as when my personal relationship with the Mubaraks possibly caused me to back them too long during the Egyptian Revolution. Until after the Benghazi catastrophe, I even retained personal support from some Republicans. In mid-2012, Republican Senator Lindsey Graham came out and said he thought I represented the U.S. well and that I handled myself and situations in a very classy way. And that from a Republican, no less! P.S. I loved being called classy! I don't really see myself that way."

"How *do* you see yourself, Hillary?"

"As a woman who has no intrinsic talent for dressing or acting like a society woman, but is smart enough to figure out how to do it anyway."

I smiled and said, "I think that is a pretty realistic appraisal."

"It doesn't matter how I dress anyway," she continued. "The media just love to attack me on it, no matter what I wear. Sexist attitudes are clearly apparent in the ridiculous questions journalists ask me about my favorite clothing designers. Would you ever ask a man that question? In response to that inquiry in a 2010 interview, I famously labeled the question as what it was: a demeaning and irrelevant jab at me because I'm a woman."

"Good for you, Hillary!" I said. "It is about time someone took the media to task for its sexism and superficiality."

"As the first Secretary of State to visit such countries as Togo and Timor-Leste in the electronic age, I believe personal visits are still more important than ever. As I said shortly before leaving office, 'I have found it highly ironic that in today's world, when we can be anywhere virtually, more people than ever want us to show up in their countries. Somebody said to me once, 'Just look at your travel schedule! Why are you knocking yourself out? Why Togo? Why the Cook Islands? No Secretary of State has ever been to Togo before.'

"Well, I wasn't like any other Secretaries of State. I did what I thought was best for the security of the whole world. It just so happens that Togo is on the U.N. Security Council. Even if nobody has ever heard of it, Togo is full of people who are important."

May 6, 2014

Hillary came in and sat silently for a few moments. Then she began this way: "I said in an earlier session I'd tell you about my Burmese friend, Aung San Suu Kyi. It'll give me great pleasure to do so now.

"I have Bill and Chelsea to talk to about the important personal matters of our life. I know many women who I can chat with about our children and the events of daily living. I even enjoy talking to you. But I must admit it gets a bit lonely up at the top. I don't have a single woman friend at my political level with whom I can mull over the circumstances and events of the day. I sometimes doubt if there are any others like me in the whole world. Most of the daily events are classified, and I am honor bound to keep silent about them. It is a heavy load to carry alone. The world of the Secretary of State is a closed universe, which is difficult to understand if you are not deeply involved in it. My closest aide, Huma Abedin, who was practically my right arm, helped to fill the void. She assisted in planning policy, prepared me for events, and even carried my luggage when it was necessary.

"But for me it was difficult, with an employee, to feel the kind of intimacy I needed. There were things even she could not know, and we did not have the same level of security clearance.

"Although Barack is wonderful to talk with, he was rarely available to me. And he is a man. I must admit that there is something about a close woman friend that I need in order to feel at my best. Nevertheless, although I crave understanding from a female equal, I long ago gave up looking for one, and learned very early in my political career that if I were going to be at the top of the political world, loneliness is the price I would have to pay."

I understood very well. I am in a lonely business, too. For reasons of confidentiality, I am unable to discuss my patients with anyone. There was nobody I could tell that the most powerful woman in the world is my patient, although I would have liked to shout it from the rooftops.

"On December 1, 2011," she continued, "that was to change forever. On the shore of the vast and glorious Inya Lake directly across from the former home of General Ne Win, the ruthless dictator who ruled Burma with an iron fist for half a century, is a two story villa set in the middle of a ragged, unkempt garden overrun by weeds and unmowed grass. On our state visit there, we approached the villa, which was well known to me and the world through photographs. Like most buildings in the area, it was in a state of disrepair. Its stucco walls were stained black with mildew, and looked as though they wouldn't make another year in an upright position. The home was surrounded by a blue fence with delightful green figures of dancing peacocks painted on simple white disks.

"The house, which had become the symbol of the democratic movement of Burma, was the residence of Aung San Suu Kyi, the fifty-four-year-old Nobel Peace Prize winner and world-renowned political dissident, who is almost always called 'The Lady,' a respectful title given her by the people of Burma who are reluctant to mention her full name for fear of reprisals by the military regime, the SLORC (The State Law and Order Restoration Council).

"We arrived in Rangoon as the sun was setting upon the oldest Buddhist pagoda in the world. With its gold plating and thousands of diamonds and rubies, it lit up the sky on the darkest of nights. As an important visitor of state, I was permitted to ring one of the glorious forty-ton bells, which resounded throughout the countryside. Sometimes when I can't sleep at night, I listen to the glorious tones of the pagoda bells in my head. They will remain with me as long as I live. What an auspicious beginning to the experience of a lifetime! I felt a surge of excitement quite unusual for me, I who spent my days hobnobbing with the most important people in the world. That evening, I was scheduled to meet a woman who had been a heroine of mine for many years.

"When I first entered the home of 'The Lady' at her lakeside villa in Rangoon, where she had been held under house arrest for six years, I ran my eyes over the huge living room, which seemed almost empty. Nearly lost in a distant corner was a woman with a flower in her long dark tresses and a wisp of hair across her forehead. As she approached me, I felt overwhelmed by her elegant beauty. I thought her features were as delicate as a carved cameo. No photograph or description has captured her unique essence, which was evident immediately on meeting her.

"A branch of yellow flowers hung from the bun at the base of her neck. Although almost my size, five feet four inches tall, she possessed the commanding presence of a taller woman. Like me, she must have liked what she saw, for we first greeted each other with a mutual smile that reached as deep inside as a smile can go, and I knew immediately that I had found my equal in this famous activist and that she would become the friend I had long sought. We then greeted each other with a kiss on the cheek and a warm embrace, and slipped into easy conversation as if we had known each other for years.

"Although we had spoken only once on the phone, we already knew a great deal about each other. Suu Kyi had read both Bill's and my autobiographies, and I had watched *The Lady*, a film about her life. We spent over three hours talking about our lives, and our hopes and dreams for ourselves and our respective countries. To those people in the United States who opposed engagement with Burma because of its cruel military dictatorship, Suu asked me to explain that the Burmese people themselves would like democracy and close contact with our country.

"Already Suu and I were best friends, and spoke together of things no one else in the world knew. I gave her a rare and precious set of books written and signed by another heroine of mine, Eleanor Roosevelt. Suu gave me a silver necklace she had made herself. I immediately put it on, and knew I would always regard it as one of the great treasures of my life.

"After dinner, as we strolled hand in hand in the garden, her dog happily jumped for joy around the two of us, seeming to understand that something phenomenal was taking place in his mistress's life. The 'garden' was now little more than a pile of mud, for Suu's release from imprisonment had come at the high point of the monsoon season, when torrential rains turn huge expanses of the countryside into a foggy water world, from the shores of the Andaman Sea to the bottom of the Himalaya foothills. Suu explained apologetically that on the day they placed her under arrest, her garden had been very beautiful, overflowing with exquisite fields of Madonna lilies, orange frangipani, and fragrant yellow gardenias and jasmines. She loved working in the garden; it was one of her great pleasures, but it required a lot of money, and she could no longer afford it. She spoke in an elegant British accent she had acquired at Oxford University.

"Sometimes she couldn't even pay for food. She became so malnourished, her hair fell out, and she could barely climb out of bed. She feared she would die of heart failure. Her eyes went bad, and she developed spondylosis, a deterioration of the spinal column, which made moving painful. After telling me all this, she was quiet, apparently taking in my sympathy, and then pointed to her head and said proudly, 'But I never let them get me up here, where it matters!'

"All her life, Suu has been obsessed with her father, the great General Aung San, who was assassinated when she was two years old. It was a loss that determined the course of her life, for she felt impelled to live out his life for him, for herself, and for the sake of their country. Aung San was a Burmese revolutionary, a nationalist, and the founder of the modern Burmese army, who was considered to be the father of modern day Burma. The great man was responsible for achieving Burma's independence from British colonial rule, but was assassinated six months before independence.

"Imagine losing your father at such a young age! I was a middle-aged woman when my father died, but at least I had him while I was growing up. He was the biggest influence of my life, and I still mourn him every day. How Suu does so well without ever really having had a father is incomprehensible to me. I'm sure I couldn't have come as far as I have without my father's influence during my growing-up years."

I suspected she would have, but didn't say so. Besides, who really can know such things for certain?

"'I always felt close to my father,' Suu said. 'It never left my mind that he would want me to do something for my country.' When she returned to Burma, she thought a life of politics wasn't for her, but the people were demanding democracy, and she felt compelled to stand in her father's place.

"A colleague of Suu's said to me that she and her father are very much alike. She was inexperienced in politics when arriving back in Burma, but she had her father's gift.

"We looked up at Aung San Suu Kyi, who was then speaking to a surrounding crowd. I remember her speech clearly: 'We must avoid having extreme ideas,' she told them. 'Think before you do anything. The struggle for human rights and democracy in Burma is a fight for life and dignity. It is a battle that includes all our political, social, and economic aspirations.' When Suu finished speaking, the crowd remained silent for a long moment, and then burst into applause for fully ten minutes.

"It was time to end the evening with my friend. First, we said our political goodbyes, Suu thanking our country for all its help and its attempt to connect with the government of Burma. Then we spoke our personal farewells and all that the meeting meant to both of us—words I will keep in my heart forever. As we reluctantly took our leave, we embraced warmly and agreed to stay in frequent touch by phone and mail, which we have done. When we waved goodbye for the last time, my eyes filled with tears, and I saw that Suu's did, too. I felt like I was leaving my long lost sister.

"Suu's outreach to Burma balances unwavering support for human rights with the promise of support to a previously suspicious regime and has opened that country to the world for the first time in decades. I am happy to tell you, Doctor, that Aung San Suu Kyi is now free and her party is actively participating in the reform efforts in Burma. We stay in touch as we promised, and there isn't a day that goes by that I don't miss her, and long for her to visit the United States."

Hillary and I were both too moved to speak. She got up and left without either of us saying a word.

May 7, 2014

"Well, Doctor," she said the next day, "you never answered my question: Do you think my tenure as Secretary of State was successful?"

"How would *you* sum up your tenure?" I asked.

She considered the question carefully before answering. "There are good and bad things about it," she finally said. "First of all, what I didn't accomplish. To my great sorrow, I failed to bring about peace in the Middle East. I wasn't entirely unsuccessful in setting Afghanistan on the road to prosperity and stability. I didn't permanently prevent Iran from continuing the development of their nuclear program. But the twenty-first century has seen a great change in the nature of power. The United States' power is larger than the total of our successes and failures on the problems we tackle. We no longer are in a position to define for other countries what their goals should be and how they should go about enforcing them. Like a parent sending her child off to college, we have to let them develop in their own way, come what may.

"I was the first Secretary of State to implement the concept of 'smart power.' Under me, budgets now include money for issues of gender. Foreign Service officers are now stationed at the Pentagon, and economic management is now part of diplomatic responsibility. I am proud of these accomplishments and am determined that my work continues now that I've left office. I expect to invest a lot of time following it up and advising my successors if they'll let me.

"But I would say that my finest contribution as Secretary of State was not in these separate actions, important as they may be, but in repositioning our country as the top leader in a changing world. I have helped the United States to become a great global chairman who can help navigate crises yet to come, which there certainly will be, from economic upheavals to climate changes to sociological disturbances.

"We are presently occupied in creating the world of a new century. Part of what I was committed to was introducing the United

States to every country, government, and group of people that matter to our ideals and our security. Things are more complicated than they used to be. We may not be under the same danger of a nuclear attack that we were when I was a little girl and told to get down under my desk for protection (as if a little wooden desk could have protected us from a fallen tree, let alone an atom bomb)—when we were at a Cold War crossroads with the Soviet Union. Instead, we now live with the fear of suicidal terrorist organizations obtaining nuclear material and nuclear weapons.

"We are on the threshold of doing something unprecedented, the results of which are unknown. Years in the future, people will look back and say, 'They did it right, or they did it wrong. They should have done this, or they should have done that.' But the fact is that this is uncharted territory. We can only do the best we can to make the world advantageous for our grandchildren and great-grandchildren.

"America undoubtedly remains the foremost political, economic, and military power in the world, and I expect and count on it remaining so because I think that's absolutely in our best interest as well as that of the whole world. While America is not in a position to solve every worldwide problem, I don't believe there is any major difficulty on earth that can be resolved without us. So we still retain the status of top dog.

"By the end of World War II, we were unquestionably in that position, and first began to understand the importance of alliances. As a result, NATO was born. We signed mutual defense treaties with Japan, South Korea, Thailand, and the Philippines in Asia, as well as with other countries. With the demise of the Soviet Union, there was a premature, false assumption that, 'Well, that's finished! Communism has been defeated! The Soviet Union is no more. Hooray! We are an even more dominant power and therefore don't have to keep building these relationships.' Not true. A house of cards can always tumble down and be constantly rebuilt all over again by many hands.

"At the same time, it is time we understand that we cannot take on the obligations of doing everything by ourselves. No person or country is that omniscient or omnipotent. We cannot bear the psychological burden or the financial responsibilities. We want a world in which both existing and rising powers are responsible stakeholders, and we don't have to go it alone. So it is in our deep and profound interest to build worldwide alliances and networks."

I looked at Hillary with awe, admiring her dedication to humanity, her brilliance, and her creativity. "Hillary," I said, "you have so much energy. Why didn't you continue as Secretary of State during Obama's second term?"

"Because *I* know how tired I was. I may look like Superwoman on the outside, but being Secretary of State is a very intense experience. It requires a 24-7 commitment. I could be called up in the middle of the night every night and be asked about something important. The survival of humanity could depend on my being wide awake. I often operated on an around-the-clock schedule. I might be traveling, be twelve hours away, and be asleep, but Washington was awake. I wanted to give the job my all or nothing at all; I didn't want to hold anything back. I wanted to do my very best to support the president and help our country. I thought it was expedient and important personally for me to say, 'I'm going to do this fully for four years and then move on to other things, because I am a human being and can do no more.'"

She looked up at me and said, "Well, Doctor, are you going to answer my question? Do you think my tenure as Secretary of State was successful or not?"

"What do *you* think, Hillary?" I asked.

"Yes!" she exclaimed, her eyes all aglow.

She slowly got up from the couch and walked over to me. We both cried.

May 9, 2014

Today was to be Hillary's last session. I wondered how it would go. Would she be happy? Would she be sad? Would she cry, as so many patients do on leaving? Would I be sorry to see her finish?

She came in much as she had for most of her other sessions, with not much expression on her face. To my surprise, she said with deep feeling, "Doctor, I need to thank you for all you have done for me. You have given me a lot, and I love you for it. But I think I can hack it on my own now." Her eyes filled with tears. One of my questions had been wordlessly answered.

I expressed my professional judgment that this seemingly frozen person was now able to express her love for me. Neither of us spoke for a while, as we shared the moment of intimacy.

"I think you are ready to leave too, Hillary," I finally said. "You have come to terms with your biggest conflict, the one that brought you here, and resolved your ambivalence about staying with Bill. You also have improved greatly in what I considered your biggest problem, your difficulty in accepting your feelings and the ability to express them."

"Still, I hate to leave you, Doctor," she said. "Before I came here today, I thought that I must be crazy to leave this wonderful woman, the only person I've ever known who accepts me as I am, warts and all."

"You will never really leave me, Hillary," I answered, "any more than you have left your parents. My teacher, Dr. Theodore Reik, once said, 'People who love each other don't have to stay together to be together.' You will take me with you wherever you go."

"Wherever that may be."

"You can tell me now, Hillary," I said jokingly. "Where is that? Are you going to run for president? I promise I won't tell anybody."

She threw back her head and laughed her raucous, guttural laugh, which held nothing back. "You know me all too well, Doctor. I'll let you answer that one yourself."

"Aw, shucks!" I said.

When the time is right for a patient to terminate therapy, I generally feel good about it. I listened to what my instincts had to say about Hillary and, although I knew I would miss her honesty, her political genius, and even her sense of humor, I knew it was time for her to leave.

I got up and extended my hand to her. Ignoring my outstretched hand, she threw her arms around me in a warm hug. I hugged her back, as I would a dear friend. She left the room as she did everything else. She didn't turn back.

That night I had a dream that answered my fundamental question, and that of most of the people in the United States. I dreamt I was at Mount Rushmore, and saw there was a fourth mountain with a human face on it. The face was Hillary's. The unconscious is prescient, I thought. It was telling me that Hillary indeed will run for president.

It was also saying she would not only win the election and become President of the United States, but be among the greatest presidents our country has ever known. An old song, "You didn't have to tell me; I knew it all the time," ran through my mind.

I turned over and went back to sleep, secure in the knowledge that I knew the truth about Hillary, and that our country would be well taken care of in her competent hands. After all, who would know that better than I?

Bibliography

Note: The author asked for an interview with Hillary Clinton. The request was not granted.

BOOKS

Anderson, Christopher. *Bill and Hillary: The Marriage*. New York: William Morrow, 1999.

Bernstein, Carl. *A Woman in Charge: The Life of Hillary Rodham Clinton*. New York: Knopf, 2007.

Bond, Alma H. *Jackie O on the Couch*. Baltimore: Bancroft Press, 2011.

Bond, Alma H. *Marilyn Monroe on the Couch*. Baltimore: Bancroft Press 2013.

Carosella, Melissa. *Hillary Rodham Clinton: First Lady, Senator, and Secretary of State*. California: Teacher Created Materials, 2012.

Chafe, William H. *Bill and Hillary: The Politics of the Personal*. New York: Farrar, Straus, and Giroux. 2012.

Clinton, Bill. *My Life*. New York: Knopf, 2004.

Clinton, Hillary Rodham. *An Invitation to the White House: At Home with History*. New York: Simon & Schuster, 2000.

Clinton, Hillary Rodham. *Hillary Rodham Clinton: Living History*. New York: Simon & Schuster, 2003.

Clinton, Hillary Rodham. *It Takes a Village, and Other Lessons Children Teach Us*. New York: Touchstone, 1996.

Doak, Robin S. *Hillary Clinton*. New York: Scholastic Inc., 2013.

Estrich, Susan. *The Case for Hillary Clinton*. New York: HarperCollins, 2005.

Ghattas, Kim. *The Secretary: A Journey with Hillary Clinton from Beirut to the Heart of American Power*. New York: Times Books, 2013.

Harris, John F. *The Survivor*. New York: Random House, 2006.

Heilmann, John and Mark Halperin. *Game Change: Obama and the Clintons, McCain and Palin, and the Race of a Lifetime*. New York: HarperCollins, 2010.

Klein, Edward. *The Truth about Hillary*. New York: Penguin, 2005.

Krull, Kathleen. *Hillary Rodham Clinton, Dreams Taking Flight*. New York: Simon & Schuster Books for Young Readers, 2008.

Kuiper, Thomas. *I've Always Been a Yankees Fan: Hillary Clinton in Her Own Words*. Los Angeles: World Ahead Publishing, 2006.

Levin, Robert E. *Bill Clinton, the Inside Story*. New York: Shapolsky Publishers, Inc., 1992.

Limbacher, Carl. *Hillary's Scheme: Inside the Next Clinton's Ruthless Agenda to Take the White House*. New York: Crown Publishing, 2003.

Maraniss, David. *First in His Class: A Biography of Bill Clinton*. New York: Simon & Schuster, 1995.

Marton, Kati. *Paris: A Love Story*. New York: Simon & Schuster, 2012.

Noonan, Peggy. *The Case Against Hillary Clinton*. New York: HarperCollins, 2000.

Osbourne, Claire G. *The Unique Voice of Hillary Rodham Clinton: A Portrait in Her Own Words*. New York: Avon Books, 1997.

Rodham, Hillary. *There is Only the Fight: An Analysis of the Alinksy Model*. Wellesley College Archives, 1969.

Reik, Theodore. *Listening With the Third Ear*. New York: Farrar, Straus, and Giroux, 1983.

Shambaugh, Rebecca. *Leadership Secrets of Hillary Clinton*. New York: McGraw Hill, 2010.

Sheehy, Gail. *Hillary's Choice*. New York: Ballantine Books, 1999.

Victor, Barbara. *The Lady: Burma's Aung San Suu Kyi*. Thailand: Silkworm Books, 1999.

PERIODICALS

Hillary Rodham's Shocking Drug Diary! Posted by Frank Marafiote on February 13, 2013 in *Life*.

One on One with Hillary Rodham Clinton, by Richard Wolf, *USA Today*, May 19, 2012.

ACKNOWLEDGEMENTS

I gratefully acknowledge the following people for their help with various aspects of this book:

My wonderful publisher and editor, Bruce Bortz, the answer to every writer's dream, and his knowledgeable and hard-working interns, Raychel Rapazza, Michael Stabile, and Hayley Turnbaugh;

Bancroft Press' supremely artful and patient designer, Jen Herchenroeder;

My son Jonathan Bond and his lovely wife, Rebecca, for supplying me with enough books to fill the Library of Congress, and for generously helping us afford to properly publicize this book;

Eli and Eileen Brill for their assistance in obtaining books on Hillary Rodman Clinton;

My cousin and friend Sylvia Williamson, for using her eagle eyes to spot my frequent errors;

Linda Figueroa, for her illuminating discussions about Condoleeza Rice and the Bengazi attack;

Michael Monahan, librarian and friend, for his generosity in forwarding books and articles about Hillary Clinton;

Afton Monahan, for taking the burden of household activities off my shoulders, to give me more time to write. Without her help, this book never would have been finished;

Jeffrey Monahan, who keeps my computer running at any hour of the day or night I need help;

And the librarians of Bosler Library in Carlisle, Pennsylvania for their dedicated assistance, and for the great lengths they've gone to obtain books that I needed.

While I have read many books and articles on Hillary Rodham Clinton, I particularly want to thank Wikipedia, the free encyclopedia, for its careful and detailed study of Hillary Clinton as Secretary of State. In this book, I have followed its time line closely.